THE NPR INTERVIEWS
1995

THE NPR
INTERVIEWS
1995

Edited and with an Introduction
by ROBERT SIEGEL

HOUGHTON MIFFLIN COMPANY

BOSTON · NEW YORK 1995

For information about permission to reproduce
selections from this book, write to
Permissions, Houghton Mifflin Company,
215 Park Avenue South, New York,
New York 10003.

For information about this and other trade and
reference books and multimedia products, visit The
Bookstore at Houghton Mifflin on the World Wide
Web at http://www.hmco.com/trade.

ISSN 1078-0211
ISBN 0-395-73055-4
ISBN 0-395-73054-6 (pbk.)

Printed in the United States of America

Book design by Robert Overholtzer

QUM 10 9 8 7 6 5 4 3 2 1

"Blacksmith Shop" from *Provinces* by Czeslaw Milosz and
Robert Bly. Copyright © 1991 by Czeslaw Milosz Royalties
Inc. First published by The Ecco Press in 1991. Reprinted
by permission. "A Confession" from *The Collected Poems
1931–1987* by Czeslaw Milosz, translated by Robert Hass.
Copyright © 1988 by Czeslaw Milosz Royalties Inc. First
published by The Echo Press in 1988. Reprinted by permis-
sion. "Adieu, George Bush," copyright © 1993 by Calvin
Trillin. Originally appeared in *The Nation. The Waste
Land* rejection letter used by permission of the author.
"My Life as a Doggerelist" excerpted from *Deadline Poet*
by Calvin Trillin. Published by Farrar, Straus, & Giroux.
Copyright © 1994 by Calvin Trillin. "Hamlet" from *The
Compleat Works of William Shakespeare (Abridged)* by
Jess Borgeson, Adam Long and Daniel Singer. Reprinted by
permission of Applause Books, 211 West 71st Street, New
York, New York 10023. 212-496-7511.

CONTENTS

WASHINGTON

AMERICA TALKING

ENDERS

INTRODUCTION

The story of the year 1994 did not so much break as erupt during the night of November 8. The Republican party took control of the United States Senate, where it had been in the minority for a decade, and the House of Representatives, where it had spent a biblical forty years in ineffectual opposition. By dawn on Wednesday, November 9, Republican candidates had achieved gubernatorial victories in New York, California, Texas, Michigan — in every big state except Florida. In describing the election of 1994, politicians and political writers strained the limits of hyperbole. With "landslide" now commonly applied to roughly every second presidential election, the Republican sweep was dubbed a "sea change." Republican leaders in the House, having triumphed through the audacity of committing themselves to a Contract with America, were still more audacious in declaring a "revolution." Other observers of the political scene detected more of an anti-Washington, anti-tax, and anti-Bill (and Hillary) spasm than a Glorious Revolution.

The true extent of the impact of the 1994 vote will become more clear with time, but some things were already clear that Tuesday evening: the habits and assumptions of politicians were broken and disproved. Congressional power was no longer wielded by tenured Democrats with an expansive view of government and often deeply sympathetic to such causes as civil rights, consumerism, and environmentalism — and, I suppose I should add, public broadcasting.

While we public broadcasters did not merit a clause of our own in the Contract with America, we were soon given the treatment reserved for the ancien régime in time of (contractual) revolution: a ride to the financial guillotine. The Corporation for Public Broadcasting, which distributes money to public radio and television stations, and provides some direct support to National Public Radio, was slated for deep cuts, if not eventual elimination. The CPB's funding of public radio accounts for about one dollar in six. It is, however, quite often the dollar designated for the purchase of national programming. The depth of cuts contemplated by the 104th Congress was feared likely to prove fatal for many public radio stations, and injurious to NPR. In our news reporting, we endeavored to cover the debate over federal funding of public broadcasting as we might cover another legislative issue presumed to be of special concern to our listeners. NPR corporate officers spoke on our behalf in Congress and elsewhere; on-air personnel left heavy lifting advocacy to Big Bird, Bert, and Ernie. Our job, we reasoned, was to describe and measure the eruption, not protest that we might be burned in the shower of embers. As of this writing, the future of federal funding for public radio, the changes NPR will be obliged to make as it adapts to a new system of funding, and the extent and meaning of our privatization are unknown, and all the unknowns make an always precarious existence in public radio shakier than ever. While it is true that journalists enjoy a perverse exemption from the Chinese saying that it is a curse to live in interesting times, the past year has been entirely too interesting for journalists at National Public Radio.

In compiling the second annual volume of *The NPR Interviews*, I have occasionally wondered, in this season of our financial trials, what sort of document the book makes in support of the case for federal funding of public radio. I think it is a strong one. It represents the breadth of interests pursued on *All Things Considered*, *Morning Edition*, and *Weekend Edition*. We are, as a network news and information programming division, both more serious and more frivolous than most other programming on the air. Like a good sound system, we exhibit high fidelity to both the high and low ends that are filtered out of the compressed mainstream of American broadcast journalism. I doubt that the homogenized blur of commercial radio could accommodate Daniel Zwerdling's conversation with the

Polish Nobel Prize–winning poet Czeslaw Milosz. Nor would much of the content of the "Enders" chapter — items of the sort that end segments on our shows — rate more than ten or fifteen seconds on a network TV news show. Some are, frankly, silly.

While some of the people interviewed here are more familiar on commercial airwaves than on our own, there are also many who would not be broadcast at all, but for public radio. The actors Richard Harris and Julie Andrews, prime examples of the former type, both spoke with Scott Simon, whose interview with the novelist Henry Roth opens the "Arts and Letters" chapter and, hence, the book. Andrews and Harris are frequent interview subjects, questioned marvelously by Scott. Roth published his critically acclaimed first novel, *Call It Sleep*, in the 1930s and waited until the 1990s to publish his next. I doubt that his whereabouts or his reasons for becoming a literary MIA would rate much time with Regis and Kathie Lee. But I don't think that its distance from the popular culture makes the Roth interview inherently superior or inferior to Richard Harris's resigned acknowledgment that he is too old to play Hamlet, or to Julie Andrews explaining her one topless moment on-screen. What distinguishes all three is the intelligent curiosity of the interviewer and the time that NPR permits him to devote to each subject. All three interviews reflect our aim to describe the country and the world. That includes wars and floods, books and movies, animal trainers and the woman who designs figure skaters' costumes for the Winter Olympics.

Our devotion to such pedestrian stories might be seen as weakening our case for federal support, or financial support of any kind. Why subsidize a program that eulogizes a dead rooster whose owner claims he could pick basketball games and presidential elections? Would we not be on firmer, higher ground if we stuck to Milosz and V. S. Naipaul? My answer: higher perhaps, firmer no. The aim of a great radio network, like that of a fine newspaper or magazine, should be to integrate the disparate events and ideas around us into accessible, regular programming: not just the classy events and elegant ideas, not just the natural concerns of aesthetes and charitable worthies. The result should be a mix of words and voices in which those listeners who never read *Call It Sleep* might sense an invitation to do so and those who never heard Richard Harris sing "Mac-Arthur Park" might hear the most famous note he sounded and how he did it. It should include the voices Noah Adams captured in Northern Ireland and in an American prayer group. We should hear Ed Wilson telling Alex Chadwick of how bugs came to fascinate him and lead him to a career in science. We should hear Liane Hansen interview the cellist Elsa Hilger during the week that she turned ninety, as well as the considerably younger members of the rock group Phish. And we should hear, in the news of the world and the nation, the rumblings of eruptions and forecasts of those to come.

I think these interviews further substantiate an already strong case that NPR makes an invaluable contribution to American broadcasting, one worthy of survival and continued support.

Some notes on NPR personnel who appear in this edition: Scott Simon returned full-time to *Weekend Edition, Saturday* in 1994 — hence his substantially greater presence in this volume than in the first. Conversely, Scott's return meant fewer hosting appearances by Susan Stamberg and Neal Conan. Also, Bob Edwards spent the entire year at *Morning Edition;* during the previous year he was on leave for several months writing his book. Daniel Zwerdling took over at *Weekend All Things Considered,* backed up by Jacki Lyden. Linda Wertheimer, Noah Adams, and I continue to host *All Things Considered* on weekdays. As ever, the interviews included reflect the labors of bookers, editors, producers, cutters, and engineers, as well as hosts. As with last year's book, the judgment of what to include and what to leave out was subjective, imperfect, and entirely my own.

For assistance in compiling *The NPR Interviews 1995,* I am indebted to Gail Ross of Lichtman, Trister, Singer and Ross, and at NPR to Mary Morgan, as well as Ori Hoffer, Asha Cornelio, and Necola Deskins-Staples. At Houghton Mifflin, I am grateful to John Sterling for launching this project and getting this second volume under way before leaving to assume new challenges, to Hilary Liftin for picking up where John left off, and to Jayne Yaffe for her superb editing (although I do think that any self-respecting resident of the city of the Celtics should know what "driving the lane" means). Finally, this book could not have been written without the tireless and inspired efforts of Doug Lemov, as fine a research assistant as one could ever want. May he emerge from graduate school as wise as he enters.

ARTS AND LETTERS

The novelist HENRY ROTH speaks with Scott Simon about the sixty years between publication of his novels. In 1934, Mr. Roth wrote *Call It Sleep*, a critically acclaimed book set in the tenements of New York City's Lower East Side around the turn of the century. He did not publish again until 1994, when *A Star Shines over Mt. Morris Park* appeared. Once again, the novel's setting is New York City in the early twentieth century. February 12, 1994

SIMON: Well, there's no other way to begin except by saying, "What took you so long?"

ROTH: Yes, that's a good question. I think what happened to me is what happened to a whole generation of my contemporaries in the thirties. It's a little earlier than Salinger and Ellison, and some of the other guys, but the guy who wrote *Call It Sleep*, even though he was already somewhere between twenty-four and twenty-eight, was essentially a precocious adolescent. There was a sixty-year interval. Well, I would say it took sixty years for me to grow up.

SIMON: Mr. Roth, the report that used to surface in the literary world over the last sixty years was that you were at your typewriter, and maybe later at a word processor, trying to turn out the great proletarian novel.

ROTH: Yes, that was the great disaster, the proletarian novel. There was nothing worse. I had to give that up. I had a contract with Scribner's to do it. They had already paid an advance.

SIMON: Let me get some idea of the span of your career. As I understand it, the man you signed that agreement with was Maxwell Perkins.

ROTH: That's right.

SIMON: The famous literary agent who handled Ernest Hemingway and F. Scott Fitzgerald.

ROTH: That's right. I tried to write the novel, but at the same time there was something in me that recognized the falsity of my view that the Communist party was going to be the great liberator of mankind, even if I was stupid enough to think so. I couldn't do it as an artist and I didn't go any further.

SIMON: You did an awful lot of things during those sixty years.

ROTH: Oh yes.

SIMON: Like what?

ROTH: I worked in the woods. Firefighting after a while. I worked four years in a hospital as an attendant.

SIMON: You were an attendant in a psychiatric hospital?

ROTH: Psychiatric hospital. I sometimes wondered who ought to have the keys.

SIMON: You were a waterfowl farmer?

ROTH: I raised ducks and geese.

SIMON: Mr. Roth, all those years that we say that you weren't writing. You know —

ROTH: Yes.

SIMON: What we really mean is that you weren't being published. Were you sitting down to the typewriter or a tablet of paper every day and writing?

ROTH: No, not every day, but every once in a while I would be seized by an urge to put down something that I had seen or heard.

SIMON: Yes.

ROTH: And finally, at age seventy-three, I guess the pressure had gotten so high I just blew my top, and once I started it was like a dam breaking. I couldn't stop.

SIMON: Mr. Roth, why is it that after taking on so many professions over sixty years, when you returned to being a novelist, you still wrote about immigrant Jewish life in New York City in the early twentieth century?

ROTH: Well, I think it's really a continuation of what I should have been doing way back sixty years ago.

ALEX MELAMID describes the perfect American painting, based on a public opinion poll and focus groups that he conducted with a fellow Russian immigrant artist, Vitaly Kolmar. They asked people their preferences in genre, style, medium, and color. Alex Melamid tells Jacki Lyden that it's a perfect painting by the numbers. February 26, 1994

MELAMID: Everything is scientifically correct in this painting. Of course there's some interpretation, but still I can explain some of the features of this painting.

LYDEN: If you would, please. What does it look like?

MELAMID: It's a landscape with a lot of skies and a lot of sea and a lot of blue because forty-four percent of the American people like blue color. Then eighty-eight percent wanted a seascape, and that's what we basically painted.

LYDEN: A seascape?

MELAMID: A seascape, yes.

LYDEN: I thought you said it was a landscape.

MELAMID: It was a landscape with the sea, OK?

LYDEN: [laughs] All right.

MELAMID: It was a compromise between the seascape and the landscape because American people like wilderness. That's for sure. Most people prefer to have wild animals as opposed to domestic animals in this picture, so we have a group of two deers and one small hippopotamus.

LYDEN: I have to tell you, Alex, everyone I spoke to and showed this painting to was really surprised that you put George Washington in the middle of it.

MELAMID: Yes? That's no surprise. George Washington is the father of the nation. He is a very important figure. Since a majority of the people didn't have a certain opinion if they wanted a historic figure or not, we felt at liberty to put in a historic figure.

LYDEN: Well, let me ask you, Do you like it?

MELAMID: I've been staring at this picture for the last month, and the more I stare at it, the more I like it.

LYDEN: Well, Alex, you could mass-produce this painting and offer it at a discount.

MELAMID: The price which the people want to pay for the painting is from two hundred to five hundred dollars.

LYDEN: Sounds pretty good.

MELAMID: It's good for the people. Not very good for the artists.

The jazz musician WYNTON MARSALIS, author of the book *Sweet Swing Blues on the Road*, tells Noah Adams about touring more than two hundred nights a year. The book weds the trumpeter's text with the photographs of Frank Stewart, who traveled with Marsalis's septet. December 13, 1994

MARSALIS: I remember once I sat in with Mel Lewis at the Village Vanguard when I had first come to New York. Everybody was saying, "Man, we got to hear this young trumpet player that's supposed to be so hip." I waited until the end of the set and then Mel called me up, and they played a shuffle in E-flat minor. I had never played in E-flat minor, and I played something that was thoroughly sad, and when you play something that's sad, even the silence around it is sad. So every time I would stop playing, what I heard in the silence was so bad that I would keep playing. When the tune was over it was like you heard everybody saying, "Oh no." Erroll Garner said, "Well, man, at least you read the part." He was trying to find something to tell me that would make me feel better. Mel just looked at me, and shook his head like, You got a long way to go. So I went back to my apartment. I really was depressed. I didn't know what I was going to do. The next morning I got up, and the first thing I started playing was that E-flat minor scale.

ADAMS: Chapter 3 of the book is all about what it feels like to be playing onstage. Do you ever have a moment in which you do not feel fully confident these days?

MARSALIS: Many times right before a show I'm nervous, and that's part of what makes it exciting. A lot of times you depend on other members of the band to carry you. They can tell when you're not confident. Like Russell, he'll say something like,

"It's cool." You always have those jitters before you play a little bit.

ADAMS: You sometimes get strange looks from the other players. Do surprising things happen onstage?

MARSALIS: All the time. Surprising things happen all the time because you never really know what somebody is going to play, especially when you're improvising. The art of jazz is the process of improvisation and group negotiation.

ADAMS: You say whoever is playing the most music at any given moment is the leader on the bandstand.

MARSALIS: Yes, the bandstand is an arena of true democracy because your skills determine who you are. That's why I like to leave a lot of room for the men in the band to play, to take the music in a direction. If you can't hear what they're playing, you have to figure out how to hear it. Eric Reed, our pianist, likes to play chord substitutions all the time, and if you can't hear the substitution, you have to work on your ears. He'll tell you, too: "I think you need to figure out how to hear these substitutions." When Jeff Watts was in the band, he liked to go in all these different times and he would always come out right. If you had a ground rhythm, he would superimpose another beat. Now, you would still be playing in the first time, so it would be very hard to keep your place. If you got lost in the form, he would start laughing. Musicians are always trying to throw things out at you, and say, "OK, can you deal with this?"

ADAMS: How much chance do you get to think about what's going on in the audience? Here you are imagining, in Chapter 3, people in the audience. There's a couple who are out on a date. There's Professor Fernandez, who has brought his high school band to this concert?

MARSALIS: Right.

ADAMS: And a young man, their best trumpeter, first-year all-state player, Nathan. He's got all of your records and he's out there watching.

MARSALIS: Right. You plan for people. They're part of the dialogue. It's difficult because an audience is always comprised of many different types of people who like different things, but there's a certain rhythm and a tempo that goes through an audience, through any group of people. When people are confined in a space for a certain amount of time, there's a rhythm and a tempo. It's my responsibility to figure out what that is and try to touch a chord in that.

ADAMS: I had not realized that trumpet players — that there's a bit of pain here.

MARSALIS: Yes.

ADAMS: You write, "I hit a high one and hold it, lips swollen, cut by teeth, head bursting, heart straining, past the point of pain"?

MARSALIS: Boy, it hurts, too! Anybody who plays trumpet will tell you. I saw a picture of Louis Armstrong once, his embouchure, all the scar tissue around it. I thought to myself, Man, that's all those years of hitting all those high C's. You know, when you have something really high to play, you're taught not to use pressure, but you always do. To get those notes to come steaming out of the trumpet requires a lot of force and power. Your teeth are against your lips and your lips are very soft and your teeth are hard, so you have your lips in between two hard things. If you don't have perfectly straight teeth, then they're going to cut into your lips. Just the breathing — sometimes you can play with such power. Some pieces I have to sit down and play or I'll hyperventilate and faint. The trumpet is not to be played with.

OSCAR PETERSON and ITZHAK PERLMAN talk about making music together. The album *Side by Side*, a collection of such standards as "Blue Skies," "Makin' Whoopee," "Mack the Knife," and some Peterson originals, is a collaboration of the legendary jazz pianist and the great classical violinist. The recording marks Peterson's reunion with his quartet — the guitarist Herb Ellis, the bassist Ray Brown, and the drummer Grady Tate, as well his first recording since suffering a stroke the year before. As they tell Robert Siegel, it was a chance for Perlman, a longtime fan of Peterson's, to try improvisation. September 28, 1994

PERLMAN: I said to myself, "Well, if he's willing, I'm certainly willing to try." Because both our languages are music, but it's a different kind of music that we're talking about. And, of course, the question of improvising, to a classical musician, is extremely foreign. So I said to Oscar, "Listen, are you going to trust me with this?" He said, "Yeah, sure, everything will be fine."

SIEGEL: Oscar Peterson, how do you think he's coming along as a jazz musician?

PETERSON: Fantastically well. He has an innate sense of harmonics and rhythm which falls right into our grooves, so there's been no problem at all.

PERLMAN: Well, I'm really flattered that you say that. [*laughs*] I was having real trepidation. Just before every chorus, I said to myself, "What am I going to do now?" But it was a wonderful experience for me, and everybody in the group was extremely nice to me and very patient with all the stuff that I did.

SIEGEL: Do you have to play the violin differently and strive for different kinds of sounds out of it when you're playing jazz?

PERLMAN: I found that I did. In a sense I found that I had to really concentrate on the purity of the tune and play it without the traditional things I have in my head when it comes to classical music. That was a change that I had to get used to. At the end of the recording sessions there was one selection, I don't remember which it was, where we heard a playback and I didn't recognize who it was.

PETERSON: Playing with someone like Itzhak, that (A) I've never played with before, and (B) because of his background and from whence he comes, puts a different insight into the playing, means that I had to listen a little more carefully to where he was going and to try and track him so that there were no clashes and no divisions in the playing.

PERLMAN: That's for sure.

PETERSON: And it meant that because he is a different player, because he comes from a different realm, a lot of things that I played behind him — never mind on my solos, but behind him — were quite different than I might have played with someone like the late Dizzy Gillespie or Roy Eldridge or someone of that kind.

SIEGEL: I came across a review of a Canadian radio documentary about you, Oscar Peterson, that said quite definitively, "After years of failing health and a stroke that robbed him of some use of one hand, it's doubtful that Peterson will ever perform again."

PERLMAN: That's funny.

PETERSON: Well — [laughs]

PERLMAN: That's very funny.

PETERSON: I'm very pleased that my first performance since the stroke was with Itzhak, and not only was it a challenge, but it was great encouragement.

SIEGEL: How recovered are you from the stroke? I gather it was not a major stroke, but it robbed you of some use of your left side, from what I've read.

PETERSON: Yes. Actually, my whole left arm was in pretty bad condition after the stroke, but thanks to therapy and a very dedicated therapist I feel I've been able to overcome it. So I'm back in contention again. [laughs]

PERLMAN: That's for sure. The second day I came to the recording studio, Oscar, you said, "Do you know 'Making Whoopee'?"

PETERSON: Yes, right.

PERLMAN: I said, "How does it go?" You said, [hums the tune], and I said, "OK, let's do that."

PETERSON: That's the beauty, the spontaneity, of this kind of music. You take these kinds of chances. Itzhak certainly took them, and he met the challenges beautifully.

PERLMAN: Thanks.

SIEGEL: Had you known "Making Whoopee" before that?

PERLMAN: I kind of knew how it went.

PETERSON: I'll say.

SIEGEL: So when do you do the Beethoven sonatas together? When does the collaboration break the other way, Mr. Peterson?

PERLMAN: Do you know how it goes, Oscar?

PETERSON: [laughs] I have a bad left arm.

PERLMAN: Very funny.

SIEGEL: I see there are occasions when you'll plead that.

PETERSON: That's right.

WILLIAM STYRON'S *A Tidewater Morning* was the first work of fiction he published in fifteen years. Styron's 1967 historical novel, *The Confessions of Nat Turner*, won a Pulitzer Prize. His next book, *Sophie's Choice*, became a bestseller and was made into a movie. Then came a nonfiction account of his battle with clinical depression, *Darkness Visible*. Styron talks with Bob Edwards about the three semiautobiographical novellas contained in *A Tidewater Morning*, and his narrator, Paul Whitehurst, a white boy growing up in southern Virginia during the 1930s. February 1, 1994

STYRON: [*reading*] "There was a pleasant geometric neatness about the village with its alternating stucco and clapboard houses, linear intersecting streets, straight flagstone walks. It bore a traditional Tudor look but was too contemporary to be quaint; the ordered angularity was softened by raggedy oblongs of shade trees, hedges, shrubbery, and the whole should have been a model for the legion of bleak Levittowns and Daly Cities that were its descendants. It was the first true housing development in the nation, built by the shipyard for its white-collar workers during the Great War. The dwellings were diminutive but very well built. I insert this comment, perhaps a bit gratuitously, in order to reassure myself that the village, whatever its cramped drawbacks, was a more agreeable, far prettier place to grow up in than the mass-produced high-tech eyesores that overwhelmed the landscape in later decades."

EDWARDS: Aside from your coming from the Tidewater region, what does it do for you in a literary sense? How is it as a setting for fiction?

STYRON: I have always felt that I've been drawn back to my

origins as a writer, even when I have been dealing with far-flung subjects, subjects that are not relative to that region of the country. I think writers are often very much a product of their roots and tend to gravitate backwards toward those roots, and therefore, I have always felt that in most of my work there was a reflection of my first twenty years or so.

EDWARDS: Paul Whitehurst is a young man coming of age. He's having to deal with a lot of difficult times, with a dying mother, with his first realization of the race issue in the South. How do you describe Paul Whitehurst?

STYRON: Well, I think he is unabashedly a reflection, at least in part, of my own sensibility, my own personality, and, indeed, aside from the fact that the title story, *A Tidewater Morning*, is about the death of my mother, the other thing you mentioned, the so-called race problem, was very, very important to me growing up. I was absolutely obsessed as a boy by the puzzle of race, by the fact that I was living in a strange, bifurcated, totally apartheid society, and I think that's later reflected in my other work.

EDWARDS: Why were you puzzled? Why weren't you just expected to continue the attitudes of white males at the time?

STYRON: Well, I don't know. I don't mean to claim a special refinement of sensibility, but I do think that I was more aware, for some reason, than my contemporaries of the paradox of this segregated society in which I grew up, and of its injustices and of its overriding tragedy. It embedded itself in my personality. I know that because I was intensely responsive to the nature of black experience even though it was remote from me. I wanted to find out about it, I wanted to know more about it, and I was immensely moved by certain aspects of what in those days we called "the Negro experience," which was their music and their religion and that sort of thing. And I think that later became reflected in a great deal of my work.

EDWARDS: You had enormous success with two historical novels, *The Confessions of Nat Turner* and *Sophie's Choice*, but you had to endure criticism from people who felt you didn't have the right to be addressing those subjects.

STYRON: Yes, but I don't buy into that criticism at all. I think it's totally invalid. A writer has the right to deal with virtually any experience. It can be totally alien to him in terms of the way it actually happened in his life, or did not happen, but there is no, to my mind, area of experience which is off bounds to a committed serious artist. Therefore, the criticism I got about *Nat Turner* I find ludicrous and offensive, still, to this day.

EDWARDS: Have you done everything you've wanted to do?

STYRON: I don't think anyone's really done everything they want to do. I would like to have done a lot more, and I'm still in the process. I don't feel that by any means there's a foreclosing of the possibilities, but for me, writing has always been such a difficult proposition that I'm — really, without being immodest or vainglorious in any sense — I'm very pleased to have done what I've done, given the fact that for me writing has always been a great, great source of real pain. And I'm glad that I've gotten what I've gotten done.

The novelist TOM ROBBINS tells Liane Hansen
how he writes such dazzling and wildly titled books as
Jitterbug Perfume, Skinny Legs and All, and *Even
Cowgirls Get the Blues.* His most recent book and the
subject of this interview is *Half Asleep in Frog Pajamas.*
September 4, 1994

ROBBINS: I always begin with the structure and it's the only thing I begin with. I have no outline. I have really no idea where the book is going. I have no real intentions. I prefer adventures to intentions, so I try never to take a ride if I know where it's going to end up.

I do a lot of useless reading and read a lot of science magazines. Every Thursday night is magazine night for me. I subscribe to about thirty magazines, and every Thursday night I put on a satin smoking jacket that I bought in a secondhand store on Melrose Avenue in Los Angeles, and I light up a big Cuban cigar and read magazines. It's as if your mind is a Geiger counter. Every now and then, something makes a loud ping. When I discovered an oblique reference to a tribe in Africa that has this astronomical knowledge, my Geiger counter began, *ping, ping, ping, ping,* and I went on from there.

HANSEN: Some critics of your previous works talk about your encyclopedic knowledge. Just a little thing at the very beginning of the book from the *Encyclopaedia Britannica:* "It has been demonstrated that some amphibians are able to use celestial bodies for navigation." Certainly that must have been another ping for you, right?

ROBBINS: Yes, well, I had already gotten interested in frogs because frogs are disappearing from our planet, and I write about that in the book. It's a fact that they are disappearing at alarm-

ing rates all over the world, whole species. I tried, in a somewhat oblique, I hope nondidactic, fashion, to establish a correlation between the disappearance of the frogs and the disappearance of the middle class, because the middle class is
also disappearing from the planet, and I guess the one of the
connections is that just as frogs are a bridge between water
and land, between fish and reptiles, and maybe between the
stars and planet Earth, so the middle class is a bridge between
abundance and scarcity. The economic world, the world of the
equities markets, just seemed like a perfect foil, the ideal back-
drop against which to contrast this story about legendary amphibians from outer space, because everything these days is all
about money. In this book I'm hoping to illustrate that there not
only are far more important things than money, but there are far
more interesting things.

HANSEN: I read a brief quotation from you in the *Detroit
News*: "I am an ordinary, sweet, witty guy who happened to
possess a luminous comic vision and a passionate appreciation
of fine sentences." I don't think we've given enough play to this.
On page 136, you talk about "the essence of a Henry James
sentence weaving in and out of prepositional phrases, dependent clauses, and parenthetical asides (periodically hitting the
brakes to avoid misplacing a modifier)." You allude to it being
like driving a Porsche in and out of rain-slowed traffic. To a
certain extent, is that your own sentence construction process?

ROBBINS: Yes. I guess when all is said and done, what I'm
really interested in, what really throws the logs on my fire, is
language, is messing around with language. The language a
writer uses may be ultimately more important than his or her
message. Certainly Shakespeare thought so.

HANSEN: Does it come to you easily? Let me give you just an
example that I've repeated endlessly to people around here. You
write, "Belford is lying on the bed, eyes closed, and an expression on his face that could end three Italian operas and still have
enough anguish left over to butter an existentialist's toast."
Was it a long struggle to come up with that one?

ROBBINS: Sometimes they come easy. Sometimes they come hard. I don't walk around with a notebook full of those phrases. I guess what I try to do is to create situations, spaces in which language can take place. I sit there and create the situation and sooner or later that little green man who's chained to a wooden stake in the bottom of my brainpan will squeeze out some of this stuff.

HANSEN: And then you put it down on paper.

ROBBINS: Yes. It's situational. I sit there with my eyes closed and think about the situation and sooner or later it makes its splash in the pond of language, so to speak.

HANSEN: This might be a sensitive question, but do you think this book would make a good movie?

ROBBINS: I think it's filmproof, Liane.

DOMINICK ARGENTO talks with Robert Siegel about his new opera, *The Dream of Valentino*, which was commissioned by the Washington Opera. Although the great silent film star Rudolph Valentino seems an equally appropriate subject for a Broadway musical, Argento emphasizes the difference between that genre and contemporary opera. February 3, 1994

ARGENTO: *The Dream of Valentino* would not play on Broadway. I think the music is not that kind of music. It does not strive to have hit tunes in it. It does not strive to do the sort of thing that [Andrew Lloyd] Webber does. The music in an opera should percolate up through the drama and even percolate up through the characters. In a Broadway musical, I always find the music extraneous, that is, pretty. It's attractive and it does what it's supposed to do, but it doesn't particularly advance the drama or interpret the characters for us. It's just ancillary to the whole thing, and that for me is a very fundamental distinction between those two forms. Neither one being superior to the other because of it, but nonetheless, I think it's a valid distinction.

SIEGEL: When you say that you're not striving for pop show tunes, does that mean that in the process of composition, you are veering away from the hummable aria? Are there moments when you think you might do that but decide instead, No, I don't want to do that?

ARGENTO: You almost have to, I believe, Mr. Siegel, because the moment it becomes whistleable and the kind of thing you can take out to the intermission and hum, it means, in effect, that you've failed because it has distracted from what the music ought to be doing in an opera. If it's found a little niche in the audience's brain as a separate entity, as a distinct piece, then I think it hasn't worked. Some of your listeners will know the story of Verdi, when *Rigoletto* opened in Venice. The night before, they allowed all of the gondoliers to attend for free. That was their way of getting P.R. All of the gondoliers the next day would say, "You have to go see Mr. Verdi's opera." But what they did was to sing the "La donna è mobile" all over town, so that by the time people arrived at the theater it was an old tune. I think it makes a nice anecdote, but what it really proves is that there is something that you can take away without perhaps understanding the drama, understanding what the whole point of *Rigoletto* is about, seeing none of that attack on nobility which the story is all about and which got Verdi into trouble. If you come out just whistling "La donna è mobile," in a sense, the rest of the piece has failed for those particular gondoliers and other audiences.

SIEGEL: That the very accessible, catchy tune, you're saying —

ARGENTO: Yes.

SIEGEL: Becomes separated from the whole, from the very idea of opera as all of these media integrated into one experience and then is undermined —

ARGENTO: That it's distracting. Because how many people today go to hear an opera in which Mr. Pavarotti has been contracted? They're waiting to hear him sing "Vesti la giubba." They're waiting to hear him sing "Una furtiva lagrima," which would indicate to me that they haven't been paying an awful lot of attention to the second tenor or the *seconda donna* and they're really not following the opera as a drama. And I insist upon that. My whole outlook is geared to the opera as a drama.

SIEGEL: So what does a contemporary opera composer make of his audience humming and whistling "La donna è mobile"? The patrons of the Washington Opera, which commissioned the work, are after all the same people who attended the company's production of Georges Bizet's *The Pearl Fishers*, an opera notable to most for one great duet.

ARGENTO: No one knows anything about *The Pearl Fishers* except that it's got a great duet in it. And that's sort of sad. I have a feeling that that same subscription audience you're speaking of couldn't tell you what the story was about. They probably sat there the first half of the evening waiting to hear *The Pearl Fishers* duet and the second half wondering if it was worth coming out for. Whereas, I think the other approach, the reason Washington commissioned me, was that they had a great success with an earlier opera of mine four or five years ago called *The Aspen Papers*. And nobody came out of *The Aspen Papers* whistling anything. I think many of them were captured by the drama, Henry James's drama, not mine, and the way the music supported everything without ever intruding on their consciousness. For that reason, that same subscription audience is the one, I suspect, that came back for *Valentino*. And they came back with no expectations of finding, you know, a gem here or there. They came back thinking that they were going to see a drama that had been articulated by this music.

MARGARET ATWOOD, the author of eight novels,
several collections of short fiction, and many volumes of
poetry talks with Jacki Lyden about her women and
villainy. Atwood's most recent book was *The Robber
Bride*, a twist on the Grimms' fairy tale called "The
Robber Bridegroom." The protagonist of the book
is Zenia, an unabashedly evil woman who robs three
very different women, including one named Roz, of
their men and more. February 5, 1994

LYDEN: Margaret, why a novel about such an evil, evil
woman?

ATWOOD: Well, she's not as evil as she could be. She's not a
serial killer and she doesn't do mass warfare. She's a con artist.
Literature used to have quite a few con artists and some of them
were women, and then they just disappeared for about twenty
years. In the fifties, we had characters that were more like Deb-
bie Reynolds or, if worst came to worst, Marilyn Monroe, but
not like Marlene Dietrich in the von Sternberg film *The Blue
Angel*. And then in the seventies, I think it became sort of a
no-no to say that women could be bad because that was supposed to be male projection. Somehow, out of that notion came
the idea that you couldn't, or shouldn't, say bad things about
women. Real life, on the other hand, kept producing female con
artists and manipulative persons just as it produced male ones.
So I felt it was time for this character to make a comeback.
Besides, I've always been interested in stories in which people
are taken in.

LYDEN: Where people are deceived?

ATWOOD: For instance, right now we have *Schindler's List*,
and Schindler is a con artist. He lies, he cheats, he steals, he

corrupts, he bribes, and it's his talents in these directions that allow him to also be heroic. If he weren't a con artist to begin with, he could never have done what he did.

LYDEN: Let me take you back to the idea of the villainess. I've read that one of your inspirations for her character was Lady Macbeth, certainly one of the classics. I mean, Shakespeare has lots of evil women.

ATWOOD: Yes, he has quite a few, but he's not the only one. I would say my character is probably a little bit more like Delilah in the Samson and Delilah story. Lady Macbeth is not a seductress particularly. She does that Margaret Thatcher thing of "I'm more man than you are, so I'm going to kill these guys," but she's not thought of as a particularly sexual being. In fact, she says herself that in order to do these bad things, she has to divest herself of her female nature and then she goes crazy. So although she's an evil woman, she's not as close to my character as some other, previous evil women.

LYDEN: Is it more fun writing about bad women than good women?

ATWOOD: I think probably. John Keats said that Shakespeare got as much pleasure out of creating an Iago as he did out of creating an Imogen. I would say probably more, because you can remember what play Iago is from, and I bet you can't place Imogen.

LYDEN: That's right. *Othello*, and I have no idea where Imogen was from.

ATWOOD: There you go. If you create a completely good person, nobody is going to believe it. Because we all know ourselves, I would hope, a little too well. We know our temptations and we know the places where we fall down and our lacks and shortcomings and our envious feelings and all of those darker sides to us. We may not act them out, but we know that they are there. So if you create a person who is spotless in thought, word, and deed, nobody is going to believe it. And I've never met such a person anyway.

I know of only one novelist who set out to create an entirely good person, and that was Samuel Richardson when he created *Sir Charles Grandison*. Have you ever read it?

LYDEN: No, I have not.

ATWOOD: Well, there you go.

LYDEN: I was thinking of Jonathan Livingston Seagull, though, for a minute.

ATWOOD: But he's a bird.

LYDEN: True. Point.

ATWOOD: And anybody who knows anything about real birds knows that it's quite fraudulent anyway. I mean, if you've ever studied seagull behavior, you know that they're absolutely greedy and very aggressive.

LYDEN: You took your title from the Grimms' fairy tale "The Robber Bridegroom." One of the characters in your book reads a story to her daughters, and the daughters only want the pronouns to be female. Did you find that fairy tales read a very different way when you started putting *she* in the roles?

ATWOOD: They did. The one in the book is "The Three Little Pigs." Roz's children insist that everything be female, that the three little pigs be female and also that the wolf be female, so what you have is three female pigs and one female wolf and that reads very differently because we just aren't used to the wolf being female. Possibly that's why wolves in females' clothing do so well, because they're unexpected.

LYDEN: And I had thought that you had Zenia facing off against three women because they were like the three witches in *Macbeth* or the Three Graces. I didn't think of "The Three Little Pigs."

ATWOOD: Well, there's also "The Three Little Pigs." Three is a very significant number in our culture. You can have three of lots of things. Why stop with the Graces? There's also the blonde, the brunette, and the redhead that were always in the Clairol ad.

LYDEN: Right. The Breck girls.

ATWOOD: That's it.

CORNELL CAPA and his brother, the late Robert Capa, were both great war photographers. Robert, who captured one of the classic war images of this century — a soldier dying in the Spanish Civil War, his body arching in the air — died in 1954, killed by a land mine while photographing the war in Indochina. After Robert's death, Cornell Capa took up the camera and worked for *Life* magazine for twenty years in Europe, Latin America, the Middle East, and the United States. In his office on New York's Upper East Side, Cornell Capa, now in his seventies, thumbs through the images of his career with Jacki Lyden. February 6, 1994

CAPA: Wars, revolutions, uprisings, the overthrow of Perón, political prisoners —

LYDEN: When you look at these pictures of these political prisoners behind barbed wire —

CAPA: They are ageless. They are timeless and ageless.

LYDEN: It could be a recent picture from Bosnia. It happens to be an old picture from —

CAPA: Nicaragua after the killing of Somoza. These are the people accused of being against Somoza.

LYDEN: The pain in these faces! When you look at it, do you think back to the moment you took that picture?

CAPA: Of course. I remember every picture that I have ever taken. Pictures are a terrible load to carry.

I like the idea of the word *eyewitness*. All writers want to be eyewitnesses, but the true eyewitnesses are the photographers. A writer can unobtrusively watch a scene and make notes or not make notes; a photographer cannot be unobtrusive. And a photographer has to be there. My brother's famous motto is "If your pictures are not good enough, you're not close enough."

LYDEN: It's always that decision between being obtrusive and unobtrusive for a photographer, isn't it?

CAPA: Passive or impassive, subjective or objective. To be objective is one thing, to be subjective is something else, and to really be an impassioned person, you can't really be objective. If you're objective, your pictures will not be very passionate. War, poverty, crime, drugs — the world is going around the same axis all the time, and the concerned photographer is going to make the world visible to everybody. [We thought] maybe we were going to end wars, end poverty, end all kinds of famine, because the power of photography can do all that. It hasn't quite worked out that way.

LYDEN: We're still looking at images of famine. We're still looking at images of war. Is it —

CAPA: Frustrating! It's frustrating. The concerned photographers, caring about the survival of the human race in spite of all the plagues that confront it, we can't fix it. Of course we can't, because nobody can fix it. But we make you aware of it, and we're eyewitnesses to bring it to you so maybe you'll realize what it's all about.

CZESLAW MILOSZ, eighty-two, the Polish poet who
won the Nobel Prize for Literature in 1980, joined the
resistance in Poland during World War II and went
into exile after the communists took power. He now
lives in California but still writes in Polish. After giving
a reading of his poetry in Washington, Milosz speaks
with Daniel Zwerdling about poetry and language.
April 17, 1994

MILOSZ: Occasionally, I write essays or articles in English,
but I write poetry only in Polish because I feel that poetry
should be written in the language of your childhood.

ZWERDLING: Why? What does it matter?

MILOSZ: Because it's a different, much more sensual approach to the language. You have a very intimate relationship
with words which you know since childhood.

ZWERDLING: On the one hand, you choose to write your
poems in Polish. On the other, you get frustrated at translating
them.

MILOSZ: Relatively, yes. Because a poem translated is never
the same poem, and some poems cannot be translated at all.
And that's a compromise, but if not for translations, I could not
have had any contact with American audiences. Now I have a
double life because I read poetry in America and I publish in
America, but also I go to Poland and read my poetry in the
original, and I publish in Polish.

ZWERDLING: You say that the poem never sounds quite as
good in English as it does in the original Polish. I was thinking
that, last night at the poetry reading. I loved the poems you read
in English, and when I've read them they've sounded wonderful
to me, but when you read one poem in Polish, I thought, That
sounds better. Would you read a poem for us?

MILOSZ: I could read "Blacksmith Shop." This is a poem about a childhood adventure. The working of a blacksmith's shop, for me, was a fascination.

> I liked the bellows operated by rope.
> A hand or foot pedal — I don't remember which.
> But that blowing, and the blazing of the fire!
> And a piece of iron in the fire, held there by tongs,
> Red, softened for the anvil,
> Beaten with a hammer, bent into a horseshoe,
> Thrown in a bucket of water, sizzle, steam.
>
> And horses hitched to be shod,
> Tossing their manes; and in the grass by the river
> Plowshares, sledge runners, barrows waiting for repair
>
> At the entrance, my bare feet on the dirt floor,
> Here, gusts of heat; at my back, white clouds.
> I stare and stare. It seems I was called for this:
> To glorify things just because they are.

ZWERDLING: I think Americans have this image of poets as tortured, hunched over the table, thinking profound thoughts, and obviously your poetry does have wonderful profound explorations in it, and people speak about the dialectical power of your poems — the moral weight and conviction — but what I love about your poetry is how sensual it is.

MILOSZ: Yes.

ZWERDLING: It's so accessible, it's so earthy. This "Blacksmith Shop" poem, I think, is an example. Your poetry is almost sexy sometimes.

MILOSZ: Yes, it's very erotic. That's not for the first time I hear that, but I have very, very few really strictly erotic poems about women. My attitude to the world is erotic.

ZWERDLING: What do you mean?

MILOSZ: To the world, namely to things, various things of this world.

ZWERDLING: I guess that's what you're saying here. "It

seems I was called for this: / To glorify things just because they are."

MILOSZ: Precisely, precisely.

ZWERDLING: You write a lot about food in your poems, too. Maybe that's one of the things that makes them erotic. Would you read this one, "A Confession"?

MILOSZ: Aha.

> My lord, I loved strawberry jam
> And the dark sweetness of a woman's body.
> Also well-chilled vodka, herring in olive oil,
> Scents of cinnamon, of cloves.
> So what kind of prophet am I? Why should the spirit
> Have visited such a man? Many others
> Were justly called, and trustworthy.
> Who would have trusted me? For they saw
> How I empty glasses, throw myself on food,
> And glance greedily at the waitress's neck.
> Flawed and aware of it. Desiring greatness,
> Able to recognize greatness wherever it is,
> And yet not quite, only in part, clairvoyant,
> I knew what was left for smaller men like me:
> A feast of brief hopes, a rally of the proud,
> A tournament of hunchbacks, literature.

ZWERDLING: The last couple of days, I keep saying those two lines to myself. "My lord, I loved strawberry jam / And the dark sweetness of a woman's body." To what extent do you think that it's important to have a rich, sensual life in order to have a rich, spiritual life?

MILOSZ: For me, it's very important not to be disembodied. I studied philosophy, but I forgot. [*laughs*] The problem is, I guess, to write philosophical problems without using the language of philosophy, but using the language of poetry. And the language of poetry is, by necessity, very sensual.

ZWERDLING: In "A Confession," a couple of other elements come out that I see in your poems, and maybe they're connected. One of them is the sense of inadequacy you express. At the end, you say, "I knew what was left for smaller men like me: / A tournament of hunchbacks." That's sort of a self-deprecating vision, isn't it?

MILOSZ: Modesty, not necessarily false modesty, because it extends to literature, to all writers.

ZWERDLING: But has that been an important part of your psyche, wondering from time to time, Am I wasting time?

MILOSZ: Yes, I would like to be somebody bigger than just a poet.

ZWERDLING: How would you be bigger? You won the Nobel Prize. You're one of the most famous poets in the world. What's bigger?

MILOSZ: A late friend of mine said, "You know, Czeslaw, every tragic actor dreams about a comic role and every nun would like to be a prostitute and every prostitute dreams about being a nun." Maybe I would like to be a saint, or a hero or something like that.

....

Liane Hansen interviews the cellist ELSA HILGER
during the week of her ninetieth birthday, an event she
celebrated by performing on the campus of St. Lawrence
University. Born in Prague and schooled at the Vienna
Conservatory, Elsa Hilger came to America in 1919.
In 1934, she was the first woman (aside from harpists)
to become a permanent member of a major symphony
orchestra. She was invited to join the Philadelphia
Orchestra by the conductor Leopold Stokowski.
April 17, 1994

HILGER: I knew his first wife, Olga Samaroff, very well, and
she called me up by phone, and said, "Elsa, dear, Mr. Stokowski
is looking for a first cellist, and he would like to hear you play.
Will you come, please, to Philadelphia" on the same day! I said,
"Look, this is an hour and a half drive from where we are, and
I'm in my housedress and slippers." She said, "Come as you are
but come right away because he's waiting for you." I played for
him on the stage of the Academy of Music for two hours, all solo
pieces. After the two hours, he says, "Fine, you're in. You're
engaged." That was it!

HANSEN: This was a big deal!

HILGER: Oh, it was.

HANSEN: Did you get a lot of attention because you were that
first woman?

HILGER: I had no idea what I was in for! Because then we gave
a lot of tours with the Philadelphia Orchestra, all the way to
California and back, everywhere. And always they had a big
article, usually in the front of the paper, about the first female
in any major orchestra, so I think they got their money's worth
out of that!

HANSEN: Were you accepted by the other members of the orchestra?

HILGER: Oh yes. Most of them heard me playing in solo concerts and recitals. They said, "Oh, we all know you're a wonderful cellist, but will you be able to hold up physically?" At that time, the Philadelphia Orchestra was the most touring orchestra in the whole world. We went everywhere. Every week, at least two, three days: Washington, Baltimore, New York, every week. They had no idea that I had traveled with my sisters from the East Coast to the West Coast, sometimes three times a year, and I did all the driving. I was used to driving two, three hundred miles a day and playing a concert in the evening. So I never missed a rehearsal or concert.

HANSEN: In thirty-five years, you never missed a rehearsal or a concert until you retired from the orchestra in 1969?

HILGER: Yes.

HANSEN: You did have stamina!

HILGER: Oh yes. Yes, they were amazed. They said, "We needn't have worried. You're better than us men!"

HANSEN: Tell us about your debut with the orchestra when someone behind you was playing a cello.

HILGER: Oh yes. Our first concert in Carnegie Hall. There was still Stokowski conducting. Just before he came out, the man behind me tuned a cello, and I didn't know him at all. So he tuned it, and I looked around, and I said, "Mmmm, that sounds nice." Then he played a few notes on it, and then I really turned around and looked at it, and said, "By God, that's my Guarnerius!" So I asked him about the cello. He said, "Miss Hilger, I really don't know. I'm only trying it out for somebody else who didn't want to play it this evening, not knowing the instrument." I said, "Well, look, you see it's a Guarnerius," and, of course, he gave me sort of a dirty look, but he did look. And there it was. He said, "How could you have known?" I said, "This is the cello that I had from the age of twelve, and it was stolen from me." I said in the intermission, "Please don't get away. I must play on the cello to make one hundred percent sure it is mine." So in the intermission I went to the artist's room and he brought the cello, and I played on it all the cadenzas that I could think of, most difficult stuff, and all the cellists stood around, and said, "It must be your cello. You couldn't possibly play like this on an instrument you don't know." So that was it. That was the cello.

HANSEN: Did you get it back?

HILGER: Yes!

HANSEN: Do you play that cello today?

HILGER: No, my grandson has it.

HANSEN: You've also played with Albert Einstein?!

HILGER: Oh yes! That was very interesting.

HANSEN: Was he a good musician?

HILGER: Wonderful. We were surprised because we never even heard that he played. We played several Beethoven string quartets. We had such a good time. We had dinner with him, and we were invited back and all that. And he heard about my cello being stolen and he was absolutely enraged. Do you want to hear a few words of what he writes?

HANSEN: Yes, sure.

HILGER: Here we go. "Dear Ladies, With pain and outrage I see from your letter what a difficult robbery, a dreadful robbery, was practiced upon you. I wish for nothing more longingly than for you to obtain your beautiful instrument back soon," and so forth. He writes more, and then he says, "In friendship with the best wishes," personally signed, "Albert Einstein."

HANSEN: What a nice friend to have!

HILGER: Yes!

HANSEN: Are there things you still wish to accomplish on your instrument?

HILGER: Well, I'll tell you, my manager tapes every concert we play. Sometimes we don't even wait, we listen right after the concert to what we did, and then we try and hear what we didn't like too much and try to do it better the next concert. We do that every time. So you try to get better and better. That's the only way.

HANSEN: Even after playing the instrument for over eighty years?

HILGER: Oh, yes, you can always learn something. For instance, Bach. Especially Bach. You're never finished with Bach. There's so much in his music that it has to be brought out because he just wrote the notes. He didn't even put dynamics in, or bowings or anything.

HANSEN: Do you think you're close to being able to bring it out?

HILGER: I think so. I think I'm getting better at it.

In the novel *A Way in the World*, the Trinidadian-born writer V. S. NAIPAUL employs both historical characters and fictional ones so convincing that readers have difficulty distinguishing between the two. In an interview with Robert Siegel, Naipaul reads a passage about the work of a fictional novelist, an English writer named Foster Morris. Naipaul attributes to Morris a book about Trinidad in the late 1930s called *The Shadowed Livery*. And in the passage, Naipaul faults the fictional Briton for what he fails to understand about the people of Trinidad. May 23, 1994

NAIPAUL: [*reading*] "He wrote of them with the utmost seriousness. He gave them families, backgrounds; he treated what they said without irony. Nothing like this had been written about local people before. He wrote of them as though they were English people — as though they had that kind of social depth and solidity and rootedness.

"It was well-intentioned, but it was wrong. Some of the people he wrote admiringly about, like certain lawyers and teachers, were even embarrassed by Foster Morris's misplaced social tributes. What was missing from Foster Morris's view was what we all lived with: the sense of the absurd, the idea of comedy, which hid from us our true position. The social depth he gave to ordinary people didn't make sense. That idea of a background — and what it contained: order and values and the possibility of striving: perfectibility — made sense only when people were more truly responsive for themselves. We weren't responsible in that way. Much had been taken out of our hands. We didn't have backgrounds. We didn't have a past. For most of us the past stopped with our grandparents; beyond that was a blank. If you could look down at us from the sky you would see us living in our little houses between the sea and the bush; and that was a kind of truth about us, who had been transported to that place. We were just there, floating.''

SIEGEL: "We," in this case, were the people who lived in Trinidad. In your case, Asian Indians, but also the descendants of slaves and Spaniards who'd settled.

NAIPAUL: Yes.

SIEGEL: New World people.

NAIPAUL: New World people, yes.

SIEGEL: It seems that this is something about the people of this hemisphere. You're saying that we're new. We don't have the solidity that an Englishman might expect to find in everyone.

NAIPAUL: In his own country, yes. In Trinidad, after the destruction of the aboriginal people, there was wilderness, and then on that wilderness, late in the eighteenth century, there began to be created a plantation. I fear that is how we have to think of the place. It can't be a country in the way you would think of Persia as a country or Turkey as a country or even Kazakhstan as a country. The place is a plantation, and I think this is where all inquiry must begin, with that fact.

SIEGEL: I'd like to ask you about something that a few of the New World characters — or Old World characters who come to visit the Western Hemisphere — do in your book, which is, when not in Trinidad they invent things about themselves. They lie. They make up stories of ranks they held in armies, and universities they studied at, and gold they found. Is that part of what's happening there? Was this a place where people could come and make elegant fictions about their lives?

NAIPAUL: I think this is one of the most noticeable features about that part of the world. It's not only the Europeans who did that. When I was growing up, I was aware that people like us, who were not conquistadors or travelers, who were just there as workers, whose ancestors went there as workers, we too could begin to manufacture stories of our ancestry. People could claim to be of noble origin, although their ancestors had come from India as indentured agricultural workers. In a way it is the human wish to escape. There are certain circumstances in which the only way you can be human and proclaim your humanity is by lying about yourself, by having such regard for yourself that you create a lie for yourself. It's very odd. The truth is wonderful in certain societies, but in some places it isn't wonderful. I mean, why tell the truth in a work camp? In a gulag? There's no point in telling the truth.

SIEGEL: Your background, as someone born in Trinidad of Asian Indian family and then having gone off to Oxford and having taught in Africa, makes you in many ways a very inconvenient witness to events. You had to witness the East African oppression of Asians, for example. The people who stood in the way of nationalist ideologies, both in the Caribbean and in East Africa, were people, very broadly speaking, of your ethnic —

NAIPAUL: That's true, absolutely. Yes, especially in the two important ones, Trinidad and Guyana.

SIEGEL: You have a character who is asked why he doesn't "write about the Negroes," but to many of us in America it's the Asians who are much more ignored, forgotten. We can more easily understand black and white than we can understand the people who came from families like your own to work in tea plantations.

NAIPAUL: Yes. We're too small a community. The world is such a big place. We can't afford to pay attention to all communities everywhere. Our capacity is limited, after all. Our capacity of knowledge and interest is limited.

But a point about what you said earlier: "inconvenient witness." I would say rather fair witness, as it turns out. You mentioned East Africa. I went there sixty-five, sixty-six, and the book I began to write three years later blended elements of Rwanda, Kenya, Uganda, and Tanganyika.

SIEGEL: Was this *In a Free State*?

NAIPAUL: Yes. I was very disturbed by what I saw there. I

saw dictatorships and I saw all kinds of political absurdities and lies. I saw disaster to come. And the book I wrote was an extraordinarily prescient foreshadowing of someone like Idi Amin. If that book had been taken more seriously, if people in 1970, 1971, weren't dealing with this other fantasy of Africa, they probably wouldn't have encouraged Amin so much, and that terror, that mass murder that went on in Uganda, might not have taken place.

The people who ran down that particular vision as being inconvenient have said nothing about Uganda. I think that what is wrong about the running down of this independent vision is that people seldom stay with the story. They feel that their principles are being violated by what the writer is saying and then they stop listening. I met a West German woman who told me with some pride that at one time she had been a communist, although living in the West. She said this with pride because it was for her a mark of intellectual attainment, and when she was faced with things that were inconvenient, she ignored them. If someone began to talk about what had gone wrong with Castro's Cuba, she would leave the hall. She would close her mind. There is a totalitarian attitude in people who have views about the glorious future of, shall we say, Islamic Fundamentalism or African territories. So I'm not an inconvenient witness. My work lives according to how true it is, and if twenty years or so after I've written something it still can offend people, largely because it appears to attack certain things, I wouldn't call that inconvenient. I would call that comforting in that there was a witness who saw it. It didn't go by unnoticed.

Liane Hansen interviews the bassist MIKE GORDON and
the singer-guitarist TREY ANASTASIO, who, together
with the drummer Jon Fishman and the keyboardist Page
McConnell, form the Vermont-based quartet Phish, a
group whose fans are so dedicated they are compared to
the Deadheads, who follow the Grateful Dead. Anastasio
and Gordon talk about how they try to stay fresh after
playing together for ten years and about their 1994
album, *Hoist.* October 23, 1994

ANASTASIO: Tom Marshall had written a long poem, and
the last line was "God never listens to what I say / That you
don't get a refund if you overpray." We got on the phone one
day, and we said, "Let's write a song together, written from the
point of view of someone who would be saying that line," and
the whole thing grew. We were on the phone for hours, and it
was a teamwork kind of thing. We were bouncing ideas off each
other, and after the phone conversation was over, the song was
written, music and lyrics. Bela Fleck played on that one, and we
wanted to put him in an atmosphere where it would be the last
song that you would expect to hear banjo on, banjo being such
a happy instrument, and it's such a sad song. It was a real challenge for him to fit the banjo into that very slow, sad, sweet kind
of song, and he was incredible.

HANSEN: There's so much interesting music on this album
and the other ones you've done. It's a very eclectic mix of music. Trey, you've been quoted as saying it's "East Coast rock-
a-suey"? I'm afraid to ask what that means.

ANASTASIO: It's kind of a cross between that and rock-
donkey-dunkle.

HANSEN: Rock what?

ANASTASIO: Rock-donkey-dunkle.

HANSEN: Yes.

ANASTASIO: [*laughs*] It's a little country, a little — the thing was that the four of us all had very different influences when we got together, and none of us were willing to give them up, so instead we decided to try to meld them.

HANSEN: How much were you all influenced by Frank Zappa?

ANASTASIO: Lots, particularly myself and Fish, our drummer. I remember following Zappa around for a week or so at one point back when he was still touring a lot. I always liked any kind of improvised live music, be it Frank Zappa or the Dead or jazz, and I think that's the one love that we all shared.

HANSEN: The thing about Frank Zappa's improvised music is there was a certain control to it, a certain discipline, whereas a lot of improvisation can end up being rather self-indulgent.

ANASTASIO: Yes, absolutely. We actually have exercises that we do where we work on improving our improvising as a group. It's an exercise to get rid of the ego, and the more we do it, the more we find that our improvisations are less concerned with showing off flashy solos and more concerned with making a group sound. There's the feeling that we talked about when we toured with Santana. He had brought up this thing about the hose. I don't know if you've heard about that.

HANSEN: No, I haven't.

ANASTASIO: It's where the music is like water rushing through you and, as a musician, your function is really like that of a hose. The audience is like a sea of flowers, and you're watering the audience. The concept is of music going through you, that you're not actually creating it, that the best thing that you can do is get out of the way. When you're in a room full of people, there's this kind of group vibe that seems to get rolling sometimes.

GORDON: It really starts to seem like it's not the audience or the band. This thing that gets rolling is its own thing. When things are going really well and a jam has taken off, there's this feeling of motion that is created by the rhythm and at that point my bass feels like this sort of vehicle or a hitch for me to hold on to.

HANSEN: Sounds like water-skiing.

GORDON: Like if you were on a ski lift maybe, a chair lift or something that would hook you on to the motion that's going and pull you along with it.

ANASTASIO: And I think the proof of it is that there are times when you just can't pull it together, and you try and try and try, and you're beating your head against the wall, and it's just not happening, and that kind of shows right there that you can't pull it. It's got to pull you.

HANSEN: Is this true: Do you allow people who come to your concert to actually bring a tape recorder with them?

ANASTASIO: Oh yes. We sell special taping tickets through mail order, and people can bring their gear, and they tape, and they have been for the whole ten years.

HANSEN: So there are bootlegs of your concerts, but it doesn't bother you? It doesn't matter?

ANASTASIO: No, as a matter of fact, it's been the key to our existence, I think, because the live show has always been so much a part of what we do, so much a focus of our energy, and the shows are different every night. People have been trading tapes and before we ever even signed with a major label. We were touring the whole country just in our van, and there were no records available of Phish at all. It was purely through tapes being traded and word of mouth. It's always been a real underground phenomenon, and the taping has been such a big part of it that it would be pretty strange for us to stop it now. It keeps you on your toes. You can't do the same show twice. You can't tell the same joke twice. You can't do anything twice because everybody knows. They use the computer networks, the Phish.Net, to start tape trees, and you might play a show in South Carolina or something like that, and a week later you're playing in Phoenix, Arizona, and everybody there has heard the tape: "Oh, I heard you did such and such a thing in South Carolina." So you can't do it again.

HANSEN: That's bound to keep you fresh, exciting, energetic, alive.

ANASTASIO: It really does. That's why I say it's the key to what we are, because I'm sure there are times when we would have just fallen back on our past successes. "Oh, well, it worked last time. Let's do that again." But you really can never do that, and that's great. You just have to keep thinking of something new.

TELEVISION, RADIO, AND FILM

....

On the fortieth anniversary of one of Edward R. Murrow's
most historic broadcasts, Bob Edwards interviews the
producer of the March 9, 1954, CBS program *See It Now*.
The program exposed the tactics of Senator Joseph
McCarthy and led to his downfall as the most vocal and
unscrupulous anti-Communist in Washington. The
producer of *See It Now*, FRED FRIENDLY, went on to
become president of CBS News.
March 9, 1994

FRIENDLY: Everybody was scared of Senator McCarthy. Senators were scared. Congressmen were scared. Politicians were
scared. The people were scared. A friend of Murrow's jumped off
a building and died because Senator McCarthy, who didn't
know what he was talking about, said he was a Communist.
That was the world of 1954.

EDWARDS: When did you and Murrow decide you had to go
after McCarthy?

FRIENDLY: In the early part of 1954. Murrow and I began
making film wherever Senator McCarthy went. If he went to
Baltimore, we got that. If he went to New York, we did that.
If he went to California, we photographed that. We were developing a big library of Senator McCarthy, his meanness, his
anger.

EDWARDS: You did so with no small risk. You had a sponsor.
You had network executives like William Paley and Frank Stan-
ton, who probably were not terribly pleased with what you were
doing.

FRIENDLY: Well, they didn't really know what was going on.
We had a budget number of everything that we photographed of
Senator McCarthy, and one day in early January somebody

came down to us and said, "What is this budget number?" I said, "I can't tell you." We didn't want anybody at CBS to know we were doing it because we were fearful that somebody would say stop.

EDWARDS: The program is largely McCarthy himself. It's not a lot of narrative. It's McCarthy in various speeches, doing what McCarthy did.

FRIENDLY: I remember Murrow saying at the beginning of the program, "This is a portrait of Senator McCarthy told in the words and face of Senator McCarthy." It was a picture of McCarthy for the people to judge for themselves, a half hour long.

EDWARDS: With a close by Murrow.

FRIENDLY: Best closing ever done by Murrow.

EDWARDS: A very strong statement, much stronger than any reporter or even a commentator has been heard to say on television since.

FRIENDLY: That's a very interesting point. People don't do what Murrow used to do. Murrow explained what the terror of Senator McCarthy was, and the American people listened to Murrow. There was nobody like Murrow in those days, and there has not been since.

EDWARDS: You gave McCarthy time for rebuttal, and he went right at Murrow the way he did a lot of other people: past associations and the like and implying that — well, he didn't imply; he said they were Communists.

FRIENDLY: There's an interesting moment I'd like to tell you about. We edited our programs and put them on the air from 550 Fifth Avenue, and I remember Murrow and I turning to our staff of editors, and saying, "Senator McCarthy is going to attack us tomorrow if we do this program, and he's not going to attack the staff, he's not going to attack Friendly, he's going to attack Edward R. Murrow. Now, if any of you know anything about yourselves that Senator McCarthy would grab on to, this is the time to tell it to Ed so he knows what the ambush will be." We went around the room. One person said he had a wife who had been a member of the Communists, but they were divorced. I said I grew up in Providence, Rhode Island, and my name was Ferdinand Wachenheimer, and when I got into broadcasting in Providence, I changed my name to my mother's name, and I became Fred Friendly. Imagine me having to explain that to Murrow and the other people. And every reporter talked about his anguish. Finally, it came to Murrow. He had a cigarette in his mouth, both his hands on his knees, and he looked up, and he said, "The terror is right here in this room. Let's do the program." And that was that. I remember that moment forty years ago.

Scott Simon interviews RICHARD HARRIS, the Irish-born actor, aged between sixty-one and sixty-five (depending on the biography), about a career that included such roles as King Arthur in *Camelot*; the foppish gunslinger English Bob in *Unforgiven*; Macbeth; King Richard the Lion-Hearted in *Robin and Marian*; and Bull McCabe in *The Field*; as well as recording the 1968 song "MacArthur Park," regarded by the humorist Dave Barry as the worst record ever made. Harris also discusses his 1994 role as the Old Testament patriarch Abraham in a TNT television film. March 26, 1994

HARRIS: If there is any slight regret in my life, it's that I think I would have been a great Hamlet, one of the great Hamlets.

SIMON: May I ask, are you too old to play Hamlet?

HARRIS: No. *Hamlet*'s not about age. It's about the reading. It all depends how you approach it. Yes, of course, I would appear to be far too old. Who would play my mother?

SIMON: I've got to ask, Mr. Harris, and I don't mean this facetiously, did you read the book before you took the part of Abraham?

HARRIS: Well, yes, I knew it. I was a Catholic brought up by the Jesuits, which is somewhat of a classical education. But even apart from that, I knew the story of Abraham, maybe not as well as I knew it by the time this picture was over.

I wasn't overly enthusiastic to accept the part at the beginning. In fact, I wasn't going to do it at all. I was asked why, and I raised all the reservations I had against it. I didn't want to make it a political document, which the Bible could tend to be, nor to make it a religious document, which Abraham's story was not because religion didn't exist then, because it was a polytheistic society. I wanted to make it a spiritual experience. That's two points. Three points was that when Hollywood ventured into the Bible, the actor playing Abraham would either play him as a rebel, a hero, or a saint. I said I would do none of that. I wanted to play him as a simple guy who was chosen, and he had doubts all his life that the visitation, the voice, was God. It could have been the devil or could have been hallucinations. I wanted to make sure. I wanted to play him as a man not born to greatness, but a man whom greatness was thrust upon.

SIMON: Let me ask you a few questions, while I have the chance, that have sort of been accumulating for years.

HARRIS: Yes.

SIMON: That last note in "MacArthur Park" —

HARRIS: Yes.

SIMON: How did you hit it and how did you hold it?

HARRIS: The secret of electronics. They can take your voice and lift it up and hold it there. But I think in those days I could hit notes.

SIMON: But did they electronicize it somehow?

HARRIS: Yes, they did, of course they did.

SIMON: They do everything.

HARRIS: Yes, of course they did. They can do anything they like now.

SIMON: You've had an extraordinary run in recent years between *Unforgiven* and *Wrestling Ernest Hemingway*.

HARRIS: And *The Field*.

SIMON: And *The Field*, of course.

HARRIS: My favorite.

SIMON: When you played English Bob in *Unforgiven*, was any of your depiction based on the fact that you were an Irishman who had grown up observing Englishmen?

HARRIS: Totally. You know, our history is based upon people like that: out of jails, the Black and Tans. The English opened up their jails and sent over murderers and rapists to Ireland to fight the battles against the Irish resistance. The whole history of our country was, you know, giving away large portions of land to really illiterate slobs like English Bob. So I knew exactly how to play him and what a fake he was. And what a coward I made him. I was determined to do that.

SIMON: Did you take some satisfaction in that?

HARRIS: I did. I wish Hackman had beat him up more. I loved the part, hated the character, though, which is good. The worst thing for an actor is to be indifferent. So there was no indifference to that.

SIMON: I heard from a director once that if you're going to play an ogre you make a mistake by playing the hate. You have to play the hurt.

HARRIS: I don't know. There is a terrific tendency in America at the moment, in the American cinema, in the American theater, when playing a character who's evil, if you like, the actors, in doing their method background, want to emphasize the fact that they're really human beings, you know, and they're really nice. It's their own ego intervening in the creative process. There are evil guys in the world.

SIMON: Over the years you've made somewhat more than fifty films, but I've read that you've only really liked a few.

HARRIS: I would have thought about six. I did six, five or six, great pictures and the rest were really rubbish. *Sporting Life* I liked, *The Molly Maguires* I loved. *The Snow Goose* for television, *The Field, Hemingway,* I adored. I fought just to make *A Man Called Horse.* Every actor in Hollywood turned it down, and I said, "No, I'm going to make it," against the advice of all my agents who said "Don't." I said, "I'm going to make it." Why? Because I understand the oppression, being Irish, and I know what they went through, and I think that it's about time that the American Indian was dignified. For that alone, I'm happy I did that. *Cromwell* I thought was a great movie, and maybe *Camelot.* I don't know, it was a bit romantic. I don't even classify that as a great picture. But that's about it. The rest were rubbish.

SIMON: Why did you make rubbish?

HARRIS: We were working. We'd jobs to do. We've got children to educate and so forth, and also there came a stage, really, in my life when I think living was my vocation and acting became an avocation.

SIMON: Living?

HARRIS: Living. I was going to have a good time. Drinking as much as I could, making the girls as much as I could, enjoying life. This is not a rehearsal, this is it, and I wanted to get it all in, take it all in. I wanted to savor everything that was possible. And acting was was one of them, but not a priority either.

SIMON: Now, I hate to sound like a parson, but do you regret any of that, looking back?

HARRIS: No, not at all. Some guy said to me today, "Well, that was odd casting. Casting you as Abraham after the life you've lived." He said, "That Rabelaisian runaround that you gave every bar and every girl in town. That was a strange casting." But the point is, Did I pull the part off? Did I convince you? Did I make you believe in the dilemma that this man had, the fears he had, the weaknesses he had? I think so. I think I pulled it off.

SIMON: Do you want to work more now than you have in recent years?

HARRIS: No. I'm definitely not going to do any more of, you know, that period in my life about ten years when I just did anything. I didn't care about it, but those days are over. I'm not ambitious the way I was. I don't need to work anymore. Let's put it that way.

SIMON: When you say, "I don't need to work anymore," are you talking just financially or —

HARRIS: Yes, I don't have to work.

SIMON: But I'm wondering. A man who says, "I might, on the surface of things, be too old to play Hamlet," you must be wondering a little bit about what kind of reputation you finally rest with as an actor?

HARRIS: I've got to tell you, I'm not into it. Why would it worry me after I'm gone? I won't be around to observe what people say about me. Look what they say about me now, for God's sake, and I'm alive! A lot of it's not very complimentary, you know, so why would I worry about it after I'm dead?

Daniel Zwerdling examines a British television rendering of American television in *The United States of Television*, a series on Britain's Channel 4. The series coproducer FENTON BAILEY says he wants to give British viewers a glimpse of the wonders American television has to offer. March 19, 1994

BAILEY: In England we really only have four channels, and TV there is supposed to educate and entertain the audience. We don't have anything to compare with the sheer abundance and variety of American television.

ZWERDLING: So what you're telling me is that the British are intellectually impoverished. Right? You can't channel-surf.

BAILEY: In America people watch television in a completely different way than they do in England. In England the idea is that you watch a program from beginning to end. It's like the idea that you should read a book from beginning to end. But in America you have five hundred channels. Well, you don't have quite five hundred, but hundreds.

ZWERDLING: OK, but in this show, you are not just skipping around. You're finding stuff I've never seen. One group of TV excerpts that you have are ads for guns.

BAILEY: That's a clip from a home video, which is called "Sexy Girls and Sexy Guns."

ZWERDLING: Bikini-clad women wearing spike high heels. They're firing machine guns. As the women are firing away, the screen is flashing vital statistics. "Adrienne, five-four, 105 pounds," it says. "Thirty-four, twenty-four, thirty-four."

BAILEY: We weren't looking for the everyday. I mean, we didn't take clips from American football. We have American football in England. The idea is that we do the zapping for you, and we're going to search out the bits and pieces, the nuggets that you might not find yourself.

ZWERDLING: Here's another nugget I've never seen, a hate-mongering talk show. I guess that's a judgmental phrase, but let's call it what it is, a hatemongering talk show, starring a guy named Wally.

BAILEY: The *Wally George Show* is fascinating because it's been on the air now for ten years, and the interesting thing about that show is that it precedes the ultraright TV of Rush Limbaugh.

ZWERDLING: You also found TV evangelist preachers rather interesting, especially one selling his videos. When these evangelists get on stage and make their pitch, how does the average British brain react to them, do you think?

BAILEY: The average British brain believes that their television is the best television in the world. What inspired us to make this series was to show them that this, in fact, wasn't the case. The average British brain takes great pride in the fact that it doesn't have a great deal of choice. In England, they tend to believe that less television is more television.

ZWERDLING: I wonder if showing a lot of these really bizarre clips, though, is going to prove the British nationalist point that their television is better?

BAILEY: I don't know if it really plays into the hands of that argument. In the end, people have enjoyed watching this show tremendously. I think that that's always worth remembering. No matter how much one pours scorn or contempt on some-thing, people at the end of the day like to watch it, and that's what really counts.

ZWERDLING: I would be doing a terrible disservice to our listeners if I did not mention the aerobics show of a woman in a black leotard. Her hair is dyed orange, and she's praising the Lord as she does leg lifts.

BAILEY: Yes, the interesting thing about that show that struck us was that most workout shows are huffing and puffing and doing the moves, but she's giving a workout for the soul at the same time as the workout for the body.

ZWERDLING: Where can I see that one?

BAILEY: You know, you've got me there! I'm not quite sure. We have something like 250 clips, which we whittled down from about 1,200 different possibilities. Somewhere along the line it becomes a bit of a blur. But she's out there.

Scott Simon — making no attempt to conceal his intense admiration — interviews JULIE ANDREWS on the occasion of the release of a new recording, *Broadway: The Music of Richard Rodgers*. Simon asks Andrews about her career, the characters she has played and — with great delicacy — the one film in which she bared her breasts. October 29, 1994

SIMON: The Mary Poppins, Maria Von Trapp image notwithstanding, you were not a governess but a child of vaudeville.

ANDREWS: Right. It was extraordinary that those two roles very nearly gave me an image for life of a snippy lady who looks after the children and so on.

SIMON: Oh, not snippy. You were a lot of fun.

ANDREWS: Well, Mary Poppins was a little snippy. Let's face it.

SIMON: Is it true you began singing during the Blitz in a tube station?

ANDREWS: No, that's a slight P.R. overstatement. It was during the Blitz. My school had closed down, and for a while we were evacuated to the country and so on.

SIMON: I've seen this movie.

ANDREWS: No, I was underfoot and a real pest. I had a fairly new stepfather. My mother had remarried, and he was a fine singer. My mother played the piano, and they were in vaudeville.

SIMON: He was called the Canadian Troubadour.

ANDREWS: That's exactly right. Gosh, you have done your homework. As much to keep me quiet, so to speak, and shut me up and give me something to do — I think he also wanted to try to get close to this stepdaughter, who was very wary and not welcoming at all — he started to give me singing lessons, which I hated. To everyone's surprise, including mine, they discovered I had a freak adult voice, and it sort of went on from there.

SIMON: You had and, I imagine, still have, this extraordinary range that people write about.

ANDREWS: I don't know if it's that extraordinary anymore, because as you grow older your range does shift and alter and so on, but, in all honesty, I'm enjoying my voice these days because I know better how to phrase, better how to present a song, I hope. Certainly that's what I've been hoping to do is to grow and learn and improve.

SIMON: I do have to ask you about this image of purity and innocence, if I might. Did it take a director to whom you happened to be married, Blake Edwards, a director with that special knowledge of you, to put you into films where you could portray the tougher, more glamorous but more determined side of you?

ANDREWS: That's a hard question to answer. It's a lengthy question, and I'll try to make it as short as possible. Yes and no is the answer —

SIMON: Thanks for clearing that up after all these years.

ANDREWS: It's as simple as this. I was aware that great roles, wonderful scripts, don't just come across your desk every day of the week, and I was lucky enough to get *Mary Poppins* and subsequently *Sound of Music.* In between that, I was trying to change my image. I did a little black-and-white movie called *The Americanization of Emily.* The thrill for me is to do as much that is as varied as possible. It's such fun to embrace new things. But because of the enormous profile of those first two blockbusters, people were inclined to bracket me, and even though I was trying to not just be put into one little pigeonhole, it did take Blake Edwards — I guess he does know me better than anybody else — to allow me to do some other things.

SIMON: He hasn't spent twenty-five years married to Maria Von Trapp?

ANDREWS: Oh God, I hope not.

SIMON: What a discovery to make.

ANDREWS: You'll have to ask Blake, but, boy, based on our everyday existence, I don't think it's quite that.

SIMON: Well, when you made the film *S.O.B.* for your husband, Blake Edwards, which I thought was —

ANDREWS: That's a slightly different image right there, you know.

SIMON: You know the scene I'm thinking about.

ANDREWS: No, I don't, Scott. Which one could you possibly be thinking about?

SIMON: I cannot bring myself to say this to Julie Andrews. I'm sorry. There's a special spot in hell for the man who talks this way to Julie Andrews.

ANDREWS: That's funny.

SIMON: I will explain for the benefit of people who haven't been fortunate enough to see the film. It's a very dark, edgy satire of Hollywood and the film business, and you portray filmdom's sweetheart. Let's put it that way.

ANDREWS: I'm just keeping quiet here and letting you drown, Scott.

SIMON: Thank you. Who has a dark, edgy side. And at one point in the script, you are — everybody in the control room, by the way, is hoping I drown before I get this question out. At one point, you, portraying a character, open your blouse.

ANDREWS: Oh, come on. I expect better of you than that.

SIMON: Your breasts are seen on camera.

ANDREWS: Right, exactly.

SIMON: And I remember Roger Ebert wrote, "If you love Julie Andrews, prepare yourself for a shocker when she bares all." I don't know if that was supposed to deter us from going to the film, but I want to tell you, I went to the theater as fast as I could.

ANDREWS: That's my boy. Good for you.

SIMON: Well, was that supposed to be some sort of, I don't

know, declaration of independence? Was it supposed to be a shockeroo?

ANDREWS: No, listen, for about ten years, he had been trying to get that movie made, and when he first wrote it, I thought, "Well, we'll just see how that turns out. It may get deleted from the script. Who knows?"

SIMON: Did he write it for you?

ANDREWS: Yes, he did. Well, it was about me and my image, if you think about it.

SIMON: Yes, of course.

ANDREWS: A goody-goody lady who tries to change her image by doing a sort of pornographic movie. And you know what? It wasn't gratuitous. It was part of what was really needed for the character. It really was an acting chore as much as anything else. And at the preview, the whole audience broke into this huge round of applause, and I wasn't sure if it was for my boobs or my performance, you know.

SIMON: Oh, I'm sure it was for your performance.

ANDREWS: Well, of course, yes. Yes, we know that.

SIMON: Could you tell me the story about being a young actress? I forget if it was in London or New York at that point, but you met Richard Rodgers, and he asked if you had anything on your plate at the moment.

ANDREWS: Oh, that's right. I was auditioning for a show he was about to do called *Pipe Dream*, and I sang for him. I wasn't sure what he thought, and he said, "Have you been auditioning for anything else? Is there anything else out there?" And I said, "Oh, well, they're making a musical of Shaw's *Pygmalion*, and they're going to call it *My Fair Lady*. And, yes, I have auditioned for Mr. Lerner and Mr. Loewe." And he was quite quiet for a moment, and then he said, "I'm going to say something." He said, "If they ask you to do it, I think you should, but if they don't ask you to do it, will you please let me know because we would like very much to use you?" And I thought that was so incredibly generous. So thank you, Mr.

Rodgers, very, very much for guiding me to do *My Fair Lady*.

SIMON: Of course, you know I'm going to ask this. Does a spoonful of sugar really help the medicine go down?

ANDREWS: Do you know, I think it does. To my surprise and delight, I've discovered that when you have to take something awful, for God's sake, take a bit of honey or something with it.

....

Sister Wendy's Odyssey, the most successful BBC arts television program after Kenneth Clark's *Civilisation,* was followed by *Sister Wendy's Grand Tour: A Visit to the Great Art Works of Europe.* Sister WENDY BECKETT, a South African–born nun, lived a cloistered life in an English convent for twenty-two years before going to observe and reflect on the art she had studied in books. A book accompanies the television series and prompts this interview with Scott Simon. March 19, 1994

SIMON: You wrote about art for years, but is it true that you had only seen postcards before the BBC took you off to see the great artworks of Europe?

BECKETT: Yes, that is true, postcards and books. And let me assure you it's a very good way to get to know great art.

SIMON: How so?

BECKETT: Well, think of the ordinary museum experience. Your feet hurt, you're hot, there are lots of other people there. There are other artworks crowding round. Whereas, if you have a postcard, you can sit in your own room in silence and in peace and really contemplate the work seriously.

SIMON: I want to ask you about a number of paintings, for example, Botticelli's famous *Birth of Venus.* It hangs in Florence, and it is Venus coming out of what nowadays we'd identify as a seashell, beautiful in her nakedness, except her nakedness is covered by her long russet hair.

BECKETT: But what makes that picture to me so poignant is that she's moving towards the shore, and waiting for her on the shore is a nymph with a cloak, because we are afraid to look at naked beauty. We're frightened of beauty.

SIMON: What is beauty?

BECKETT: I think beauty is a reflection of the light of God. I can't give you a better definition than that. It's one of the ways in which we can come close to understanding the numinous mystery in which we have our being.

SIMON: There are some of us who find it difficult to see in our own nakedness, much less anybody else's, something of beauty. We welcome that cloak.

BECKETT: It's not so much that the body has to be clothed, it's that beauty has to be clothed. T. S. Eliot said, "Man cannot bear very much reality." In that sense the beauty, the holiness of life, is something so overwhelming that we wrap it up, we diminish it. It's not the nakedness we can't see, it's beauty as such. Is that clear, or have I put it clumsily?

SIMON: No, you've put it very well. You certainly realize that there are people in your audience that think it's very humorous to hear a nun talking about nakedness.

BECKETT: This has puzzled me because, after all, who made the body? I mean, if God didn't think the body was a good and beautiful thing, He wouldn't have started it in the first place. He would have joined our head to our feet and stuck hands where our ears were, or something like that, but He lovingly crafted this delicate piece of machinery, and I think it's very irreverent not to praise Him for what He's done.

SIMON: Why is it, Sister Wendy — the question is irresistible — that your Church, then, will put nuns of your order in a habit that deliberately, near as one can gather, deemphasizes the contours of the body?

BECKETT: Well, the Church doesn't do it. It's the choice of the individual orders. And I can tell you that I'm very, very grateful for the habit, because its main function is it saves us from having to bother about what we're going to wear every day. All your psychic energy can be given to loving God instead of having to think out, What skirt, what coat, how will you do your hair, what shoes? It's a great simplifier.

SIMON: You write in the introduction to your book — and, of course, the grand tour on which you went to see the great artworks of Europe is, for many, the fruition of a dream — but you write that delightful as it was, "It did not improve on the joys of solitude and prayer."

BECKETT: Yes, very true.

SIMON: You actually have the audacity to write that Paris somewhat disappointed you.

BECKETT: Yes, everyone was disappointed in me being disappointed, I'm sorry to say.

SIMON: I'm not sure I've ever asked this question before. What was there about Paris that disappointed you, Sister Wendy?

BECKETT: I found it so noisy and crowded. There seemed to be a lot of big, heavy buildings everywhere. We couldn't get taxis easily. I did a lot of painful walking and trying to get tubes. I'm sure I was wrong. Also, perhaps, I had had too glorious an idea of Paris, you know, the sun-dappled light and the green trees and all the young love around. It just seemed to be a hardworking city with anxious people. I saw the wrong Paris, obviously.

SIMON: Well, I hope you don't see New York.

BECKETT: I have been to New York.

SIMON: And?

BECKETT: It was a lovely city. What I would love in New York would be for somebody to get some kind of little wagon so I could lie down and be drawn through the streets so I could really enjoy the skyscrapers properly.

SIMON: [laughs] Just look up at the skyscrapers?

BECKETT: Yes, because they're beautiful buildings.

SIMON: Let me ask you about a few more works of art, if I can. *Peasant Wedding*, Pieter Brueghel the Elder: it's a wedding, and you detail the idea that it's an arranged wedding. This is not a moment of great happiness, necessarily, so much as it's a business transaction.

BECKETT: That's right. It's a sale. The young woman — the poor, pathetic little creature, her face lit up with a kind of almost imbecilic smile — this is her great day, and she has no concept of what's actually happening. It's a very, very sad picture. And it has always fascinated art historians that you can't see the husband anywhere, and I think that's one of Brueghel's subtle points, you see. It doesn't really matter who she is marrying. She's just getting married.

SIMON: Now, there is a man holding a set of bagpipes, looking longingly over at the food as it's being borne to the table, and I must say the first time I saw a print of this I had something of a comic reaction, "My, that man looks hungry." But you have a different reaction.

BECKETT: Is it funny that somebody should be hungry?

SIMON: No, it's not, but I thought —

BECKETT: You see, he was really hungry. And if you look at what's being served at the marriage banquet, it's some kind of porridge or custard. It's the food of the very poorest. And the people at the table are eating with avidity. These are the peasants who don't get enough to eat. And the poor bagpiper will probably be paid for his bagpiping at the end with a dish, and, to me, it's one of the most poignant looks in the whole of art, the way the eyes on that dark, unshaven face follow so longingly the pathetic plates of porridge being carried past him. I think that the more you look at it, the more it gains a kind of moral stature. He does smile, but he smiles with that kind of twisted smile of somebody who knows these people are poor. And we are not poor and we're responsible. He's a deeply moral artist, Brueghel.

SIMON: Sister Wendy, how do we open ourselves up to the appreciation of art in our lives?

BECKETT: I think we have to feel that it matters, that this is something that can make us more truly human. Because we get what we want in life, you know, and if we want to be more truly human, then we'll seek every way of becoming such. And art is a very real way. It may not be everybody's way, but it's a great way for many people, if they only knew it. So it comes down to desire. What do you want?

The documentary filmmaker KEN BURNS was so highly regarded after making the renowned PBS documentary series *The Civil War* that he had guaranteed backing and his choice of any subject for his next project. Burns tells Bob Edwards why he chose to make the the 1994 series *Baseball*. September 16, 1994

BURNS: This was a way to understand the country that we became after this conflagration of the Civil War had defined us. Not in its totality, but in the sense that the poet William Blake meant when he said you could find the universe in a grain of sand, that it was possible to study a detail and know an appearance, an aspect, of the whole. And, indeed, the story of baseball became the story of our country, the story of race, of labor, of immigration, of the exclusion of women, of the rise and decay and rebirth of great cities, of the nature of heroes and villains and fools. All of the great themes that preoccupy us and occupy our attention, the game manifests, besides being the greatest game that's ever been invented.

EDWARDS: But, at eighteen and a half hours, aren't you giving it a stature that it doesn't deserve? To put it on parallel with the Civil War?

BURNS: I don't think so. It's not so much what your subject is as how you treat it. The Civil War covered four years in our nation's life, and we found, as documentary filmmakers formally trying to understand that moment, that the way we could take apart, say, the Battle of Fredericksburg, was to look at all the photographs, and we ended up with about a ten-minute section. It is no less important as a filmmaker to give ten minutes to the Merkle Boner. We know that the Battle of Fredericksburg has much more importance in the scope of American history, but to understand the Merkle Boner and, by extension, the time in which it took place — 1908, the Polo Grounds, a rookie's simple base-running error which cost the New York Giants the pennant and helped deliver the Chicago Cubs their only World Series victory, filled with magnificent characters, Tinker-to-Evers-to-Chance, Three-Finger Brown, great baseball action — to tell that story you need ten minutes. If you're covering the scope of two hundred years of American history, you need to take that time. You could do eighteen and a half hours on the Brooklyn Dodgers and the story of Jackie Robinson alone.

EDWARDS: And you almost did. Race is a huge part of this film.

BURNS: Race is a huge part of the American story and, as you begin to delve into baseball and begin to accept this notion that it is a kind of mirror on the tendencies and the character of the country, you begin to realize that in baseball, as in our larger republic, race is the central question. We are a country founded two hundred–plus years ago on the most noble idea yet advanced, that all men were created equal, and yet we tolerated slavery. In that fault line has been the story of our central tension as a people. Baseball's finest moment, in my opinion, is when Jackie Robinson, a grandson of a slave, began playing major league baseball on April 15, 1947, at Ebbets Field in Brooklyn. His heroic moment was the first real popular progress in civil rights since the Civil War. This comes before lunch counters; it comes before Rosa Parks; it comes before *Brown v. Board of Education*; it comes before a practical integration of our armed forces. So I began to realize that this moment was charged with symbolic importance, and Jackie's heroic action — this combination of forbearance in the face of racial abuse and, yet, the militancy that underlay it — characterized and inspired a generation of civil rights leaders.

EDWARDS: Even when we come into the era of motion pictures, you pretty much stick with your style of stills.

BURNS: Well, we've got a lot of moving pictures in this, but I still think that the still photograph is kind of the DNA of our process. If you've got newsreel footage of Babe Ruth rounding the bases, you can basically only talk about Babe Ruth rounding the bases and his prodigious skill as a home run hitter. But if you've got a photograph of Babe Ruth and you can look into his eyes and have some sympathy for him, you can talk about that prodigious skill but you can also talk about his childhood. You can talk about his parents, his troubles in school, his reform school experience, you can talk about his early years, you can talk about his off-the-field excesses, all the aspects of him. And so the still photograph becomes an empty vessel in which meaning can begin to be constructed. If you look at these old photographs, and also listen to them at the same time, they give up an essence of the moment that they were intended to represent. That helps to kick-start an understanding of the past. If you trust the past, if you don't treat it as if it was diminished and somehow less than us, but as if the people back then lived lives as full as ours, then you have that rare moment when the past comes alive. That's all we look for in the editing room, this excitement, so that in the Merkle Boner, and seventy-five other moments in this film, you can feel for a brief moment not that history was, but is, as Faulkner said.

....

MARV ALBERT is one of the best-known sports broadcasters in America, calling professional football, hockey, and basketball games on network television and on local radio and television in New York City. Albert talks with Bob Edwards about his book, *I'd Love to But I Have a Game,* in which he chronicles his nearly thirty years of professional broadcasting and his childhood experiences, as well. As a boy, he created a fantasy sports radio station, WMPA, for Marv Philip Albert. March 15, 1994

ALBERT: I'd be broadcasting P.S. 195 against P.S. 136 and bring all the exciting action to a very select audience. That's all I ever wanted to do. I played a lot of ball. I mean, I was an average athlete playing baseball and ice hockey and also quite a bit of basketball, but I was more interested in the broadcasting phase and the writing phase.

EDWARDS: Your third-grade teacher told you you were dreaming.

ALBERT: Yes, Mrs. Lipowsky, who was a wonderful woman. However, when she saw the composition, the usual what-do-you-want-to-do-when-you-grow-up composition, and I wanted to be the voice of the Knicks and the voice of the Rangers and have a regular column in the *New York Times* — that's what I was aiming for at the time — she thought it was a little out of reach, and was very nice about the way she handled it. I think that she did not want my expectations to be wild-eyed. In fact, after I began doing network at NBC, I got a very nice note from her, saying congratulations, and she remembered that, not that she discouraged me, but that she did not encourage that it would happen.

EDWARDS: A man named Sid Borgia also had an enormous, albeit unintended impact on your career?

ALBERT: Sid Borgia was a very colorful referee in the NBA, I would say in the fifties and the sixties. He was a very animated referee, had a number of key phrases and really took charge of a game when he called fouls. When I was playing schoolyard basketball in my grade school and high school days, there was a friend of mine who was always — I'm sure everybody's experienced this — always some kid as you were playing a sport who was doing play-by-play, imitating some announcer, and he would actually do the games while we were playing. I was kind of a shy kid so even though I was so interested in broadcasting I would not do that. But he used some phrases, such as "Yes!" and "Yes, and it counts!" He was imitating Borgia, who, when a player would score and would be fouled, would go, "Yes!" or "Yes, and the basket counts!"

So I kind of incorporated that eventually into my play-by-play after several years of doing Knicks basketball. And people started repeating it back to me at games, and I started to use it more and more. It's one of those phrases that just happened to catch on, and now I use it all the time in the NBC telecasts and Knicks broadcasts and I get a kick out of it because you hear it in the schoolyards now when kids are playing ball.

EDWARDS: It's everywhere.

ALBERT: It's scary, Bob. I'd like to put a stop to it.

EDWARDS: Lots of people feel they have to do their impressions of you.

ALBERT: I have people coming up to me from time to time at very unique places and who will just break into a so-called Marv Albert impersonation. I've had people come up to me, for example, at O'Hare Airport in the men's room. And it's very difficult to explain that perhaps you can wait a few moments, but, you know, we'll be standing side by side and someone will just go into an impression. What I usually say — I'll rate it. I'll say, "Hey, that's a strong six," and, you know, they're usually satisfied. But it's very nice that people do it. It's very flattering.

EDWARDS: You were doing a boxing match in a prison once and someone favored you with an impression.

ALBERT: Yes. One of my early boxing telecasts was at Rahway State Prison. There were several telecasts from Rahway because there was a boxer, a light heavyweight by the name of James Scott. Scott was ranked prior to going into prison for, as it turned out, armed robbery. At any rate, I was there a week before the fight to do a feature from the cell of James Scott, and one of his buddies, a fellow by the name of Malcolm, started to tell me how he had always enjoyed my broadcasting over the years and how they had radios and televisions in the cells and they had followed things. And he did a great impression. And, you know, he went into his play-by-play and seemed like a real nice fellow. I said, "By the way, what are you in prison for?" He said, well, he was in prison for life. He was part of a religious cult, and apparently they were charged with chopping heads off people. Very pleasant. I said, "Malcolm, very nice to meet you."

EDWARDS: How was his impression of you?

ALBERT: His impression? I told him he was great. He was outstanding.

Noah Adams interviews the movie director ANG LEE
of Taiwan about his film *Eat Drink Man Woman,* the
central character of which is the master chef at a Taipei
restaurant. According to the show business newspaper
Variety, Ang Lee's 1993 low-budget film, *The Wedding
Banquet,* was the most profitable film of the year.
His films include many scenes of sumptuous meals
being prepared and consumed, which literally whet
the appetite of his audiences. August 22, 1994

LEE: I prefer they go with empty stomachs.

ADAMS: Do you really?

LEE: Yes, because hunger is the best sauce. Just add flavor.
It's like when you scream over bungee jumping. It just adds
excitement. It's my obsession to put good food and cooking,
especially Chinese cooking, on the screen. It's pure cinema.
It's very suggestive. If you have a full stomach, you're not
hungry anymore.

ADAMS: What was it like shooting this film in Taipei for
you?

LEE: Ordeal. It is very difficult to film in Taiwan. It is totally
director-oriented. That is to say, in the States, it's the producer
who is producing. As a director, it's studio and artistic choices,
but in Taiwan, you have to generate everything. There's not
much sense of producing. The director has to push everything,
everyone, and that's exhausting.

ADAMS: Do you mean that people in the crew are afraid to
make their own small decisions about what they should be
doing?

LEE: Yes. You have to organize in detail. You don't sleep very
well because you're in constant fear something may go wrong

or somebody didn't remember something, or they don't fully understand. It's very scary.

ADAMS: What sort of movie industry is there in Taiwan? How many films are coming out? Are they very good? What are they about?

LEE: Nowadays, mostly festival-type films, good quality or art films. There are about ten like that made every year in recent years, partly due to the declining of film industry. We used to produce 200 to 250 melodramas or kung fu movies a year. Now that's declining. It was taken over by Hong Kong, and there's not much industry there anymore.

ADAMS: Hong Kong can do it cheaper?

LEE: Well, more entertaining, more commercial.

ADAMS: Could your new film be considered in any way a Taiwanese film?

LEE: *Eat Drink?*

ADAMS: Yes. Does it relate to life in Taipei the way, for example, *Manhattan* would speak about life in the United States? Which is to say, it's not really that descriptive.

LEE: You can make that comparison. It's just about the same as *Manhattan* is to the States. It's very middle class, bourgeois, a dramatized movie, where the scenery you're seeing about Taipei is whatever the drama demands. If the scene is about the conflict between modernization and tradition, I find an old Japanese house, where they're living. The old maid daughter, to match her mood, I give her a job as a teacher in a high school, where the color is very low-key. All that is according to what I want in the drama, but I think you can also have a good look at middle-class Taipei life.

ADAMS: This movie is getting great reviews. Your previous picture was the most profitable, per dollar spent, I'm told. Are you going to have a great deal of leverage in Hollywood? Do you want to make a picture that costs millions and millions of dollars to make?

LEE: If it takes that much money, yes. It depends on the material, but I will be very careful about who I work with. I don't think I'm very skilled with that kind of production yet. It's not all about making movies, a lot of it is about politics, how you deal with producers and your stars. I don't think I'm skillful enough to do that yet. You don't want to waste all that money not to make it back.

Liane Hansen interviews the director JOHN SCHLES-
INGER twenty-five years after the release of his 1969
film, *Midnight Cowboy*. The movie starred Dustin
Hoffman as the con man Enrico Salvatore "Ratso" Rizzo
and Jon Voight as Joe Buck, a young stud from Texas
seeking his fortune as a street hustler in New York City.
Midnight Cowboy was the first major studio production
to receive an X rating. After it won three Academy
Awards, the movie's rating was changed to an R.
February 27, 1994

SCHLESINGER: We never censored ourselves. We were in an
atmosphere of immense freedom, working for United Artists,
who were a great group of people to work with. I think that you
must remember, that X certificate meant something very different then. The category has totally changed. Now it's a hard-
core porn kind of certificate, and ours was an adult certificate in
those days, and it was quickly changed to an R after it had won
the Oscars.

HANSEN: Did you fight the X rating before the film was released?

SCHLESINGER: No, we didn't. It didn't occur to us. We knew
X meant adult film of a serious kind and we felt this was an
adult film and we weren't put under pressure by the studio to
change it. It was a memorable film for me to make. It was my
first American film. I came to Los Angeles for the first time
with *Far from the Madding Crowd*, which was a terrible flop,
and I had to recover from that. The best thing to do was to
plunge into work, and work for me is not just working on a
script. It's observing; it's looking around; it's recording in my
mind all sorts of details of life that I see, and the States are

certainly very rich in that. I come from a culture which is more closed in, and one doesn't see so much. The British play it close to the vest, and in America you see characters and their stories quite publicly in the streets and all-night cafés. So I spent a great deal of time wandering around and observing life here, both in Los Angeles and New York. And it was immensely gratifying to do that.

HANSEN: Was Dustin Hoffman always a part of the package in the role of Enrico Salvatore Rizzo from the Bronx?

SCHLESINGER: He was as soon as I met him. I'd only seen him in *The Graduate,* and I said, "Well, I can't judge him from just that. He's certainly not Ratso Rizzo, looking at that movie." So I went to New York and met him, and he had the great presence of mind to dress as he envisaged Ratso, in a dirty old raincoat, and we wandered along Forty-second Street and went to an Italian restaurant somewhere nearby. He said, "I'm taking you to this restaurant because if Ratso Rizzo had been a success, I think he would have ended up as headwaiter," and there was this extraordinary character, the headwaiter, and I could see exactly what Dustin meant. Then we spent a lot of time in pool halls and all-night cafés and so forth, and by the end of the evening it was quite clear to me that he blended into the scene perfectly and there was no point in looking any further, and that's how he got the part.

HANSEN: Did he improvise at all? I mean, we all remember the scene where he's crossing the street and he's almost hit by a car and he says —

SCHLESINGER: "I'm walkin' here." That actually wasn't improvised. It looks it, but we had a stunt driver and a taxi just off camera who drove in on cue, and Dustin delivered that famous line and gesture. When I saw it the other day for the first time in a long time in front of a big audience, they almost echoed the words. It was great and it got a huge round of applause. It's almost gone into the vernacular of film, but it was set up.

HANSEN: The cast is just incredible. Brenda Vaccaro, a very young Bob Balaban getting picked up by Jon Voight on Forty-second Street, the incredible John McGiver, Barnard Hughes.

SCHLESINGER: Yes, it was a great cast. I love watching the performances. I think they're all wonderful actors and they rose to the occasion. The characters are all a bit larger than life, and I enjoyed directing this film, perhaps partly because of that. They're very rich characters.

HANSEN: I saw the movie when it was released. I was eighteen years old and very innocent at the time, I'm afraid. I missed every single homosexual reference, but I did remember the telephone being stuffed in Barnard Hughes's mouth, and in fact, watching the film again, I was dreading that moment, knowing it was coming. Did you get as much grief about the violence in this film as you did about the sex?

SCHLESINGER: Well, of course there were people that criticized the film, yes. I expect there still will be. I remember pondering about that particular moment in the film, as to whether we should include it or cut it out. I mean, first of all, this film wouldn't be made now. It wouldn't be possible, and were it submitted to the whole preview system of turning the audience to critics and making them fill out cards, I'm perfectly certain we would have been influenced to remove all sorts of things which actually give the film its power. But we certainly wondered whether this was such an antiheroic act that the audience would lose sympathy for Joe Buck. In fact, I tried [taking] it out and then absolutely knew it had to go back in, because Joe is a mixture of many things. He is strong-willed about the fantasy until such time he knows it's not working. He's vulnerable. He has a very gentle and naive side to him, which I think is one of the reasons one can accept Jon Voight's beautiful performance, which is immensely sensitive. And yet there is an enormous amount of anger, and the desperation to get his friend to Florida, and the need for money makes him violent in that scene and absolutely determined to get the money. I suppose Barnard Hughes, as the elder man that picks him up, is basically masochistic and suggests this, so in a way Jon Voight is doing his job and pleasing him, but at the same time he's immensely violent in trying desperately to get rid of the image of what he's become and get his friend onto that bus to Florida. It's an emotionally charged scene. The phone in the mouth is an act of gratification and also prevents the operator from getting through to the man in the room.

I've always believed that heroes are human, and that they do strange and violent and sometimes even cowardly things. There are people that can't come to terms with what the film is about. The content includes all the suggestions of sexual violence and rape and explicit homosexual sex. Though you don't really see anything in detail, you know what's going on. I've always believed that you suggest rather than show details. I can't bear the preoccupation with exploiting violence, for instance, and I've never really understood why in the States people are rather puritanical about sex and yet you can show anybody blowing someone's head off on television. I find that worrisome.

HANSEN: What do you think it is that bonds the two men together? Is it more than just need and loneliness?

SCHLESINGER: Well, I think it's largely need and loneliness. There isn't anything overtly sexual in it, though one wonders if the Ratso Rizzo character played by Dustin wouldn't want to be embraced by man, woman, or dog. He's a desperate character and very sick. I think it's the need and the loneliness and the fact that they realize that their concern for one another finally, through a great deal of earlier antagonism, is the thing that's going to cause them to survive. I believe implicitly in survival, even though quite often my films end with question marks or unresolved relationships and sometimes with rather sad endings. That's the way I view life. I don't think it's all rosy and hands joined together, walking into the sunset.

ROBERT ZEMECKIS talks about the intense discussion inspired by the very successful movie he directed, *Forrest Gump* — the story of the extraordinary success of a simple man. Arguments over the meaning and political implications of *Forrest Gump* moved from the nation's entertainment pages to the op-ed pages. Linda Wertheimer asks Zemeckis why people are debating his movie. September 20, 1994

ZEMECKIS: It is partly because the film means so many different things to so many different people that it creates this debate. Plus the fact that it's something the media feels compelled to put it in some sort of slot or put some label on. That's what causes the debate, I think.

WERTHEIMER: When you saw the final cut of it, did you understand that you were looking at a movie that would mean so many different things to different people?

ZEMECKIS: To be perfectly honest, no. I felt that the movie worked. I felt that I was very comfortable with it. But I knew that doesn't mean anyone's going to go see it. I was in that very hysterical point in the release of a movie, so this all just comes as a wonderful surprise.

WERTHEIMER: I'm sure you heard about the liberal-conservative debate. Pat Buchanan says that the theme of the film is "stupid is as stupid does," that Forrest Gump is always honorable and decent and chaste and full of fidelity, and he triumphs, and those are conservative values.

ZEMECKIS: My feeling is that it's not about necessarily these conservative virtues, it's basically about common things. It's common sense, common decency, which I think everybody understands. I mean, there is a lot of cynicism in the movie as well. My feeling is that everybody either can bring something to this party and take something away as well, and I think that's what's happening.

WERTHEIMER: Do you buy the notion that this film is a metaphor for the sixties, for America in the sixties — America the bumbling but well-intentioned creature, staggering through the world — that somehow this movie reconstructs our image of the sixties, the dominant image of the baby boom?

ZEMECKIS: Yes, I do. As a matter of fact that's what I saw when I read the screenplay and that was the movie I tried to make. For me the film *Forrest Gump* is in fact a metaphor for the American character in the last half of this century.

WERTHEIMER: Michael Lerner, who is the editor of *Tikkun* magazine, wrote about it in that way in the *Washington Post*.

ZEMECKIS: Yes, you know, I don't think I've read all these things, but that's great that he understood that because, you know, every aspect of the movie in my mind represents a different part of the American character.

WERTHEIMER: But he also says that you go through the movie, and this wise child, this innocent creature — somehow contact with him makes other people whole. Without working at it, without struggling with it, his presence and his innocence are transforming. In that case, says Mr. Lerner of *Tikkun*, the story slips away from us again. It is not rigorous.

ZEMECKIS: You know, I think you've got to be careful about trying to look at everything under that much of a microscope. I mean, what the Forrest character allows us to do is to go on this adventure, go on this journey, and because he is in fact innocent and has no agenda, the audience takes what Forrest says at face value. What that allows the audience to do is to bring their own feelings to the movie. When Forrest says, "A promise is a promise, Lieutenant Dan," I mean, that's a pure statement, and you're not sitting there in the audience, saying, "What is he really saying?" Which is what you would say about anyone who is "normal."

WERTHEIMER: Mr. Lerner also says that Forrest Gump in

some way personifies the civil religion of America, which is that we are Americans, we are blessed, and it's right that it should be that way.

ZEMECKIS: Again, I think that that is represented in some aspects of the movie. I also feel that the movie talks very strongly about the fact that we in this last half century as a country have gotten blood on our hands and we realize that we can't just do anything that we want. I feel that the whole film is filled with balances and counterbalances. It's not just one thing specifically.

WERTHEIMER: This film is like a box of chocolates?

ZEMECKIS: Yes, I think it is. I mean that was the thing I found very compelling about the story. You had no idea where you were going to end up in this movie, and yet it's compelling, you don't get lost. You know, that's a very rare thing to find these days.

WERTHEIMER: The other thing that you have done in making this movie is that you appear to have created some kind of an American icon here. You have entered the language or you have moved the way we think around a little bit. Does it scare you to think that you succeeded in this way and then you have to go on and do the next thing?

ZEMECKIS: You know, I can't let that paralyze me. I did what I did on this movie the same as I did on all movies, you know. I just tried to do my best. I don't have any magic formula for why these things work. This movie and the success of this movie proves what I think William Goldman said, that nobody knows anything.

SCIENCE

The Harvard biologist EDWARD O. WILSON discusses biodiversity, ants, teaching, and other subjects in an interview with Alex Chadwick. Wilson's childhood fascination with bugs led him to specialize in ants. Before publishing his autobiography, *Naturalist,* Dr. Wilson won two Pulitzer Prizes for nonfiction. In his lab in Cambridge, Massachusetts, Wilson tells Chadwick that if the world were going to lose either ants or humans, it would be much better off without us. October 27, 1994

WILSON: If all human beings were to disappear, that is, human life as a whole, we would only lose a few other species. There are a couple of species of mites — little spiderlike creatures, for example, microscopic — that live in the pores on our forehead. They would suffer. But most of life would benefit because the natural environments which hold most of the biodiversity would heal and grow back. But if ants were all to be removed, the result would be catastrophic. Thousands of species of plants and animals depend on ants. Ants turn more soil, worldwide, for example, than earthworms. They're responsible for aerating large parts of the soil of the tropical forests and savannas and they're principal predators of small insects. And they are principal scavengers: ants carry away and dispose of, mostly by eating, more than ninety percent of the small creatures, from other insects to small birds, that die.

CHADWICK: Do you have ants in your house? That is, not ants you've meant to collect, but that are there in the kitchen?

WILSON: Yes. Like everybody else, I get ants in my kitchen.

CHADWICK: Do you kill them?

WILSON: Let me put it this way, the question that I'm asked

most frequently about ants is, "How do I get rid of the ones in my kitchen?" And my answer is always, "Give them little crumbs of cookies. They like that. Bits of tuna, maybe some whipped cream, and then watch what they do. They will display to you remarkable behavior if you look at them closely that is about as close to what social life might be on another planet." I'm kidding, of course. When they get bad in our kitchen, my wife and I dispose of them like everybody else, but I'm using this little entree here to express the great interest of ants and perhaps why we should leave them alone, except maybe in our kitchen.

CHADWICK: One of the things that I wanted to ask you about was your teaching. The only course that you teach now is a freshman biology course for people who are not majoring in the sciences.

WILSON: I happily teach this course because I realize that I am addressing the future newspaper editors, senators, business leaders, and other members of society whose decisions are going to make a great deal of difference to the future and who need a strong science background. There's no better way of teaching science, I think, than through evolutionary biology, because it addresses the issues that everybody is concerned with already: for example, the basis of human illness, heredity, and ecology.

CHADWICK: If it is true that most life forms eventually go extinct, then what's the point of running around trying to save things?

WILSON: That does lead to this philosophical question, If most species are destined to go extinct, why should we worry about the extinction that is of human cause? The answer is that although most species have, through time, become extinct, that extinction has occurred over billions of years, and humanity is increasing the rate of extinction, I estimate, between one thousand and ten thousand times faster over what it was before humanity came along. So in fact we are rapidly depleting biodiversity because we are killing off species thousands of times faster than they can be created.

CHADWICK: In the close of your book, you address yourself to young scientists who may be reading the book and thinking about their own careers. You suggest that a scientist interested in the great explorations to come might consider downward scale, might consider looking down and becoming a microbial evolutionist?

WILSON: The bacteria of a forest soil are about ten billion to a single gram — that's about a pinch that you would hold between thumb and forefinger — and contain as many as four thousand or five thousand species, almost all of which are unknown to science, unknown even in the sense of having a name. We don't know what their biology is like; we don't know how they interact, and so on. If a young scientist goes down to that level, then he is in what I like to call a micro-wilderness. A handful of soil for bacteria is the equivalent of the Amazon basin for birds and mammals. But on the other hand, there's no question that there is something very deeply satisfying about exploring a world that is in meters and kilometers, and looking at large organisms. Oh, I wouldn't stop that. I suppose that if you wanted to put me in paradise, it would be to allow me to be a microbial ecologist, but to let me do a lot of my research in the remaining rainforest, where, at lunch break and in the evenings, at dawn, I would be up looking at birds and ants and all these other things. To me, that's paradise.

The work of the inventor Nikola Tesla helped to usher in the age of electricity. Tesla was born in Croatia in 1856. Twenty-eight years later he moved to New York City, where he found work with Thomas Edison. He eventually formed his own lab and developed patents that were bought by George Westinghouse. TAD WISE, the author of *Tesla: A Biographical Novel of the World's Greatest Inventor*, tells Liane Hansen about the inventor's fascination with electric power, which began when he saw a picture of Niagara Falls when he was a boy. December 4, 1994

WISE: He is the inventor of the alternating current dynamo, upon which our entire electrical system is based, and arc lighting systems. He beat Roentgen to the X-ray. He took the first photographs taken by electric light. He, not Marconi, was the father of radio. He built the first solar electric cell in the previous century. He developed the most powerful turbine ever built. He was the first creator of neon bulbs. It goes on. Tesla's overriding desire was to create power, which was a gift to mankind. He felt, as a loyal American, that one of our inalienable rights was the pursuit of happiness, and built in to that idea was the notion that a certain amount of power was the birthright of every American.

HANSEN: J. P. Morgan figures very heavily into this story because J. P. Morgan was one of the money men.

WISE: Morgan backed him to the tune of perhaps 150,000 dollars, which is probably ten million dollars today, but when Morgan found out that he wanted to actually supply power to the world, this was a complete threat to the capitalist system. All these other millionaires, Frick and Astor and Ryan, are all extremely interested in Tesla while he's the darling of J. P. Morgan. Then, all of a sudden, Tesla becomes an untouchable. He loses his lab; he loses backing. He is, let's face it, extremely eccentric to begin with. The list of his phobias would make a lunatic look like a Boy Scout.

HANSEN: When he came to the United States, one of the first persons he worked with was Thomas Edison.

WISE: Yes.

HANSEN: And at one point, they were talking about the process of illumination and Edison was talking about the different filaments he was using in light bulbs, how he tried one and then another, and Tesla said, "Well, I do this all in my head. I've already replaced flywheels. I've already replaced gears. I've already tried out the filaments." Eventually they had a falling out, and their falling out became what is known as the battle of the currents, AC versus DC.

WISE: Yes. I was talking with a gentlemen over at the Smithsonian yesterday. We politely agreed to disagree. I said that in order for the proper importance of Nikola Tesla to emerge, some of the importance of Edison would have to be sacrificed because it's kind of an either-or situation. I said that Edison is an important icon for, let's say, schoolchildren, but that these schoolchildren don't know that Edison was electrocuting small animals to defame AC power. They didn't know that Edison developed the electric chair and that the first person electrocuted, William Kemmler, was not supplied with enough power. He came back to life. He was then shot with so much juice that his spine caught on fire and various journalists were sick. The great Edison was up against the wall and using everything he could come up with to defame Tesla. In the end, he was successful.

HANSEN: Wasn't there not just the problem of his personality, but, given the time, some question as to where Tesla was going with some of his inventions? People thought it was magic, not science.

WISE: Yes. To be perfectly fair, he was responsible for a lot of this. Because he donned the cape of magician. He was six foot six. He was handsome. He was Serbo-Croatian. He had all of Hamlet and Faust in his head. He memorized whatever he wanted. He loved being high-handed, and he loved being the Houdini of science. He was supersaturating his audiences' concentration. Inside of ten minutes they'd seen as much as they could understand, and it would go on for another three hours. He was purposefully spinning circles over their head and making himself out to be the archetypal mad scientist, which is what he was. You look at the old movies, I mean, this is Dr. Frankenstein.

HANSEN: One of the reasons J. P. Morgan eventually dropped support of Tesla was that Marconi managed to transmit a wireless message across the Atlantic.

WISE: Finally. First the English Channel and then the Atlantic.

HANSEN: The letter S.

WISE: The letter S.

HANSEN: Now, Nikola Tesla had, not to this extent, perhaps, already demonstrated what later became known as radio.

WISE: Absolutely.

HANSEN: And he said that Marconi was using something like seven of his patents.

WISE: Seventeen.

HANSEN: Seventeen of his patents to accomplish it. Marconi gets the credit for radio. Why didn't Tesla get the credit?

WISE: Because he was a terrible businessman. Because he did not know how to truncate his science, make it accessible. He was, as we were just discussing, so filled with ideas. He was like Mozart, you know. He just lived and breathed science. Marconi was smart. He said, "Don't give them what they don't understand." He said, "Here's a product. This is what I'm going to do with it. I'm sending a short wave over a small distance, giving people an idea of what this can do on a larger scale." Tesla wanted to have a worldwide monopoly on radio communication, much like a radio version of CNN. That's what he promised Morgan. That's what Morgan wanted. So he thought Marconi was a small fry, which he was. But the small fry succeeded where the grandiose genius failed because Tesla could put no limits. This was his curse. When he was receiving the unparalleled praise of London engineers, Lord Rayleigh, who was one of the greats of his day, changed the tenor of the remarks insofar as he said, "Mr. Tesla, limit yourself to one of the dozens of frontiers that you are now the incontestable master of. Let us not say, as we do of Alexander the Great, 'He tried too much.' "

The anatomist RANDALL SUSMAN proposes a new meaning for the old phrase *rule of thumb*. Susman wrote in the journal *Science* that you can figure out whether a species of prehistoric hominid was capable of using tools by knowing what it was capable of grasping — literally grasping with the hand, not with the brain. Professor Susman tells Robert Siegel that one can measure a protohuman's capacity for tool use by considering the dimensions of just one bone in the body, the long bone of the thumb. September 8, 1994

SUSMAN: It's been assumed by anthropologists since the late nineteenth century that, at any one time, the one species living with the largest brain is the toolmaker to the exclusion of all others. This is pretty much what everybody thought. In the late 1980s, I described some new fossils found by C. K. Brain in a cave in South Africa, and these fossils are more than likely to have belonged to a species of early hominid ancestor called *Paranthropus*. This was a large-toothed vegetarian with a small brain. The fossils showed that these animals were very likely to be toolmakers.

SIEGEL: So your research and your study of fossils has helped redirect the search for what enables a hominid to make tools away from brain size down to not only the hand, but actually to the thumb and even, more specifically, to one bone of the thumb?

SUSMAN: Right. When I decided that *Paranthropus* looked like a toolmaker, I wanted to go back and look at all the animals that we know are toolmakers, the later hominids, Neander-thals, and animals much later in time, the sort of definitive toolmakers, to see if there's anything that was common to all of these toolmakers and exclusive to them, and things that were not present in non-toolmakers. That's the essence of the *Science* paper, and this is a diagnosis of toolmaking based on a single bone, the thumb metacarpal, the long, skinny bone at the base of the thumb. By taking two measurements on that bone and creating a ratio, you can determine whether an animal was likely to be a toolmaker or had a more primitive, sort of apelike power of grasping such as we find in modern chimpanzees or modern pygmy chimpanzees.

SIEGEL: Well before these species or hominids had the brains, some of them had the hands, and they were making tools?

SUSMAN: Yes, precisely.

SIEGEL: When you speak of tools, what are we talking about and what do we have in the way of tools that have been recovered?

SUSMAN: The things we refer to at two and a half million years ago in eastern Africa, the very earliest durable artifacts that are actually preserved in the fossil record, are made of stone and they're nothing more than river cobbles or pieces of basalt, volcanic extrusive material, that have been banged on an edge in a fashion that never occurs naturally. It isn't until much later in human evolution, probably a million years later, that we start seeing the things that we would recognize as a flint object, you know, a thing that looks like a hand ax.

SIEGEL: So which hominid should be elevated in our esteem for his or her capacities for toolmaking as a result of this study of thumbs? Who's gone up in our book?

SUSMAN: Well, I think the *Robus australopithecines* have gone up. Mainly *Paranthropus*. *Paranthropus* was one genus, and there's a number of *Robus australopithecines*, starting about two and a half million years ago. They became extinct about a million and a half years ago. I think *Paranthropus* deserves more attention at this point, and the reasons for *Paranthropus's* extinction deserve closer scrutiny, than the simple explanation that they were just too stupid to survive.

Scott Simon interviews the molecular biologist
RANDY LEWIS of the University of Wyoming about his
laboratory's discovery: how to make a genetically
engineered spider web fiber. The spider's web is made
of the strongest material known to man.
April 30, 1994

SIMON: You have not chemically reproduced it but have actually genetically created the bacteria that manufacture a spider's webbing?

LEWIS: That's right. What we've done is basically take the gene that the spider uses to make the protein and reconfigured it so that it will fit in a bacterial system and genetically engineer the bacteria that produces the protein that will make the spider silk fiber.

SIMON: Could you give us some idea of how strong spider webbing is?

LEWIS: Sure. This material has a tensile strength of probably two hundred thousand to three hundred thousand pounds per square inch. In addition, it will stretch to thirty-five percent of its length before it actually breaks. That combination means that it can absorb more energy than any fiber that's known, three times more energy than Kevlar will before it breaks, and, as most people know, Kevlar is used for bulletproof vests and clearly is able to stop a bullet.

SIMON: What would be some uses for spider webbing?

LEWIS: Certainly some of the areas that immediately look to be important are in the medical field, artificial ligaments and artificial tendons, things like that. There just really is nothing out there. You have to use natural materials. This would allow a way around that, and if we can produce it cheaply enough, I think that one may ultimately fashion clothing as well because it does have much of the attractiveness of silk, but it has that elastic factor.

SIMON: Dr. Lewis, how does a spider do it, so to speak?

LEWIS: The first thing they do is take the proteins and synthesize them and store them in a gland that's located in the abdomen. As opposed to what most people probably think, they don't actually push the silk out. They take and pull the fiber out from an orifice located on their abdomen. So, as the material is drawn from the body, it actually is formed into the fiber itself.

SIMON: And what is the improvement you make over that process? I mean, why not just put five hundred spiders together and get them to do it?

LEWIS: One of the problems you have is that spiders are extremely territorial. If you were to try and put any large number of spiders in any kind of reasonably confined space, they'd end up killing each other. That was actually tried in the 1860s in Britain. They tried to get spiders put in old barns and be able to do this sort of thing, and the end result was that, economically, it just made no sense to try to do that.

The thesis of *The Bell Curve* by CHARLES MURRAY
and the late Richard Herrnstein made it the most controversial book of 1994. Murray and Herrnstein argue that
IQ is a better predictor than socioeconomic status or
ethnic background of how well people will fare in school
and at work, and that America is an increasingly
segregated society, but not one that is divided by a color
line or by tax brackets. We are distributed, the authors
claim, along the social scientists' bell curve. The mass
of Americans huddle at the mountain in the middle.
People with high IQs form a cognitive elite at the right,
and those with low IQs form the real underclass at the
left. IQ, they say, is dictated more by heredity than by
environment. The gap of about fifteen points between
the mean IQs of whites and blacks persists even among
groups of equal socioeconomic status. Charles Murray,
having been accused in several reviews of tendentious
scholarship and racism, talks with Robert Siegel about
his book and his detractors. October 28, 1994

MURRAY: In one way, you're talking to a sadder but wiser
man. There's no doubt about that. I have been appalled by the
last couple of weeks, and a friend of mine said to my wife when
she made this point, he said, "Well, what is it? You sound like
somebody who got into World War II and is surprised that
they're firing real bullets." So I guess I shouldn't be surprised in
some ways, but I am. I expected to get hate mail, all right? And
I expected to get hate phone calls, which I haven't gotten. Please
don't take this as a request for them. But I didn't expect to see

journalists who I respected and have oftentimes known personally for many years to act as irresponsibly as I think a lot of them
have acted.

SIEGEL: But let me stand up for your friend here, who told
your wife you should have expected as much. Arguments about
genetic determination of intelligence or the lack of intelligence
have been put to some of the most obscene uses of any science
or pseudoscience in our times. Surely you must have known, in
approaching the race issue and the disparities of IQ, that you
were walking into an area where people can become deeply
offended.

MURRAY: Yes, we did know that. And I think if you read the
chapter, as you have, that we clearly say we are aware of what
we're about to do. What's going on behind the scenes in this
country and the dialogue about race is very dangerous, and what
Dick and I said is, you know, the facts are not as scary as a lot
of the misinformation out there. It is time to lay a lot of this
stuff out on the table and in a period of time we can get over it.
We are not through that period of time yet.

SIEGEL: But let me run past you something that I gleaned
from the dialogues on race that I've been party to that I think
account for some of my reluctance to accept a rigid hereditary
or inheritable theory of intelligence. When you show that
among blacks and whites of equal socioeconomic standing a gap
in IQ persists — to say that those two groups of people are the
same clashes with what I've learned as an adult. That is, that
people of the same income level, the same education level,
black and white, can find situations of employment or education remarkably different. They can find the same physical,
material, temporal experience, on the one hand, a breeze and
something you're born to thrive at, and, on the other hand,
something quite threatening and undermining. Blacks and
whites very often see things, because of their social and economic histories, quite differently. I wonder if we shouldn't put
a big asterisk onto "same socioeconomic status."

MURRAY: Well, just to clarify something, when it comes to

the role of genes in the black-white test score difference, Dick Herrnstein and I are really agnostic about what the mix might be there, and, in fact, we aren't going to go very far out on a limb saying there's a mix at all. We don't really know. But your larger point is well taken, and I would endorse it in this regard: Let's start thinking of the environment as being a whole lot bigger and more complex than we have in the past. Let's say that it could very well be an environment that, writ large, accounts for some of these differences.

SIEGEL: The environment is not just things and money, but what I think that person over there thinks of me, in what way I think they esteem me or don't esteem me.

MURRAY: But that in itself is, I think, consistent with another point that we try to make, that we've taken a hammering on, which is that when people think of the environment causing differences, there is this impulse to think, Oh, well, we know what to do about that. And we have all these little things we'll trot out that will provide for children to make up for their environmental deficits. If there is a contribution in this book with regard to the racial difference, I hope it is this: that we get a lot more realistic about how hard it is to manipulate the environment, because I think until we do that there is going to be a lot of self-congratulatory talk every time we raise the funds spent on remedial education and whatever and not a hard enough look at what we're actually accomplishing.

SIEGEL: If one were to read the book and deal with your data more than with your policy recommendations, and say, "OK, IQ turns out to be a bit stubborn." (Some social scientists who have commented in the reviews say there are other studies to show that IQ is more elastic than you would say, but it appears to be somewhat stubborn; you say it levels out about age six or eight, and it's a very good predictor of what will happen to people in later life.) "Well, at around the third grade, let's test for IQ, track like crazy, stop with efforts to create a more diverse elite, and do vocational education starting at age nine for those people who are headed for the left tail of the bell curve." Is that a sensitive reading of your book?

MURRAY: No, no, it's not. We think that, in terms of education, what people ought to do is to be able to fulfill their talents as far as they want to go, and actually we think the family is a pretty good way to have a whole bunch of people trying hard to have their kids go as far as they can go. So we do not want an eleven-plus kind of system like they had in Britain. We want, if anything, to decentralize control over education even more than it is now. I would say there is, in our book, a very strong affirmation of a traditional American ideal, which is that you treat people as individuals, you try to let everybody fulfill their potential as an individual. What Dick and I are saying is, as we go about that process, let's also be aware of the larger social phenomena that this drives. Let's be aware of the down sides that it has, which have nothing to do with race, because unless we are aware of those we are in danger not just from an underclass, or even as much from an underclass as we are from our cognitive elite, which, in our view, is becoming more and more a potential threat to free institutions.

SIEGEL: If I had told you when you were writing or researching the book that its publication would prove terribly dispiriting, let's say, to black schoolchildren, who would catch the distant drift of this thesis that's wending its way through every news weekly and op-ed page and letters-to-the-editor page, would you think twice about that? If you felt you were putting into the air a case that might make a large number of kids feel debilitated, feel like everyone thinks they're stupid. Would you say, "Well, maybe on second thought I shouldn't write this"?

MURRAY: Dick and I talked a lot about that, and I don't want to speak for him because I don't remember exactly where he came out. I know for my own part, were this the early 1960s before the advent of treatment by groups, before the advent of a lot of other problems that we've had, when there was real progress in race relations in this country, I think that I would have had other thoughts. In 1994, it is not the case that black youngsters are suddenly with publication of this book getting the sense that, Gee, whites think that we have lower IQs than they do. This is not only in the air and has been in the air continuously; it has been, we think, all the more debilitating because it's been this kind of miasma that permeates everything, never talked about, never exposed to the light of day. Everybody knows it's there.

SIEGEL: But let me call you on that for a moment. To look back on race relations in America and to say that it was never talked about that whites thought blacks were intellectually inferior is to miss decades of racist discourse in the United States which have bombarded black people in America, and this isn't novel.

MURRAY: I was referring to right now.

SIEGEL: Yes, I know you were referring to right now, but to the ears of somebody who has been raised on the black experience in America, this is compounding something that has been absolutely the argument behind segregation.

MURRAY: Well, we're going to disagree on this, but I'll tell you why I disagree. Dick Herrnstein and I both feel very strongly that the facts on this are not something that needs to make a black youngster feel bad about himself because we don't think that's the way parents and youngsters deal with their lives. When I am thinking about what I am going to be as a child, I am thinking about what I am and what I can do, and what I want most of all is a society that tells me, "Youngster, you can go as far as your energy and abilities will take you in whatever direction you have energy and abilities." That's the message we want to send, what we think this country has been doing, and again I would ask for you to have me back in three or four years, and let's see who is right on this issue.

The late Eda Schultz Charlton was subjected to radiation as part of a government experiment program during the 1940s. Mrs. Charlton lived in upstate New York and died in 1983 at age eighty-six. Details of the experiments were made public by the U.S. Department of Energy in late 1993. Mrs. Charlton's daughter-in-law, HELEN SCHULTZ, and Dr. RICHARD HORNICK, who took over the care of Eda Charlton toward the end of her life, tell Linda Wertheimer how much she knew about the injection of plutonium she received in 1945. January 4, 1994

SCHULTZ: About 1970 she came to me with a piece of paper that had "plutonium" written on it, and she said, "What is plutonium?" She didn't understand then what it was. And, of course, I didn't realize then how serious it was either. I knew what plutonium was. I understand that in 1974 they told her what it was, and she signed a consent that they pay her medical expenses. I don't doubt that she signed it, but she didn't understand it, because in 1979 she made out power of attorney in my favor so I could handle her bills, and I wasn't getting any bills. I checked with her doctor, Dr. Waterhouse, and I said, "Who's paying her bills, and why?" She said, "I don't know a thing about it." Luckily, Dr. Waterhouse left town and Dr. Hornick took over her case, and he was most cooperative.

WERTHEIMER: Dr. Hornick, you took over care of Eda Schultz in 1979?

HORNICK: That's correct.

WERTHEIMER: What did you know about why she was being carefully followed and repeatedly tested? What did you know about her situation?

HORNICK: I knew very little also. I was told that there had been some exposure to radioactive substances, and that was about the extent of it. I did know that the atomic energy group at the University of Rochester was interested in her and wanted a copy of each of the medical records, and they were the ones who were paying the bills that you just heard about.

WERTHEIMER: So you knew that you were supposed to go through some kind of protocol for her, some kind of routine of testing and so on, and turn those results over to other people.

HORNICK: Well, there wasn't any protocol. When I saw her she had hypertension and she was becoming senile. I was doing regular medical checkups on her, and there was nothing at that time that would have suggested that she had any adverse effects from the radiation therapy because I would have been surprised that anything would have turned up that late. You would have expected something to have occurred rather immediately from a dose of radioactive material.

WERTHEIMER: My understanding is that you were the one who actually told the family that she had been exposed to radiation and how it had happened.

HORNICK: I knew that she had been exposed, and I was somewhat surprised that the family didn't know because I had thought that this was something that had been discussed. As you heard, in I think 1974 the university had notified these folks. That's when they accepted the liability for the medical testing. So I was under the impression that she knew that she had had this exposure. I was surprised when we talked with the family that they didn't know that.

WERTHEIMER: Knowing what we now know about exposure to radiation and how very harmful radiation can be, everyone is horrified by what they're reading and hearing about these tests. Were you horrified when you realized that your patient had been exposed? How did you understand this?

HORNICK: As I said, my impression was that she had been exposed and I wasn't sure that how this occurred. At the time the implication was that this was some sort of accident. I was not aware that this was an intentional injection. Just looking at her general medical condition and trying to ascertain if there are any effects and not being able to make any diagnosis related to radiation, my impression was, Thank goodness, whatever she was exposed to has not caused her any permanent damage.

SCHULTZ: Except emotionally. She was very emotionally upset. She told me one time that they put her in a sealed room to check to see how much radiation she had had, and she and I thought that they thought she had been radiated some other place, and that's why she was having all these complaints. We had no idea they were checking her for what they had done to her. And then they were collecting her specimens over the years and sending them to Chicago. This woman was so confused and upset that she was sure she had cancer. She mentioned that to Dr. Waterhouse frequently.

WERTHEIMER: What was your reaction when you discovered what had actually happened? That she had been deliberately exposed to radiation?

SCHULTZ: My reaction? Well, of course, we were upset. I said to my husband, "How do you feel about what they did to your mother?" And he said, "I'm overseas fighting the Germans for doing things to other human beings, and at the same time it's being done to my mother." It's upsetting. Very upsetting.

WERTHEIMER: That's a sort of natural, normal, filial kind of reaction, a family reaction. I wonder about you, Dr. Hornick? Knowing what we know now, it seems more frightening than probably it did at the time.

HORNICK: Yes. Again, I don't know the dose she got, and certainly anybody these days participating in any study has to have informed consent, really significant informed consent. And, as you know, all the Nuremberg trials, the Helsinki code, all the new regulations regarding human experimentation, came out after the war because of what the Germans did. So what they did in the early forties obviously would be totally unethical these days. At that time, certainly, you would have hoped that informed consent would have been obtained from these patients, but the informed consent process at that time was certainly a lot different than what it is today. So, yes, what was done is totally unethical and certainly should never have been done.

The astronomer ANDREW FRACKNOY of Foothill College in San Francisco tells Daniel Zwerdling what we have learned about "dark matter" in the universe from pictures taken by the Hubble telescope. Some scientists have reasoned that the invisible stuff occupying most of space is the same basic material that makes up stars and other visible bodies but doesn't give off enough light to be picked up by conventional human telescopes. Now come the pictures taken by Hubble.
November 20, 1994

FRACKNOY: In particular, the images and the data from the Hubble show that whatever this mysterious dark matter may turn out to be, it is probably not small, dim, dark, boring stars, which would have been the simplest explanation.

ZWERDLING: So it's not the stuff some people expected to see?

FRACKNOY: That's correct. The easiest explanation is that somehow the mysterious dark matter is made of the same kind of stuff that stars are made of and that planets and people are made of and that this, in fact, just is hiding in the form of very boring stars, stars that shine so dimly that even our best telescopes have been not able to pick it up. But now with the Hubble, this incredible eye that we have above the Earth's atmosphere, we have taken the sharpest and clearest images ever of regions where such tiny stars might be expected to be hiding, and we have found far, far fewer of them than anyone expected.

ZWERDLING: In fact, didn't some of those pictures — this is the part that's supposed to send chills up our back — didn't they show nothing where astronomers expected to see something?

FRACKNOY: In certain groupings of stars, which are called globular clusters, where stars are clustered together very tightly, we did expect to see a pretty good population of these very, very dim red dwarf stars, as astronomers call them. We saw essentially none of them in those clusters.

ZWERDLING: So now astronomers and physicists have to start figuring things out. If the matter isn't the same sort of matter as we've been seeing in regular stars, what is this matter? What are a couple of the niftiest and strangest explanations?

FRACKNOY: As with any desperate problem in science, the explanations get more desperate as we get closed in by the observations. For example, bricks would do it. If the universe were filled with bricks, bricks wouldn't give off any light, and if there were humongous numbers of bricks, that would explain the presence of all this dark matter that we infer from other observations. But nobody really thinks it's bricks. So what might it be? Perhaps it's stars that are even darker than the ones we're talking about. Instead of these red dwarf stars maybe it's what we call brown dwarf stars or black dwarf stars, the colors here meaning colder and dimmer and even more difficult to see. Those wouldn't be picked up even by the Hubble's sharp eye.

ZWERDLING: That would be stars that are so old and so feeble that nobody can see them yet?

FRACKNOY: They wouldn't actually have to be old; they'd just have to be pathetic when they started. The lower the amount of stuff — or mass — in a star, the more feebly it glows. You can have a very young brown dwarf as well as an old one, as long as it doesn't have enough material to give off a lot of light.

ZWERDLING: Let's go on to a more exotic potential explanation.

FRACKNOY: More exotic explanations involve particles that haven't yet been discovered but don't interact with matter and therefore don't give off light in the ordinary sense. Some of the particles have been called WIMPs, for weakly interactive massive particles.

ZWERDLING: WIMPs?

FRACKNOY: And WIMPs would be one candidate. No one has seen a WIMP, and there isn't a great deal of evidence for WIMPs, but when you're desperate you start coming up with new ideas.

ZWERDLING: Now, this is sort of an exciting potential explanation because this would mean that there's an entire world out there. Or that there's an entire world here like in *Star Trek*, coexisting within and inside and between the spaces of the world we know.

FRACKNOY: In fact, another nice analogy for this is the iceberg analogy, that when you come across an iceberg in the ocean you only see the tip of it, which might be about ten percent. Most of it — the dangerous part to ships — is the ninety percent that's below the ocean level and invisible to the captain. In the same way, we astronomers may well only be seeing the ten percent of the universe that's ordinary matter and accessible to our instruments and below that in the ocean of space, if you will, there might be ninety percent of the universe we have never known about and is made of something so exotic it's not accessible to our present instruments.

As astronauts aboard the space shuttle *Discovery*
prepared to fly free in space with jetpacks, called Safers,
breaking with NASA's practice of tethering astronauts to
the shuttle when they ventured outside, JOE ALLEN,
one of the last men to use a jetpack, on his 1984 space
walk, describes the experience to Jacki Lyden.
September 11, 1994

ALLEN: It's as much fun as you would imagine it to be. I
should say that the device to be used in a few days is a much
simpler version of what I used. I used something called a maneuvering unit, and it's physically a rather large device that you
back yourself into in your spacesuit. You're outside, tethered to
the space shuttle, but you back into the maneuvering unit, click
into it, and once you can confirm that you're attached, you then
pull it away from its mounting device and in theory, can unattach yourself from the space shuttle, take the tethers off, and
fly it.

LYDEN: It was pretty heavy, wasn't it?

ALLEN: Well, it's physically very heavy on the ground, but of
course, in space, everything's floating, including yourself. But
it's quite ponderous, bulky. It looks like an overstuffed arm-
chair because it has arms that come out in front of you, but it
is quite easy to fly, and you can move yourself off in any direction away from the space shuttle. The device to be used later
this week is considerably smaller and it's done not with control
sticks on the arms that project out in front but rather with
something that's a bit like a joystick you might use for a video
game.

LYDEN: I'm looking at some old pictures of you. You're re-
pairing a satellite. You went up on the space shuttle *Discovery*

and you were flying around in space with another astronaut.
You look a little bit like a figure out of *The Jetsons*. You did not
have a tether, correct?

ALLEN: Correct. And that's really the difference between
what we'll see later this week and what typically is done when
people do these extravehicular activities, or space walks. In
almost every case, we're very careful to use procedures that
are like a mountain climber's. You really don't unattach from
the mountain that you're climbing. In this case, you don't unattach from the space shuttle, lest you float away. With the
maneuvering units, or with this little test device that will be
used, you can't unattach, the reason being you can actually
maneuver yourself back to the space shuttle, should you float
away from it.

LYDEN: When you were out there with the maneuvering unit
on your back, jetting around, did you feel really vulnerable? Did
you sort of worry about drifting off?

ALLEN: Jacki, I will tell you it's an extraordinary experience.
You're quite confident that you can fly yourself back to the
mother ship. On the other hand, it is literally true that you,
yourself, are a satellite. You are in orbit. The orbital mechanics,
the path that you follow, are exactly those of the space shuttle
or the moon or other objects in orbit about planets, and it's
really quite extraordinary.

LYDEN: *Discovery*'s crew this time out has practiced, I guess,
forty space-walker rescue procedures in ground simulators in
case something should go wrong. What about that? I mean, how
confident did you feel that the ship would actually be able to
reach you if the jetpack should fail?

ALLEN: Well, again, space flight is very carefully thought
through, and we always think in terms of backup systems. In
the case of the maneuvering unit that I flew, it quite literally
was two units in one. It looked like one, but there were two
separate systems there, so if one failed, you still had a second
system, and you could use that second system to return to the
Discovery. In the unlikely event that that second system failed,

the procedure would be you just basically shut it down so that you don't spin up, so that you don't tumble, you don't jet off.

LYDEN: Like at the end of *2001.*

ALLEN: Exactly. That ruins your whole day, but there are ways to turn off the unit so it cannot possibly do that, and then the crew of the *Discovery* would be expected to bring its ship over to find you, and that's quite possible to do. And in this case coming, it should be very easy to do, so I don't really think it's that dangerous a procedure.

LYDEN: Would you call that sojourn in space where you were a human satellite the high point of your career as an astronaut, Mr. Allen?

ALLEN: Yes, it was physically the high point. Mentally, it certainly was one of the high points. The privilege of orbiting Earth in a ship of any kind is extraordinary beyond belief, and I would call a space walk out from a ship frosting on that cake.

LYDEN: I don't think I'd ever be able to look up into the night sky again without thinking of my time there. Does that happen to you?

ALLEN: Every time I look, I think about it.

....

ABRAHAM VERGHESE is a doctor. Born in Africa
of Indian parents, he was educated in the United States
and in India, and settled in Johnson City, Tennessee.
His book, *My Own Country,* is the story of how that
conservative small town and the immigrant physician
dealt with the arrival of AIDS. Verghese tells Linda
Wertheimer that AIDS is a metaphor for shame and
secrecy, for furtive homosexuality. May 16, 1994

VERGHESE: [*reading*] "AIDS simply did not fit into this picture we had of our town. The TV stations and the *Johnson City
Press* did a fine job of parroting what the wire services carried
about AIDS. But they never succeeded in treating the deaths of
Rock Hudson or Liberace as being any more significant to *our*
town than famine in the Sahel or a plane crash in Thailand. You
could shop in the mall, cut your hair in Parks & Belk, pick up
milk in the Piggly Wiggly, bowl at Holiday Lanes, find bawdy
entertainment at the Hourglass Lounge — and never know that
one of my patients was seated right next to you, or serving you,
or brushing past you in the parking lot, a deadly virus in his or
her body that was no threat to you, but might nevertheless
cause you to stand up and scream if you knew how close it was.

"My problem was the opposite: I saw AIDS *everywhere* in the
fabric of the town; I wanted to pick up a megaphone as I stood
in a checkout line and say, 'ATTENTION K-MART SHOP-
PERS: JOHNSON CITY IS A PART OF AMERICA AND, YES,
WE DO HAVE AIDS HERE.'"

WERTHEIMER: You said you also dreamed about it?

VERGHESE: You know, I still dream about it. I honestly believe that the only moment when I truly understand what it is
to have this virus in your body is when you have a dream where

you've acquired it, and the sheer terror of that waking up. Those few seconds it takes to orient yourself are something that remind me that, for all my empathy and all my understanding, I really don't quite understand what it's like to have this, to be informed that you have a deadly virus in your body.

WERTHEIMER: You describe in the book both your own attempts to understand it and the town's attempt to understand it.

VERGHESE: Right.

WERTHEIMER: And all of the different kind of patients that you had and their attempts to understand it. There's one woman in your book who says that she understood that her brother was gay, but she had no word for it. I mean, people for whom this whole thing is just not a part of their world at all.

VERGHESE: Absolutely.

WERTHEIMER: And the way they came to terms with it?

VERGHESE: I asked her, "Do you remember the moment when you knew he was gay?" She said, "Well, he had these strange friends, and I told him one time, I said, 'Be careful, now. You be careful.' " I said, "Do you mean that you knew he was gay?" She said, "I don't think I ever used that word, because gay might have been what he did, but it wasn't who he was." Which I was always intrigued by, because I wondered if he had been able to address her sentence, whether he would have agreed. I don't think he would have agreed. I think gay was what he was, and perhaps it was just two different ways that they chose to view this peculiar scenario.

WERTHEIMER: At one point in the book, you come to terms with what you see in yourself dealing with the furtiveness and the secrecy when you meet a wonderful couple who have been infected from blood transfusion — he from blood transfusion, and she from him — and you notice that you're thinking about them as innocent?

VERGHESE: Yes, it was a very difficult moment. I was really drawn to this couple and feeling guilty that I should be so drawn to them. They had used the word *innocent* to describe the way they acquired the disease, and there was a part of me that fought that, because I wanted to say, "We're all innocent. Anyone who has this disease is innocent." But there was a part of me that subconsciously seemed to be pulled in the direction of agreeing with them. I think it has to do with this metaphor of guilt and secrecy that travels with the virus. In that sense, you know, they felt that they were innocent of the metaphor, but nonetheless, they couldn't escape it. I found my heart pulled in the direction of agreeing with them, but my cognitive mind wanting to say, "That is not correct."

WERTHEIMER: You catch the voices of all those people so clearly. You catch their accents. I can just hear them. Another thing that you said in the book was that you think that, as an immigrant, you are attuned to this desire to blend. You expressed it in the book as feeling that there was some kind of commonality between you and these secretly gay people.

VERGHESE: Right. We were both aliens, although we were aliens heading in different directions. Here I was an alien. My green card labeled me a resident alien at the time, and I was struggling to blend in. I was trying to learn all these rituals that would allow me to blend in. Not just the accents and the language and the choice of words, but also, literally, the rituals of what they ate and so on. And the paradox was that I was dealing with hometown boys who were aliens in their own right, inasmuch as they really never felt like they could be who they wanted to be there, and they were camouflaging in the other direction: They were hiding their alien-ness and seeking to escape from there while I was seeking to blend in. It often struck me that perhaps one of the reasons that my patients took to me, and I to them, was perhaps they felt that as an outsider, I wouldn't pass judgment on them. In fact, I'll take that one step further. I had patients like a preacher who came more than once with a sexually transmitted disease. I almost had the feeling that he was saying to me not only that I would not pass judgment, but that as a foreigner, I had no right to pass judgment on him.

WERTHEIMER: Your attitude toward yourself in this fight is interesting, too. You talked about getting a sort of a romantic feeling about it — brave soldier taking chances, being tough about it.

VERGHESE: Yes, you know, I almost hesitate to use these words in the context of AIDS. We are talking about a fatal disease with incredible suffering, but there is a strange element about it. I know I'm not unique in experiencing this when I talk to fellow physicians in this field. There's almost a heroic quality to AIDS, analogous, perhaps, to the days of World War II when London was being bombed and you went to bed every night saying good-bye to your neighbor and not knowing if this was a simple good-bye. The good-bye was always weighted down with the sense of what had happened yesterday and what was coming tomorrow. In the AIDS scare, we're always imbued with that same sense of life being lived at the edge with a heightened, three-dimensional quality to everything we do. Nurses who've worked with me and have then gone on to work at some other doctor's office for whatever reason will call me up, and say, "You know, it is so incredibly boring here compared to what we used to do." It strikes me that it's because you cannot write a job definition for people who take care of HIV. It isn't a matter of doing a job. You have to have a passion for it. You have to actually be caught up in the romance, if you will, of it. And I think everyone I have met who's committed to AIDS care is caught up in it. There is no job definition that would encompass what they do. I can't imagine doing anything else.

WERTHEIMER: But there came a time when you described being "out on the tennis court without a racket," having nothing to do, no weapon, no way to handle it. And then, about seventy or eighty pages later in the book, it occurs to you that the only weapon you have is the oldest weapon of nineteenth-century medicine. You can help people die comfortably.

VERGHESE: Yes. It was a wonderful insight, a painful insight, but the more I think about it, the more I think that this is the lesson of AIDS, that there's a distinction between healing and curing. One of the sad things that happened when penicillin came around from pneumococcal pneumonia is that all you had to do was give one shot of penicillin and the pneumonia would be cured. But in the process, we robbed the patient and, perhaps, the physician, of the whole experience of carefully percussing the lung and sounding it out and putting hot poultices on and taking the temperature every four hours and waiting for the fever to break, and all these rituals, I suspect, had their enormously important function with the patient. And when Western medicine became so conceited with all the cures that we were able to offer, we left this huge void behind. I suspect that part of the bad rap we have as physicians is because we didn't address the issues of the soul, the need for healing. With AIDS, exactly the converse happened. We didn't have anything to offer, but we began to realize that we had to offer the very things that have made the physician-patient relationship so hallowed for so many reasons, and that is ourselves, our interest, our presence. It may sound strange to say this, but I think a healing can take place even when the disease is incurable and they go on to die. That's a healing that takes place both in the patient and in the physician.

In his book, *How We Die*, Dr. SHERWIN NULAND, surgeon, teacher, and writer, recalls how, as a medical student, he held a dying heart in his hands. In the book and in this interview with Noah Adams, Nuland addresses the question, Does the moment of death bring extreme pain and distress? February 10, 1994

NULAND: The great William Osler, who died in 1919, and who was probably the greatest professor of medicine this country has ever known, describes a series of five hundred cases that he looked up in charts at Johns Hopkins and then in England. He said approximately one person in five died in agony, which is about the way most clinical physicians would put it. Certain diseases carry patients off in desperate circumstances, and as far as the others are concerned, twenty percent of people die instantly or within an hour of the onset of symptoms. Many of the others go through a long period of great difficulty until the last day or two, and then, for whatever reason, seem to be separated from the worst of it and die a relatively tranquil death.

ADAMS: Let's talk about that last day for a moment. You offer a lot of evidence that nature has a way of providing a tranquilizer in morphinelike endorphins. You tell a horrific story about the death of Katie, a young, beautiful child of nine years old in a small town in Connecticut, who was attacked by a paranoid schizophrenic with a knife at a county fair. Her mother watched as Katie died. Describe what happened and the expression on Katie's face as she was dying.

NULAND: The mother continued to talk about this throughout our lengthy discussion. I met her three years after these events, and she still dwelt on the need to have her impression confirmed. Katie had on her face a look of a little bit of surprise, a little bit of serenity. There have been a number of studies of people who die suddenly, or come very close to death, where the endorphin level in the blood is shown to be markedly elevated. There is little question in my mind that many patients faced with a sudden trauma, especially one in which there is blood loss, will shoot their endorphins up in the air, which means that they have the same effect as if we gave them an injection of morphine. My guess is that Katie's endorphins were very high and somehow she was relieved of the terror that that moment would have instilled in anyone without a high level of endorphins. The tranquility and the serenity that come with high levels of endorphins have survival value for our species. We have evolved this [ability] over millions of years. We are descended from people who spent their days hunting, fighting saber-toothed tigers or whatever. When one panics in the presence of sudden blood loss or sudden pain, one does the wrong thing. If one has a high level of endorphins and can remain somewhat serene, it is much more likely that death will not occur. The survivors then have children of their own. Just as we have evolved to have prehensile thumbs or bigger brains, we have evolved to have the ability to pour out high levels of endorphins when we're suddenly traumatized.

ADAMS: You found an example of a mountain climber falling to a certain death who survived and related his state of mind while falling?

NULAND: The mountain climber described serenity. David Livingstone, in his book, was picked up by a lion who shook him with the intent of killing him.

ADAMS: This is the British explorer in Africa?

NULAND: Exactly. He describes this wonderful serenity. He was looking at the lion's head and watching what the lion was doing. There's plenty of anecdotal material in Western literature, and there's scientific evidence that our endorphins go up.

ADAMS: Let's go back to the patient who has had a terrible time, dying painfully for weeks, and then the last day or so it becomes a very peaceful experience. How does endorphin release relate to that?

NULAND: No one has ever studied the last day of life to seek out whether or not there is an increase in endorphins or whether our bodies and our minds respond to the same level of endorphins much more sensitively than they do before we're really in extremis. It may simply be that when everything is exhausted, the same level of endorphins provide the kind of tranquility that was previously provided by a higher level. I don't know how clear I've made that, but every clinical physician can tell you of many experiences he or she has had in which the patient goes through the terrible misery of pain and nausea and vomiting and all that messy stuff that happens so often toward the end of life, and in the last day or days, sometimes in the last hours, something changes and there is a peace.

ANIMALS

DICK FRYMIRE of Irvington, Kentucky, tells Noah
Adams about the predictive powers of his late rooster,
Ted, who picked basketball and football games. Mr.
Frymire credits Ted with eighty-five percent accuracy
during the previous football season. He would place
kernels of corn in front of small signs indicating the
teams and the points, and the rooster would peck at his
choice. Ted, who was succeeded in this practice by his
son, Teddy, made his first pick in 1984, when he pecked
at Reagan over Mondale. Then it was on to sports.
March 31, 1994

FRYMIRE: Ted the Rooster brought as much or more joy than
anything I've ever witnessed in my lifetime. He was truly an
American folk hero.

ADAMS: Did you figure he enjoyed going through this routine?

FRYMIRE: I honestly think he did. Sometimes he would be
rather stubborn. I remember one time I was trying to get him to
do a Super Bowl game, and it took him three hours to finally do
the thing. I was so aggravated with him. It was almost like, as
I look back on it now, he was trying to tell me something. He
was getting tired of doing so much.

ADAMS: And he died of a heart attack yesterday?

FRYMIRE: It was Monday afternoon when he died. He had
been watching *The Young and the Restless* on TV — that was
his favorite soap opera, he and his little youngsters and his
wife — and when he died, I was in there. I was getting ready to
change pens with two of his youngsters. I was petting Ted, and
all of a sudden he made kind of a gurgling sound, the best I can
describe it, and just laid his head over on my hand and died. And

Ted, he was with me for eleven years, so I don't guess I can complain, but you're never ready for anything like this. I've never seen such an outpouring of sympathy for anything in my life. We've gotten calls from all over the country. Yesterday, we got one from London, England.

ADAMS: Had Ted made any predictions for the NCAA?

FRYMIRE: Only ones he'd done was for the University of Louisville and the University of Kentucky games, and he got three out of the four on that. That's the only ones he'd done. Now the grains of corn are going to pass to Ted Junior, or Teddy, as I call him. He just did his first this morning. Now, how it's going to work with Teddy, I don't know.

ADAMS: So Teddy's taking over?

FRYMIRE: I'm going to let Teddy try to take over. We just finished doing that a few minutes ago.

ADAMS: OK, we have coming up on Saturday, Arizona and Arkansas.

FRYMIRE: It's going to be Arkansas by six. Now, how I did that, I placed one sign with ARIZONA in front of him and one with ARKANSAS in front him. In front of each sign are nineteen numbers. In front of each number is a grain of corn. He went to the ARKANSAS sign and ate the grain of corn in front of the number six. This is the same way that Ted was doing it. That tells me that Arkansas will win by six. In the Duke-Florida game, he went to the DUKE sign and ate the grain of corn in front of the number four. So that tells me he thinks Duke will win over Florida. Then I went ahead and did the Arkansas-Duke game, and he's predicting, or pecking out, that Arkansas will win over Duke by five points.

ADAMS: Arkansas over Duke by five.

FRYMIRE: By five.

ADAMS: Surely Ted the Rooster, the now deceased rooster, was a one-of-a-kind animal.

FRYMIRE: Yes.

ADAMS: What makes you think Teddy is going to be able to do this?

FRYMIRE: Because of the way Teddy acted right after his daddy died. I've dealt with chickens all my life, and I had never seen anything like this happen before: when the rooster died that his son would crow like that. In fact, he crowed three times two different times. That's the reason I think it's possible that Teddy'll be able to do it. Now, I'll never know until we do about fifteen or twenty games, and whether he will ever reach the height that Ted did, I don't have the slightest idea about. We're just kind of going in the dark, so to speak, right now.

Linda Wertheimer interviews ROGER TORY PETERSON, who introduced millions of people to birds and bird-watching through his field guides. The occasion was the publication of the book *Roger Tory Peterson: The Art and Photography of the World's Foremost Birder*. Peterson talks about how, in his youth, he came by his passion for birds. November 21, 1994

PETERSON: The thing that hooked me on birds was the teacher who gave us a box of watercolors and a color print by Fuertes, a great bird painter. She gave me the blue jay, and I thought I did it very well. The following weekend, I went to explore new territory south of town, and there on the trunk of an oak tree was a bundle of brown feathers. It looked dead. It was a flicker, tired from migration, but I thought it was dead, and I very gently poked this bird, and it suddenly woke up and with those wild eyes looked at me and then flashed away on these bright golden wings. It was that contrast, something that I thought was dead was very much alive, and ever since, birds have seemed to me the most vivid expression of life.

WERTHEIMER: You mention in this book painting like Audubon and attempting to paint like Fuertes. You talk about the plants and things that you drew in order to make a background for the birds being influenced by Aubrey Beardsley and those curvy drawings of his.

PETERSON: Yes. I think my earlier influences were drawings that had space and balance in them and expressed the Audubonesque approach.

WERTHEIMER: What about Fuertes? You say here that you think he's the best bird painter.

PETERSON: He was the best link between Audubon and the

present lot because he gave life to birds. Audubon wired them up, he gave them a semblance of life, but Fuertes knew what we call pterylography, feathers following form. He was the one that painted them so they looked very realistic. He gave them life.

WERTHEIMER: If you define Audubon as having recorded the minute recordings of static birds and Fuertes as being the man whose birds burst into life, then where does Roger Tory Peterson fit?

PETERSON: Well, my field guides, which most people know me for, are simply a different art form to make it simpler for people to identify birds. I always thought that the old-timers, the academics, were so formal in the way they described the bird. They would describe it from the tip of the beak to the end of the tail. A robin, for example, would have a black tip on a yellow beak, three white spots around a dark eye, six black stripes on a white throat on a gray head, and it was only halfway down the page that you'd find it had a red breast. It seemed to me that you could go directly to that and save people a lot of pain and agony.

WERTHEIMER: In the book, there's a collection of your limited edition paintings. This is a beautiful one, *Blue Jays with Autumn Oak Leaves*. It's incredibly pretty, in part, I think, because of the brown leaves and the blue birds.

PETERSON: Yes, but you'll notice that I've not painted a distant background. It's just the immediate accessories, and that sort of thing would be Audubonesque.

WERTHEIMER: Looking through the book, I notice two pages of hummingbirds, all lined up. It looks a little bit like a photograph of birds later in the book, little sea birds. They're standing on a beach, all lined up exactly the same way as they would be on the hummingbird plates.

PETERSON: Well, there's a kind of an immediacy to it when you get that moment of tension, when they're all posed in the same direction. In another moment, they'll be flying. In taking my photographs, I try to get that feeling of motion or composition. Photography is my therapy. Painting is my work, and painting is very hard work, I think. Many people think of me as painting so easily.

WERTHEIMER: Dashing them off.

PETERSON: Dashing them off. You don't dash things off. There's a kind of immediacy about a photograph, capturing a moment. I do have problems at my age with my eyes, but I can still see a picture, a composition and all that, and I do bless these special lenses they have now that give you autofocus because they even get those grab shots that are gone in a moment.

WERTHEIMER: There's a two-page photograph of bald eagles. It's such a beautiful photograph. The birds are very austere just sitting on the branch not doing anything at all, the way they do; but the tree they're sitting on —

PETERSON: That's what makes the picture.

WERTHEIMER: Moves all around, all these curvy lines, and you see these very somber birds with their white heads.

PETERSON: Yes, that's true. So often it's the branch work that makes the picture — certainly with birds of prey. Now, if I were to go to one of the spots in Alaska where as many as four hundred eagles come down in the same area, you'd get great patterns in the trees. In a way, it depends on the tree branches to make the picture.

WERTHEIMER: I still love this picture of the little shore birds. What are they?

PETERSON: Those are willets. They're about to fly. The one thing about that picture that could have been improved on is the depth. I'm going to do better with some of these birds in the near future, and that's why I'm going back to the Antarctic and the Falkland Islands in December, to do some of these things better.

WERTHEIMER: You're going to photograph penguins?

PETERSON: Penguins and other birds.

WERTHEIMER: So your eighty-seventh winter you're going to spend in a frozen place?

PETERSON: Well, it will be much more frozen in Connect-

icut. Connecticut might go down to ten below zero. I won't see
anything under thirty-two down where I'm going.

WERTHEIMER: Why are you doing this?

PETERSON: Because I want to photograph some of these birds
better, and I enjoy the Antarctic birds, the penguins. Penguins
are one of my favorite families of birds.

WERTHEIMER: Why do you like them?

PETERSON: They're a bit humanistic. They've got their flip-
pers to the sides, as we do, and they are such capable birds on
land as well as in the water. I'm not quite sure — you see, I don't
really have a favorite bird. As a family, I think penguins are my
favorites. On the other hand, the blue jay is a favorite because
it was the first bird I drew. But the bird that hooked me, really,
was that flicker that I saw on the tree trunk. From then on, I was
a birder.

One morning before dawn, at the Sacramento National Wildlife Refuge in California's Central Valley, Noah Adams witnesses one of the largest waterfowl migrations in memory with Dr. FRITZ REED, a waterfowl biologist. November 11, 1994

REED: Behind us and flying overhead right now are a few individual snow geese. They're mixing up and trying to find a flock to land in. Most of the geese that we're hearing in the distance are called squeakers. They're white-fronted geese. We can hear a wide variety of different species of ducks out there. Just behind us there's some gadwall. There's a hand shoveler that just called. We can hear the whistles of the pintail. There are a large number of pintail on the water and up in the air. You can hear them whistling.

ADAMS: Can you recognize all the ducks by their sound?

REED: I can't recognize all the ducks by their sound, but there are certain species like pintail, widgeon, and teal that have whistles that differ from the quacks that you commonly hear. Gadwall have a real grunting quack. It's a real deep, deep quack. It differs from mallard. There's a male and female shoveler over there that are courting, and I think she doesn't want to be disturbed.

It looks like a tornado, and when you look closely it's actually ducks, and what's happened is, there is a peregrine falcon that's been roosting over there and it probably made a dive at some of the teal and got up the whole group of birds.

ADAMS: There's hundreds of ducks in the air.

REED: There's thousands of ducks in the air.

ADAMS: Thousands.

REED: Yes, there's probably upwards of sixty thousand to seventy thousand ducks up in the air right there. The dabbling ducks, which are many of the birds that we're seeing out here today, forage by putting their bill either on the surface or just under the surface of the water. They'll move along and act as little vacuum cleaners, sucking up the water and the plant and invertebrate material. They'll then shoot the water back out and catch the little seeds and invertebrates on their lamellae, or their toothlike structures, and then take their tongue and just whip it around, kind of like a big baleen whale.

ADAMS: What do you figure that sounds like? Does it make a noise that you can hear?

REED: When there are a lot ducks foraging it makes a lot of noise. There's a lot of splashing. They have what's called a feeding chuckle, and we've heard that a little bit here today. I don't know if you can say they're happy, but they're making this chuckling noise and foraging in a big group. [sounds of geese circling and calling]

ADAMS: Is that communication?

REED: They communicate with each other, yes, both in the calls and in signaling with their wings. You can see some of the birds coming low now. They're whiffling. Some of them are turning upside down. They're twisting around trying to drop elevation really fast.

ADAMS: How many people are you finding now are coming here from the cities in California just to watch the geese come in and land?

REED: This refuge is used by a lot of people from the San Francisco area, from the Sacramento area. This refuge is open year-round so that you can see birds, not ducks so much in the summer, more wading birds, marsh birds. But in the winter, that's when you see the peak usage here. People looking at the tremendous number of waterfowl. When you come out here on a weekend, looking at the people that are just watching the ducks, you look, and a lot of them are members of hunting groups and they have dogs in the car and they're driving around and they're really enjoying the birds out here in these marshes.

....

BEA KESLING of Sharpsville, Indiana, tells Robert Siegel how she and her husband, Irv, have trained llamas to square-dance. The Keslings own nearly 170 llamas. They sell them for pets and to other farms. April 26, 1994

KESLING: We've always trained our llamas when they wean off the mother at about five and a half months of age. We teach them to be halter broke, and we kept thinking of square dancing with llamas. And why not? Because they'll go right along with you on their lead rope. So when you dance, your partner is a llama.

SIEGEL: I'm trying to imagine the scene: you're square-dancing, your partner is a llama, and you're holding the llama by the reins, by the halter. Just how far into it can the llama get? Can you, say, honor your partner? Honor your corner?

KESLING: Usually in those two calls you're bowing to your partner. So if you take ahold of that lead rope and pull your partner's head down with you as you bow to your corner or to your partner, the llama will do the same thing you're doing. If you see it from a distance, they appear to all be going into a bow just like you want them to, and the llamas accept this and they seem to enjoy and like it as much as we do.

SIEGEL: I can imagine that a command like do-si-do would get a little complicated with a llama.

KESLING: Well, that's one of them that we have done. We have a square-dance caller who watches the action and, in the event that he needs to speed up calls, he can, or slow down in some cases. That way it keeps the music moving smoothly and it all works out.

SIEGEL: You're not going to tell me that you also swing your partner with a llama?

KESLING: No, we haven't done that as yet.

SIEGEL: When you demonstrate the square dancing, do you do it with just with four people and four llamas?

KESLING: Right, that constitutes a square. Now most of the time we've used two squares so we had eight llamas and eight people dancing.

SIEGEL: Both going at once?

KESLING: Yes.

SIEGEL: How do people react the first time that they see the llamas square-dancing?

KESLING: They love it. They're surprised the first time they hear about it, and they think, Oh, surely not, but when they see them it's fun, and a lot of the people will come up from the crowd and dance with the llamas.

SIEGEL: You mean they'll join in the square dance at that point?

KESLING: Right, we get lots of people involved.

SIEGEL: And the llamas don't mind a strange partner?

KESLING: No, they handle that just fine.

....

TED ERIKSON of Chicago swam the English Channel
three times, thirty years ago. He tells Noah Adams
of his plan to swim the channel one more time with his
dog, Umbra, alongside. They have trained together in
Lake Michigan and in the Atlantic Ocean, off the coast
of Florida. Erikson reports that Umbra can swim
between three and four miles in open water, averaging
twenty-eight minutes per mile. March 4, 1994

ADAMS: Is she slowing you down? Is her pace slower than
yours?
ERIKSON: No, no, no! I have to wear fins to keep up with her.
ADAMS: I see.
ERIKSON: She's cranking right along. I mean, a twenty-eight-
minute mile is a little tough for a sixty-six-year-old man. With
the fins I can do it, but after two or three miles I even start
slowing down.
ADAMS: Now, what happens at the end of three and a half
miles?
ERIKSON: She goes chasing squirrels and ducks.
ADAMS: Does she show signs of being tired?
ERIKSON: No. I will say this, when I first came down to
Florida she hadn't swum since since October. I brought her
down there and the first swim I gave her was a little over a mile
and a half. She was a little bit tired when she came out of the
water and she kind of stood there for a few moments, and I gave
her a couple of snackers and then she started coming out of it.
In about five or ten minutes, she was ready to roll around again.
The next day we did a mile and a half, two miles. I keep adding
a little bit more every time we go swimming. We did a three and
a half the other day and no sign of tiredness at all.

ADAMS: Umbra is what sort of dog? What's her lineage?

ERIKSON: She's a Lab-greyhound mix, I believe. She's a homeless stray from Indiana.

ADAMS: In Britain, the Royal Society for the Prevention of Cruelty to Animals —

ERIKSON: I don't know what their problem is.

ADAMS: The RSPCA says dogs are not built to spend long hours in the sea, and fifteen hours is far too long.

ERIKSON: Well, I don't know. The London *Daily Mail* gave me some information about a Newfoundland that had been authenticated to have been in the water fifty hours and swam to shore. It fell off a cargo ship. If they think I'm trying to kill my dog they're out of their minds, because I'm not trying to hurt the dog. I'm having fun with the dog. As long as the dog enjoys it, I intend to swim that dog as far as she wants to swim, and if I can keep up with her we're going to go as far as we can go.

ADAMS: Do you have any doubts about your ability to make it again across the channel?

ERIKSON: Yes, I have more doubts about my ability than the dog's. [*laughs*] I wouldn't want to swim her without me being in the water because I'm sure that I'm providing the motivation for her. It's just a love affair, that's all. Best female I've ever known.

According to STANLEY COREN's book, *The Intelligence of Dogs*, the Border collie is the most intelligent of seventy-nine breeds he evaluated. Coren ranked the poodle second, the German shepherd third, and the Afghan hound last. His rankings were based on a survey of more than a hundred obedience instructors. He reminds Noah Adams, however, that all dogs are intelligent. April 20, 1994

COREN: They are certainly a lot smarter than a number of animals that we tend to think of as being bright, like lions or tigers or even elephants.

ADAMS: Tell us about the Dandie Dinmont terrier. Now, this is a dog popularized by Sir Walter Scott.

COREN: In a book called *Guy Mannering*. The Dandie Dinmont terrier is an absolutely marvelous little dog. It tends to weigh about twenty to thirty pounds and is absolutely fearless. It will attack a badger who weighs one and a half times its size.

ADAMS: You say a couple bought a Dandie Dinmont and finally gave up, saying that training this dog would be easier if the dog was a sack of potatoes.

COREN: Yes, they are very stubborn dogs. One of the basic things which you tend to give to a dog is the heel command, which basically means the dog has to walk beside you on a slack lead. These particular dogs would not even look at their owners, and if you tried to heel them they would roll over on their backs so that there'd be less friction when you'd drag them along the floor. [*laughs*] I suppose that takes a degree of cleverness too.

ADAMS: Just as a point of history, tell us who Dandie Dinmont was, the man.

COREN: Well, Dandie Dinmont was a character in the Sir

Walter Scott book. He's a farmer who grew these particular terriers. He is modeled after a real person.

ADAMS: Well, let's look up Dandie Dinmont on the list. Do you recall where they fall now?

COREN: They're sixty-two out of seventy-nine.

ADAMS: Oh yes, sixty-two out of seventy-nine, Dandie Dinmont terrier.

COREN: So that's going to be a rough dog to train.

ADAMS: Yes.

COREN: But you have to pick a dog to match your lifestyle. If you're away from home twelve to fourteen hours a day, you shouldn't go out and get yourself a Doberman pinscher. You know, they're number five on the list, they require a lot of stimulation and that sort of thing. In order to stimulate himself, he's going to eat your couch. He's going to destroy your Ming vase collection or whatever else.

On the other hand, suppose you had a bulldog. Their processing rate is much slower. They don't bore as easily, so they don't need that additional stimulation. At the end of the day, you come in, your couch is intact, your pottery collection is undisturbed, and here is this very sweet dog, saying, "Welcome home, I remember you!"

ADAMS: I was kind of surprised to see the golden retriever up here at number four. Now, this is kind of a placid dog. The golden is a very nice pet, a pet to have around with kids, right?

COREN: Yes, yes, they're splendid. Some people say they're goofy, that they act in a silly way. Goldens want to please very much, and they're bright enough to know what you'll enforce and what you won't. If they detect in your voice tone an indication that you're not going to enforce a command, they will ignore you. And they're very playful and very sweet.

The most surprise which people have is with the poodles —

ADAMS: Number two.

COREN: Yes, that they're number two. A lot of people say they're froufrou or fancy dogs. One of the things which people have to remember is the poodle did not ask for that particular haircut. They're really derived from German water retrievers, and they're quite solid working dogs, really quite splendid.

ADAMS: You tell a story from your childhood about your grandmother Lena and her belief about the dog Skipper that you all had. Lena had the idea that dogs could see the Angel of Death.

COREN: Yes, the folklore associated with dogs: sometimes dogs will growl or bark at something which you don't see, and the belief is that if you look through the dog's ears, you know, just sight down their nose, you can maybe see what they're seeing, but that, very often, they see the Angel of Death and try to interpose in front of the Angel.

You see, we have this responsiveness for dogs which is really quite incredible. We created them in some respects. Dogs have been with human beings for — we have fossil evidence — fourteen thousand years. That doesn't sound like much, with *Jurassic Park* and all that other stuff out there, but fourteen thousand years is a long time when you consider the fact that organized agriculture didn't come about until ten thousand years ago.

Every culture seems to have stories about dogs. One of my favorites is from the Plains Sioux Indians. The Great Spirit, the creator, decided to separate the world of animals and the world of men, so he gathered all living things on the Great Plains, and he drew a line down in the dirt. That line began to expand and form into a great deep crevasse, and at the last moment before it became unbreachable, dog leapt over and stood by man.

Dr. FRANCINE (PENNY) PATTERSON talks with Bob Edwards about Koko the Gorilla, who gained renown in the 1970s for learning from her handlers to communicate in American Sign Language. Television news features and documentaries showed Koko signing, as well as playing with her pet kitten, All Ball. Dr. Patterson talks about Koko's romantic involvement, at age twenty-two, with a younger male, a three-hundred-pound African lowland gorilla named Ndume. Patterson is the president and research director of the Gorilla Foundation, the group that works with Koko. February 3, 1994

PATTERSON: We're hoping that she'll have a baby for her own satisfaction, and also because gorillas are an endangered species, but beyond that there's a scientific reason and that is to see if Koko will teach sign language to her offspring. We've seen some signs of this. She would sign to her kitten, for instance, but also she takes her gorilla doll's hands and molds them into signs. We think that she may do the same with her own off-spring.

EDWARDS: The kitten probably had a little trouble answering back.

PATTERSON: [*laughs*] Yes, the kitten didn't know what was going on.

EDWARDS: But wouldn't a gorilla be more likely to revert to gorilla ways of expressing herself with another gorilla?

PATTERSON: Well, that's a very good question, because what we're finding is that the signs that we are teaching them are not an artificial system that we're imposing on them. We have discovered that gorillas without any instruction in sign language use over sixty different gestures that very much resemble American Sign Language. What we've done is established a common vocabulary, and that's why we can get privy to what it is that they're communicating.

EDWARDS: What kind of gesture would a gorilla make?

PATTERSON: Some of the gestures we have observed at the San Francisco Zoo are in fact in common with Koko's, gestures like "take off," which is the hand running flat across the top of the head forward. It's used by the gorillas in the zoo before they jump off an object and down to the ground. Koko uses it to mean that, but she also uses it to mean, "Take off your coat, take off your contacts," you know. "Take off other things." So she uses it in two ways.

EDWARDS: How did you go about finding a mate for Koko?

PATTERSON: We worked with the Species Survival Plan, which is a group formed in Northern American zoos and institutions that house gorillas, and we put in our petition for a mate for Koko. The Cincinnati Zoo responded with Ndume. He had already fathered four offspring at the Brookfield Zoo, where he was on loan, and was available. Koko responded very favorably to him on videotape.

EDWARDS: So you did video dating?

PATTERSON: [*laughs*] Yes, Koko actually engaged in some video dating. We thought that this would be valuable because female gorillas are rather choosy about their mates. In many cases, a female or a male will be shipped to another location and nothing will happen. The chemistry won't be there. So we showed her various tapes. She was thumbs down on some of the males. A male in Tacoma, Washington — she turned her back and ignored him, and then took her toy alligator and attacked the screen with it. Whereas, a male in Italy she was wild about. She kissed the screen and stared at the screen, asked it to be played again and again. Her reaction to Ndume was somewhere in between.

EDWARDS: Well, what happened to the Italian gorilla?

PATTERSON: Well, we tried very, very hard to convince the

officials at the zoo in Italy to release him to us, at least to loan
him for a time, so that Koko could make a family, but that just
wasn't in their plans.

EDWARDS: They must get a lot of requests for this guy, right?
[laughs]

PATTERSON: Well, I don't know.

EDWARDS: A hot commodity.

PATTERSON: He certainly looked good to me. [laughs]

EDWARDS: OK, so you found Ndume.

PATTERSON: Yes.

EDWARDS: And she went for him.

PATTERSON: She likes him very much. The first day that
they were introduced, we thought, Well, this is going to take
weeks. Koko isn't going to warm up to him very quickly. She
instantly asked for the gate to be opened between them, and I
said, "Are you sure?" She insisted, and she just dashed in and
tried to chase him down.

EDWARDS: What did he make of this?

PATTERSON: He was a little shook up [laughs], taken aback,
I guess, is the word. He wasn't aggressive, except if she got too
close, and he'd sort of wing his arm to keep her at a distance
because she was so new. She had seen him before, so, you know,
maybe she felt that she knew him.

EDWARDS: Should have showed her tape to him.

PATTERSON: Right. We didn't do that. That might have been
a good idea.

EDWARDS: So then what?

PATTERSON: They have been together ever since, every day.
They don't sleep together because our facilities don't allow that
right now, but we're hoping to create a situation, a preserve in
Hawaii, where they will be able to be together all day long.
Koko, in the meantime, has stopped cycling regularly, so we are
consulting experts on fertility to see what we can do to cause
her cycle to restart. We've found a way, but we're not doing that
yet because we have still another problem. The neighboring

property owner here intends to log his property, and this could cause severe distress to the gorillas. So we're on hold right now until we find out what's happening with the logging.

EDWARDS: So the noise from the logging operation —

PATTERSON: Could be just devastating to the gorillas' well-being. That's the way we feel about it. There's research to back that up. We're trying to see if we can't get it stopped.

EDWARDS: Are you sure it's the logging, or maybe Koko's changed her mind?

PATTERSON: I don't think so. She still very much wants to go in with him every day. We feel that she's possibly feeling a little bit stressed by this new relationship [*laughs*] and needs encouragement in the form of our, you know, words, or our signs, but we think maybe also in the form of some hormonal supplements. It may also be that she is holding out for that Italian.

Why do snakes have forked tongues? In an article in
the journal *Science*, KURT SCHWENK, a biologist at the
University of Connecticut, offered an answer: the
flicking forked tongue is a delicate sensing system.
He explains how it works to Noah Adams.
March 18, 1994

SCHWENK: The snake moves along a chemical trail that
would be invisible to you or me. It touches the ground with the
fork of its tongue, and it spreads the tips apart as far as it can.
It picks up chemicals deposited on the ground by a food item,
a potential mate, another snake, for example. It picks up those
chemicals, delivers them to the sensory organs in the snout, and
assesses in what direction the trail is leading.

ADAMS: Is the snake tasting or smelling?

SCHWENK: Based on the anatomy of the system, it's much
more like smell than like taste.

ADAMS: What actually is going on with the chemical the
snake picks up?

SCHWENK: It's delivered into the mouth and, by means still
quite mysterious, those molecules make their way up into tiny
holes in the roof of the mouth and into a little paired sensory
organ like a little bulb with a sensory epithelium.

ADAMS: You also postulate that the two tips of the tongue
act as a sort of stereo sensor.

SCHWENK: Yes. That's the best analogy for understanding it.
If we hear a sound off to our left, for example, it will sound a
little bit louder to our left ear than to our right ear, and that
gives our brain a clue that the sound is coming from somewhere
off to the left — in other words, a directional sense. In exactly
the same way, the tongue, as a delivery mechanism, picks up
more chemical on one side than the other side. When the brain

gets that information, it knows that the chemical source is a little more to the left than to the right. So in that sense, it's kind of a stereo system.

ADAMS: Why does the tongue keep flicking in and out of the snake's mouth?

SCHWENK: That kind of flicking behavior they typically do when they're moving or investigating a novelty. It's a very basic and fundamental sense to snakes and lizards. That flicking is their way of exploring their environment.

ADAMS: But is that part of the process wherein the molecules are delivered into the mouth?

SCHWENK: Absolutely. With every flick, they're bringing those chemicals in, just as you and I are constantly smelling the air every time we inhale and exhale.

ADAMS: The snake does this, you're saying, when it's looking for food or looking for a mate. Any other times?

SCHWENK: Yes. One of the most important times, in some species, is during winter aggregations. Many species of snakes den up in the winter. The juveniles wouldn't necessarily know their way back to the den to hibernate, and they've been shown to follow these invisible scent trails back to the den. That's another important function.

ADAMS: When you were poking around in history, trying to figure out what theories were correct about why the snake has a forked tongue, which one seemed most interesting and most apt to you?

SCHWENK: Well, the most interesting to me was the idea of an Italian worker back in the seventeenth century who noted that snakes tended to crawl along the ground in the dirt. He proposed that this forked tongue would actually clean out their nostrils, I guess by insertion directly into the nostrils. That was the most novel idea, I thought.

SUE HUBBELL, the author of *Broadsides from the Other Orders: A Book of Bugs*, talks about insects with Jacki Lyden. Hubbell keeps bees in the Ozarks, has observed camel crickets shedding their chrysalis, and knows how dragonflies mate and how daddy longlegs smell.
June 26, 1994

HUBBELL: Two parents came over with their little girl. She was maybe four, and she was fascinated with the bees. The parents were terribly scared. The bees were in a very good mood. There was a honey flow on. They weren't interested in stinging anybody. I put a couple of drops of honey on my arm — this is sort of a parlor trick that beekeepers do — and got a bee to come and walk along and suck up the honey. The little girl was just delighted. She wanted to do the same. Her parents were inside my house, looking out the window, quaking with fear. Somewhere along the line, the curiosity gets lost.

My private feeling is that we live in a culture that has a lot of frightening things going on. We have a lot of information at hand and we know what terrible things that are going on in Rwanda or down in Guatemala. I think we feel that we're lacking control in some way. Bugs reproduce rapidly, they're foreign, they look like invaders from space. They represent everything that's wild, the things you can't control. And you can't do anything about Rwanda, but, damn it, if there is a bug on your petunias you can do something about that.

LYDEN: Tell me about gnats and midges a little bit, about why swarms of gnats follow us. I thought it was fascinating that they're relating to us.

HUBBELL: Yes. Mating swarms of males orient themselves by some marker. You often see them near a tall fence post or something like that. But a human being is a tall fence post as far as a midge is concerned, and if you start walking along they just keep flying along with you. The females stay out of the swarm at the beginning. The males are doing a dancing motion in there, and there's some thought that the group of them together, moving like that, increases the male sex hormones. The females are around, lurking in bushes and things, and when they just can't stand it, they fly in and mate with the males.

LYDEN: One of the most glorious scenes that you've written about is ladybugging in the Sierra Nevadas.

HUBBELL: Yes. Like many organic gardeners, I at one time had ordered a package of ladybugs in the mail. They come in a nice, neat, little box, and they tell you to put them in the refrigerator and let them out every once in a while. I'd let them out and they'd go away and I'd never see them again. I kept wondering how those ladybugs got in a box, so I called up a seed company. The man was very nice, after he got done laughing, and said, "Well, we get them from harvesters. I don't know much about how they do it," but he gave me the name of a company that dealt with them, and I called them up, and said, "I understand ladybugs are harvested. Is that true?" They said, "Yes, it's true," and I said, "Can I come on a harvest?" And they said yes. I was elated to be able to do it. It reminded me of the gold mining days because these guys can make up to a thousand dollars a day just harvesting ladybugs. The ladybugs come back to the same place in the Sierras during drought periods in the lowlands. I was sworn to secrecy about where I went and exactly how the procedure went, but a couple of very nice guys took me out for several days and it was enormous fun.

LYDEN: Was there a time when you could see them emerging, these bright orange bugs, through the leaves?

HUBBELL: Yes, yes. As I say, I'm sworn to secrecy about exactly how they get them to come out from the leaves, but it's awesome to see. I mean, this is like zillions of these bugs.

LYDEN: We as human beings spend a lot of time conquering each other, trying to scope each other out, but in the insect world, there's all sorts of behavior that you could never fathom. It all seems to be about preservation of the species.

HUBBELL: All animals share that. I think that's exactly the strategy, whether you're going to reproduce crazily and do it through sheer numbers or develop some sort of protection. It certainly brings it all home, doesn't it? Curiously, we separate ourselves from the world and somehow think that everything out there is other, but we're all animals and we all have to solve this problem of how to make a living.

TOM LAPUZZA of the U.S. Navy Command Control and Ocean Surveillance Center in San Diego describes to Noah Adams the mission of navy dolphins. Budget cuts led the navy to retire twenty-five dolphins from its Underwater Surveillance Program. June 15, 1994

LAPUZZA: The dolphins provide a general capability underwater. The specific applications we have for the animals are two systems that locate mines. They're systems in which the dolphins are trained to find a mine. Human divers then swim down and do whatever human divers do to defuse mines.

ADAMS: Has that actually happened?

LAPUZZA: No, we have not done mine hunting and operational systems yet.

ADAMS: OK, what else?

LAPUZZA: The other is a system in which the dolphins operate very much like guard dogs at a land base, but they're doing it at a base that's fronting on the water. The dolphin, like the guard dog, advises his handlers that there's an intruder in the area, and then the security forces move in and deal with the intruder. That system was operational and used in Vietnam in 1970 and 1971 and again in the Persian Gulf in 1986 and 1987.

ADAMS: How many dolphins do you have now?

LAPUZZA: One hundred and one.

ADAMS: And you need to get rid of —

LAPUZZA: Twenty-five.

ADAMS: Because of budget problems?

LAPUZZA: Right, exactly.

ADAMS: What's your best plan for getting rid of the twenty-five?

LAPUZZA: Keeping them. An alternative is transferring some of those animals to qualified marine parks that meet a set of relatively rigid standards of health care and so on that we've established for that process.

ADAMS: But can you afford to keep them as opposed to giving them away?

LAPUZZA: Yes. The navy's committed itself financially as well as ethically to maintain the animals for the rest of their lives.

ADAMS: How long would that be?

LAPUZZA: Thirty years.

ADAMS: Some dolphins you've had around since Vietnam?

LAPUZZA: Yes.

ADAMS: Getting pretty old?

LAPUZZA: Yes, true. Those we would probably never give to anybody because they deserve our good care for the rest of their lives. There are some in the middle stages, animals that we've had ten years, twelve years, that we would consider for the potential of transfer, but at the moment we have no imperative to move the animals away from where they are.

ADAMS: Why would you not just release the dolphins? The dolphins came from the ocean in the first place.

LAPUZZA: We think that just releasing them is the moral equivalent of dropping your dog off along the side of a country road and saying he'll probably be OK. Our belief is that you owe the animal something for the work they put in on your behalf. We did a scientific study in the summer of 1992 at the direction of Congress to see about the notion of releasing them. Our opinion was that it is not in the best interest of the animals to release them. The potential for infecting wild dolphins with some disease that the animals might have that we don't know about, the potential for the animal not doing well in the wild or being conversely affected by some disease that the animals out there had, was just too great a risk.

ADAMS: And the dolphins? Let's say they stay in San Diego. What would their life be like there if they were no longer in training?

LAPUZZA: Very much like it is now. The animals that we

have are exercised every day. They're in large enclosures, and they have the capability to swim in and out among the enclosures, so they socialize almost twenty hours a day. They have wide swimming areas. In most instances, we release the animals in San Diego Harbor, in the Pacific Ocean, and they swim essentially freely on their own for some period of time during the day to ensure that they get proper exercise.

ADAMS: You're saying they're actually turned loose in the harbor and they come back.

LAPUZZA: Exactly. We calculated the other day that the navy has released its dolphins two hundred thousand times and in all but a very, very few of those instances, the animals came back.

James Alfred Wight, better known as the best-selling author and veterinarian James Herriot, was briefly hospitalized with a broken leg, an injury sustained when he was trampled by a flock of black-faced sheep. Mr. Wight was trying to stop them from eating his flower garden. The accident was highly publicized in Thirsk, Yorkshire, the town in the north of England where Mr. Wight chronicled his life as a country vet in such books as *All Creatures Great and Small*. Robert Siegel interviews MARTIN WAINWRIGHT, the northern correspondent of the British newspaper *The Guardian* about the incident. July 5, 1994

SIEGEL: Mr. Wainwright, black-faced sheep? Are these dangerous creatures to be around in the north of England?

WAINWRIGHT: They're very independent-minded animals and also slightly stupid. They become dangerous when they're in a group or a flock and you get in their way. We just had that wonderful film *Dances with Wolves* shown on our television over here and there's a sequence when the buffalo stampede. If you can, imagine that but with sheep.

SIEGEL: Now, in Thirsk, this must be a major event when the man who has made the town famous is assaulted by animals in a way that would not be out of place in one of his books.

WAINWRIGHT: You're dead right. There's obviously tremendous sympathy for anybody age seventy-seven who suffers a broken leg, but I think there's also kind of a wry feeling that he made a living, a very good living, out of describing exactly this sort of incident in fiction. I don't think that anything like this has happened to him before, but now it has and so people's natural sympathy is slightly mixed with the feeling that, well, as soon as he is better and writing again this will appear in the next best-selling book.

SIEGEL: I see. Is this at all common that people are knocked over by black-faced sheep?

WAINWRIGHT: Yes, well, it's very common because the Yorkshire dales, which are sort of grass-covered, low-lying hills, are perfect for pasturing sheep on. The hill farmers graze the sheep up on these hills, and in towns like Thirsk there's nothing to prevent the sheep from coming into the town. There's very little fencing and very few cattle grades to stop the animals going along the roads. Just last month a teacher living in one of these small Yorkshire towns actually wrestled ten of these black-faced sheep, which were eating his flowers, and locked them in his garage and would not return them to the farmers until they paid him compensation. His neighbor was a lawyer, a solicitor, and they went into this rather carefully and discovered that he was certainly entitled to do this because the sheep had munched up all his flowers.

SIEGEL: I see. You're within your rights to lock up the rogue sheep in that case.

WAINWRIGHT: You are, and if the farmers don't pay compensation you can then take the sheep to auction at the cattle market and pay the farmers what's left from the sale of the sheep when you've deducted what you think is a fair compensation for your ruined garden. You know, English people are very, very keen on their gardens.

SIEGEL: Well, they're very keen on their sheep also.

WAINWRIGHT: [laughs] It's the great clash between two parts of our national character.

[*James Alfred Wight, known and loved by millions of readers as James Herriot, died of cancer on February 23, 1995.*]

RELIGION

JOHN SHELBY SPONG, the Episcopal bishop of Newark, New Jersey, discusses the Resurrection with Scott Simon. In his book *Resurrection: Myth or Reality?* Bishop Spong says that a literal belief that Jesus rose from the grave, spoke to his disciples, and then ascended to Heaven may be asking too much of abiding Christians. April 2, 1994

SPONG: There is hardly a detail in the Resurrection narratives that isn't contradicted in one of the other Gospels. If you take them literally and know anything about them, you're going to have serious problems. They disagree all over the place. I don't think it's fair to say that the Resurrection originally was a physical resuscitation, Jesus walking out of the grave and being seen in any physiological way. The question is, What happened to the story between whatever occurred and the first writing?

There was clearly something there that was real. It was powerful, it was life-changing, but I'm not sure that the rendition in the Gospel narratives is anything more than developed legends, and yet I'm quite sure there's something real underneath those developed legends.

SIMON: You write that we have to understand a tradition of Jewish Scripture called Midrash. Can you help us understand that?

SPONG: To me, it's the key that unlocks the Gospels. It's a concept that I hadn't engaged until about five years ago, so it's a new and fresh and wondrous sort of insight. I suddenly became aware that the Gospels are Jewish books, written by Jewish authors, and I asked the obvious question: How do Jewish people write sacred stories? They do not write them from the point of view of Western history, describing something that really happened; they write to interpret the meaning of the experience. They do this by piling layer after layer of their tradition onto the present. Let me illustrate with the story of Jesus' Ascension and the outpouring of the Holy Spirit.

In the first century, Heaven was just above the sky, so in getting to Heaven, where God lived, you simply had to rise up off the earth. But we're space age people. What does that story mean to us? I think if you go back to the Hebrew Scriptures, to the story of Elijah and Elisha, you will discover that what Luke is telling us in both the Ascension and in the Pentecost story is just a retelling of the Elijah-Elisha story. Elijah was carried up into Heaven in a fiery chariot with fiery horses, and when he got to Heaven he gave the gift of his incredible spirit — a double portion of his human spirit — to Elisha.

Imagine I'm a first-century man. I've experienced God present in Jesus. How do I expand the Elijah story to fit Jesus' Ascension? I have Jesus go up into Heaven, not with the help of a fiery chariot but on his own power, and when he gets to Heaven he doesn't pour his double portion of human spirit upon his single disciple; he pours the enormous power of God's Holy Spirit upon the whole gathered church.

Don't ask of the Ascension story or the Pentecost story, "Did this really happen?" Ask "What does it mean that Luke is wrapping the Elijah story, raised to the nth power, around Jesus of Nazareth?" That's Midrash, and that's the way you have to approach every story in the Gospel tradition. The argument that has been mounted over the years, even over the centuries, against a metaphorical understanding of the birth, the life, and the death of Jesus is the argument that if he is celebrated simply as a great teacher, a wonderful guy, an example and an insight into human character, then he joins a pretty impressive group of people, but he is no longer of God.

SIMON: He's no longer unique.

SPONG: That's right, and I understand that. I hear that, but what I think we've got to recognize is that the concept of God that was alive then was basically — I don't mean to caricature it — but it was basically an old man in the sky. God was a human being, writ large, usually a male, indeed almost always a male, and in the sky, and capable of having a will which this God would act out in human history from time to time. That was a very interesting concept of God, but in classical theological studies, that understanding of God has had a very hard time surviving the knowledge revolution beginning with Copernicus and Galileo and coming forward to today.

My youngest daughter has a Ph.D. in physics from Stanford University. One of the things I want to do as a leader of the Christian faith is to keep the literalistic, personalistic, premodern concepts of God from blocking that child, and others like her, from seeing the ultimate truth that's behind the symbols in the Christian story.

SIMON: Bishop, have you heard from people who might say to you, "My faith is real. I'm not in danger of losing it. It's not a faith in metaphors. It's a faith in an actual baby who was born in Bethlehem, an actual human being who died on the cross and ascended into Heaven"?

SPONG: I certainly don't object to that, and I'm quite content to have people be as fundamental as they want to be. I don't try to reach those people. I hope I don't disturb those people, but I'm quite sure that I do if they hear about it. They normally don't read my books. They only read reviews of my books in newspapers and they write me interesting letters. The people I'm trying to reach are quite different. I want to reach those people who say that the Church spends its time answering questions that the world no longer even asks. That's my audience. My hope is to lead people through the words of Scripture to the experience that is behind them. If we separate the interpretations of the Resurrection from the experience of the Resurrection, and lead people through the interpretations, with all of their supernatural, miraculous, fantasy language, into the power of the experience — which I do not doubt for a moment, and which I think is real and continues to transform — then I think Easter will dawn in a new way for this generation.

The living room of a house in Manassas, Virginia, is the scene of a weekly Christian prayer group. Every Wednesday night, RICK and BECKY FREER welcome their friends to pray together. The Freers and GRETCHEN TRUMP talk to Noah Adams about their own experience of prayer and their thoughts about school prayer. All three say they pray every day. Rick Freer grew up as a Catholic and went to a Jesuit college, but says he came to know God only after being saved at an evangelical meeting. Since then, he says his life is prayer; once he even heard God speaking out loud. Becky Freer says she prays for her family and also talks with God about her decorating business. June 17, 1994

BECKY: I'm trusting Him for clients. I've come to study and to learn that, as He designed and created the world, He is the top decorator that you'll ever find. I find myself relying and trusting on Him in that field. As far as color, I can hardly wait to get to Heaven to see the colors that are going to be there, because I know they far surpass anything we have here on Earth. So I have a tendency to speak with Him often.

RICK: I had a pair of shoes, and they didn't fit, and they were brand-new. I said, "God, what do I do with them? Who can I give these to?" And just as clear, I heard the name "Gary." I knew a Gary, and I knew he wasn't very wealthy, so I took him the shoes, and sure enough, they fit. And he took them. And it was just real edifying. As a result, I developed a pattern where, as an example, my flight to get back here was not supposed to leave till five-thirty, and I might not have been here yet, but Becky said, "You got to get home early." So I noticed there was an earlier flight, and it left at three-thirty. Well, I was in down-town Atlanta. It was three o'clock. I asked the fellow in the office, "Can I make a three-thirty flight?" He said, "If you really hurry." So I'm half thinking I can make it and half thinking I can't, and I asked the Lord. I said, "God, can I make it?" He said, "The plane will be late, and you can make it. You can catch that plane if you go." So I went down and got there and sure enough, exactly what the Lord said, they had been late. In fact, they didn't even leave until about twenty minutes after I got on.

I pray for my family just about every day in the morning. I pray for the church and pastor, and sometimes I pray for our nation and different things that come to mind, and I intermix that with singing some prayer songs.

ADAMS: In your car going to work?

RICK: Yes.

ADAMS: I guess it keeps you from getting angry at other drivers in traffic.

RICK: It hasn't worked a hundred percent, but I think it does help. I think it does help a lot. When I went to school we never had prayer, and I didn't think I turned out too bad as an unbeliever at the time. There are pluses and minuses to having prayer in school. If it's undirected, who knows what somebody might pray. You do have people who want to pray bad things on individuals. One of the things that I sense both in the church and out of the church is that we really don't understand the power of our words. Solomon said, "The power of life and death is in the tongue." It really impacts you. You have people who pray against you rather than for you. When you open something up that's unstructured, you have that potential.

ADAMS: Gretchen?

GRETCHEN: I agree that we need to be very cautious. One thing that I do know is that when we really came out and banned prayer in school, if you go back, you will see an increase in violent crime, in the use of drugs, in premarital sex, in un-wanted pregnancies. All of those were going up, yes, but after sixty-two, they went up sharply. There must be a correlation there somewhere.

ADAMS: But a lot of things changed after sixty-two.

GRETCHEN: Well, yes. But what takes place in the spiritual realm does have consequences in the natural. What we do in the natural also has consequences in the spiritual realm. Therefore, we need to be very cautious, and we really need to check everything that we do to make sure that we are lining up with what God's will is for us. We said to the children in sixty-two that God didn't mean anything.

Brother PETER REINHART is a member of the Christ the Savior Brotherhood, an Eastern Orthodox community in Santa Rosa, California, where he used to run a bakery-café there called Brother Juniper's Café. In his book *Sacramental Magic in a Small-Town Café*, he writes that religious feats need not wait for holidays. Brother Peter tells Daniel Zwerdling that every meal has the potential to bring us closer to understanding the mystery of life. December 24, 1994

ZWERDLING: When we sit down at the table, what should we be thinking about as we look at the bread? As we put the fork into the vegetables?

REINHART: Certainly the first step is to bless your food, because that is a very conscious symbolic act of connection, of recognizing where the food that you eat comes from. You know, I started out writing about bread because bread is used in all religions as a symbol of the presence of God in this world. The elements of bread represent that. You take flour, water, salt, and bring them together and you make a clay, a raw clay. You inject leaven or yeast, and you bring that clay to life. You actually have a living organism in your hands. As the maker of that bread dough, you shape it and cultivate that life. Then after you've allowed it to rise a few times and knocked it down, you bake it. You put it in the oven and you kill it and then you consume it. A complete life cycle takes place. This is a very shallow interpretation of the Genesis story, but it is an indication of the kind of participation that each of us have in recreating what we understand God to be.

ZWERDLING: I wouldn't call that shallow at all. I think it is quite wonderful. You say first we should pray, we should bless our food. Do we need to do it out loud? Do we need to say a certain prayer?

REINHART: I think each person has to work within their own tradition. We have all these wonderful traditions. Whether they are Christian or Jewish or Muslim, world religions all have very similar cores, but we very rarely penetrate to the practice that allows for that connection to take place. So start where you are; work with your own tradition, whether you are Protestant, Catholic, or Jewish. If the prayer is a verbal, vocal prayer, do it that way. Some people like to pray with their eyes open, some with their eyes closed. It really doesn't matter.

ZWERDLING: After we bless the food, what is the next step?

REINHART: I think the next step is to enjoy and appreciate the food. Certainly to give thanks to those who prepared it, those who brought it to the table. This is even possible when you are eating in a fast-food restaurant.

ZWERDLING: I was just going to ask you about that. Sitting at McDonald's and scarfing down a big, gooey Big Mac seems like the antithesis of the Sacrament.

REINHART: It is in one sense the antithesis. It is an obscuring of the reality of what's happening. So while the possibility of magic is still present, even in a fast-food place, there are more obstacles in the way of our being able to see it, to recognize it. It begins from within. If we understand what we are partaking, that our souls are yearning for that Communion experience and that God works through all forms, we can still bring more of ourselves to that situation. It's just a little bit more difficult to overcome because the elements that make it easy for us are not there. It's up to us to bring the things within ourselves to the various activities that we participate in.

ZWERDLING: You speak of today's fast pace and how we're all rushing around. We're always in a hurry, we're gobbling down our food too fast. That's one reason we don't take advantage of mealtime to try to reconnect with the universe. Are there some less obvious ways that we detach ourselves from the religious nature of food? I am thinking about obsession with calories, obsession with fat, obsession with fiber. I wonder if these things detract?

REINHART: Well, they both detract and they also, in a sense, reveal where we are as a society. You can look at these things as symptoms of a greater situation. We see everything separated from everything else rather than connected to everything else. When we see food strictly as a source of physical energy, as a source of calories, as a source of fat rather than as a source of life, we are already beginning a fragmentation that's very difficult to put back together. We're not going to put that back together simply by being more conscious while we eat. There are a lot of other kinds of healing that need to take place, but this is certainly one area where we can take a stand. Who knows, in the great act of taking this stand, we may begin in our chemical process within ourselves to, as the author Thomas Moore might say, "care for our souls," and in caring for our souls our bodies will follow.

Professor BRUCE BROOKS of the University of Massachusetts tells Bob Edwards that many of the sayings attributed to Confucius, the Chinese sage who lived in the fifth century B.C., actually were the words of others, recorded several centuries later. Brooks says Confucius' followers built on and significantly altered his rather small body of work. June 8, 1994

BROOKS: To later ages he's a grandiose figure. If you get down to the bottom, you find a rather modest and short beginning. What we have been trying to do is get back at that beginning.

EDWARDS: Well, what do the historical records tell us?

BROOKS: The best source is the *Analects*, which is a series of sayings, pronouncements on various public and personal issues. This has always been regarded by the tradition as the closest source to Confucius, and it seems that not all of these can be from the same person. The *Analects* contains opposing sayings on the same subject, even about the same historical figure. For example, Gwan Jung, an earlier minister of a neighboring state, is both praised and blamed for the same action. At one point, Confucius says that a certain personal quality which the Chinese call *run* is the most important value. At other times, ritual propriety, proper behavior, is said to be the most important thing. Philosophy in China has been divided ever since on which of those is the real emphasis, the real core, of this value system. Inconsistencies in the text make you want to find which version goes back the farthest, which one is the beginning point of Confucianism.

EDWARDS: What do we know about Confucius? Who was he and how did his words and philosophy become so widely known?

BROOKS: He seems to have been a member of the military-governmental elite in the small state of Lu in eastern China, born around 550 B.C. and died, we're almost certain, in 479 B.C. He probably had some kind of position at the princely court of Lu. He had followers, not exactly disciples but protégés, whom he was grooming for office in their turn and who, when he died, made a written record of important sayings they recalled him telling them. It's that record which is the germ of the later book.

EDWARDS: Can you boil down Confucianism to one definition?

BROOKS: Confucianism, in the sense of the societal belief pattern, is about social order in my opinion. Confucian values sustain the family structure, the social peace and quiet. Imperial Confucianism is a very strong part of why China is still around. What's impressive about China is that it's still here after all these thousands of years, whereas its contemporaries, the Roman Empire and the Egyptian Empire, have long since gone in their original form. Certainly this sense of solidarity and mutual obligation is very much part of that.

EDWARDS: Do you have a favorite quotation?

BROOKS: Sure. "The master said, 'Everyone wants to succeed in the world, but if you only can do so at the cost of your principles, you will not occupy that success.' " You're not concerned with what you get, but what you give. I wouldn't call it Camelot — that would be a cheap comparison — but it strikes that same note: Ask what you can give, and let the getting take care of itself.

Dr. MAHNAZ AFKHAMI, the executive director of the Sisterhood is Global Institute, talks with Liane Hansen about the restricted role of women in Islam. Dr. Afkhami says the problem of a woman's place in Muslim countries is not rooted in the religion, but in the patriarchal structures of society. November 20, 1994

AFKHAMI: Professional women participating in their society's public sphere have often been able to reach an accommodation between their religious, spiritual life and their professional, economic life. What we're hoping to be able to do is not to convince the women — I think the women are for the most part convinced — it is to convince groups of men who hold power in their hands, especially in societies where the more conservative Islamists are coming to power or are in power. We're trying to get the possibility of women taking part in this discourse brought forward. In Islam, there are to be no intermediaries between a person and God. Therefore, each person should be allowed to interpret, to understand religion and its values for himself or herself.

HANSEN: I read the transcript of an interview that David Frost conducted with Benazir Bhutto in which he asked if she had any conflict between being a fully committed Muslim and a fully committed feminist. She said she didn't because Islam provides certain rights for women: the right to divorce, for example, the right to alimony, the right to child custody. It sounds as if many of us are not aware of what Islam really is.

AFKHAMI: Yes, I agree with Benazir in this. The way the laws are, in practice, in Muslim societies, I don't think is conducive to equal participation of women, but the spirit of the religion, the essence of the religion, is egalitarian, and allows for justice and allows for participation of all individuals in their community. There need not be a contradiction between feminism and Islam. What has brought about the conflict is not religion, but the seeking of power by certain groups who use religion in order to enhance or sustain their power in the hierarchy of society.

HANSEN: How can the women themselves effect change in their own lives, on a personal level?

AFKHAMI: Well, that is actually the main component of change on the larger level. Each woman within her own life, within her own concept of self, and within her own family unit, that's where it all starts: individual women feeling that they need to assert themselves as individuals. They need to have a role, they need to have a say in what they want to be and how they want to lead their lives and how they want to relate to other members of their family and their society. It's not necessarily the same answer for everyone. It's not the same answer for every society. But the fact that they are making that claim and that they are aware of the importance of that claim is the most important element in the coming changes that we're going to witness.

In the days prior to Easter and Passover, Daniel Zwerdling speaks with two Washington, D.C., clergymen,
a Christian and a Jew, about the shared concept of
sacrifice. Rabbi BARRY FREUNDEL was making his
home ready for Passover. For Father BASIL KISSEL
of Saints Constantine and Helen Greek Orthodox
Church, it is the second week of Lent.
March 27, 1994

FREUNDEL: This is a time when life begins again, when life
begins anew. There's a sense that you can start over, that you
can create a better world, that you can create a new freshly
flowering world, and you can make a difference as you go on
about your life.

ZWERDLING: In both Passover for Jews and Easter for Christians?

FREUNDEL: Yes, I think that is clearly true. For Jews, Passover is a springtime holiday, and there are symbols at the Seder
that are springtime symbols. We eat a green vegetable as a symbol of the renewal that comes at this time of the year. We eat an
egg because it represents the cycle of rebirth, the cycle of new
life. Within Christian doctrine, this is the time of Resurrection.
Resurrection by definition means new life, renewal of life, a
second chance at life.

ZWERDLING: And to prepare yourself for renewal, if you're
Jewish, the Passover rituals call on you to place yourself back in
the times of the pharaohs to remember when Jews were enslaved, when Jews suffered, when Jews sacrificed animals to get
closer to God.

FREUNDEL: Sacrifice at one time was the central activity of
the Passover celebration. The sacrificial experience was one

that brought people much closer to nature, to the fact that we're all products of nature. If you have an animal that has been born in your barn and raised on your farm, if you invest in that animal — and in many sacrifices you were required to literally lay your hands on the animal before it was offered as a sacrifice — you see yourself, a part of yourself, being offered to God. The belief was that you could be raised God-ward as the smoke and the fire moved heavenward when the sacrifice was being offered on the altar.

ZWERDLING: Really? You would be part of that smoke rising toward Heaven?

FREUNDEL: That's correct. It would affect you in that way. Now we're very far from that. People who lived with this sense of the sacrifice, who offered this animal on the altar, were very much in tune with their physical and natural origins and were making a statement about raising their very physical nature heavenward.

ZWERDLING: Do you think that the fact that people no longer sense the life of the animal ebbing, the ashes going up toward Heaven — toward God, as you say — does that mean that it is more difficult for people to feel that somehow a part of their souls is reaching up toward God? Can you still get that sense of union with God?

FREUNDEL: I think it's more difficult because you don't have the visual symbol in the experience. We have tried to recreate the experience with substitute experiences: the words that we say, the songs that we sing, the music that we use, and the various rituals that we go through that hopefully give us that sense.

In mystical Judaism, in particular, the ritual of removing the leaven doesn't just mean taking the physical leaven, the bread, out of the house. It also means removing the internal leaven, that element of our personality which is negative, what is called "the evil inclination" in Jewish thought, those things within us that drive us to act less than the way God would want us to act. As we remove the physical leaven from the house, we're supposed to symbolically purify ourselves and therefore renew our commitment to God, to spirituality, and to living the kind of life that we are supposed to live.

ZWERDLING: Is there some connection, then, between the swelling of bread and the swelling, perhaps, of our egos?

FREUNDEL: I think there's precisely that parallel. Yeast is something which bubbles up, which causes, as you said, this swelling type of reaction that, internally, is personified as ego, as desire, as lust, as that which would lead a person to act beyond the strictures laid down by God and by law and by expectation of morality and ethics.

KISSEL: When you enter an Orthodox church, you're transported out of this world, hopefully. You hear sounds you don't normally hear; you see things you don't normally see; you smell things you don't normally smell, and that is purposeful. The church is decorated with icons, remembrances of saints, of Christ Himself, of the Virgin Mary. These are windows to Heaven.

ZWERDLING: In Judaism, of course, there is an emphasis on sacrifice. Orthodox Christians are sacrificing, celebrating the sacrifice in Lent, yes?

KISSEL: Correct. We are sacrificing ourselves to God, but we fast. We don't eat meat, we don't eat fish, we don't eat oil. There are no dairy products. There are no eggs. It is a strict fast. The sacrifice of the fast is not unto its own end. It is to reestablish us with the sacrifice of Christ himself. He is the lamb. You mentioned the lamb bone on the Passover plate. Christ is the lamb of God. He is the one who is sacrificed. We try to emulate that. We try to deny ourselves as Christ did in the garden, in Gethsemane, where he knelt, and prayed, "Lord, let this cup pass me by." We have to deny that humanity and crucify with Christ our ego, the thing that keeps man apart from man.

ZWERDLING: So you are sacrificing, also, to get closer to God, to give up your ego so that you may get closer to God, but yours is not the sacrifice of an animal, it's the sacrifice of Jesus himself?

KISSEL: It's the sacrifice of the self as Christ sacrificed Himself.

ZWERDLING: Something that strikes me about both Passover and Easter is that this is a time which seems quite unusual in both religions. You're not just praying, you are reenacting the original event.

KISSEL: Absolutely. On the Saturday before Holy Week begins, we reenact the raising of Lazarus. I, as the first priest, the Priest Dominus, the pastor, carry the cross. I read, "Today is hung upon the tree he who hung the clouds from the heavens." It's a very beautiful poem, and it's chanted in a very beautiful tone. You cannot do that without tears, because they are the words that were written for Christ, and you sing them. Your own iniquity, your own lack of humility and sinfulness, try to push all of that away, and they can't, because you are carrying this cross with Christ on it. You are reenacting his trial, his passion.

ZWERDLING: Can you talk about it from your own perspective? You're the one who's carrying the cross. Can you put it in your own words?

KISSEL: I cry. I cannot not cry. I know me, and between Christ and me, there is a tremendous chasm that separates us. And I try to bridge that chasm. And He will accept me.

ZWERDLING: It's really a nice ceremony.

KISSEL: It's beautiful. It is a magnificent ceremony. Holy Friday is even more beautiful because it brightens a little bit. Christ is in the tomb, and we sing a group of hymns called "E Zoe En Tafo" ("Life in the Tomb"). And on Saturday night, we read the Gospel of the Resurrection, and the church is absolutely dark, and I light a candle, and then everyone in the church lights a candle by that light. The altar boys carry it up into the balcony and out into the courtyard and into the parking lot, where people will be. The church becomes very bright with just candlelight, no electric lights, and we read that Resurrection Gospel, and then we sing "Christos Anesti" ("Christ Is Risen"), and all the lights come on, and it is so joyous. I'm getting chills talking about Saturday night, because the Resurrection has happened, because the hope is realized. The hope of the Resurrection has been realized, and Christ has risen so that we may conquer death with Him. He has destroyed death by being first into hell, and destroying the bonds of the devil, and coming out and raising us with Him. What we need to do to participate in that is to accept that and move on with Him.

FREUNDEL: What both religions are saying is that in the story of where we come from and in the time of year is implicit the idea that the human condition can get better. Whether you embody it in Passover or you embody it in Easter, the fact of the matter is that we're really saying the same thing. Whatever problems we see in the world are at least somewhat soluble, and we can build a world that's a whole lot better than the one that we have presently.

KISSEL: If we all come to the realization that we are sons and daughters of the Father, then how can we war against each other? When we were created, there was no mention that God created the white man, and then the red man, and then the yellow or the black. There was no mention of that. If we can begin to see past the color of a person's skin, past his ideas, then we see only God in each person, and that will mean that we won't need to have a defense budget. We won't need to be worrying about North Korea. We can worry about each other.

Dr. Bernice Johnson Reagon, as the founder of the women's a cappella group Sweet Honey in the Rock, a curator at the Smithsonian Institution, and as the host of the NPR series *Wade in the Water*, has documented the hymns and spirituals of African American sacred music. She discusses her work as a scholar and performer with Linda Wertheimer. January 6, 1994

REAGON: It's my responsibility to pass to my generation and to future generations the things that have been passed to me. I do it as a singer and as a scholar, but in addition to passing on the old, you have to create the contemporary document. I am as responsible for documenting what I experience as I am for passing on something that was somebody else's document of an experience, and time will tell whether this document is selected.

Charles Albert Tindley is the first gospel composer in the twentieth century that we study. We study him not because he wrote songs, we study him because people liked some of the songs he wrote. And black people are picky; black people don't do all of Tindley's songs. There are about thirteen that almost any African American growing up in church — and many, many white Americans growing up in Protestant churches, especially Methodist — could actually sing.

WERTHEIMER: Name some.

REAGON: "Stand by Me," "The Storm Is Passing Over, Hallelujah," "Nothing Between," "We'll Understand It Better By and By." He wrote his songs for his sermons, and he would sing these songs to his congregation. It feels as if the community picked through the offerings of this composer and passed on what really resonated to us. The song has to be of the moment, but it also has to have the possibility of flying free of the moment and of being suited for another time.

WERTHEIMER: One of the other composers whose music has moved down through time is Thomas Andrew Dorsey, who wrote "Peace in the Valley" and "Precious Lord." There are several things, I think, that are surprising about that body of work, and one is that it is relatively recent work. You'd think that song had been around forever, but it hasn't.

REAGON: One of the exciting things about doing *Wade in the Water* was that I ran into so many young people. If I asked them to sing a spiritual, they would sing "Precious Lord." The interesting thing about Dorsey is that he symbolizes so much about the African American experience. He was born in Georgia. At sixteen, he was in Chicago, a successful blues writer and piano player — but the pull of the church was always there and he began to create songs that had sacred text but musically had the range of music he could hear in his head. In the thirties when he began to really push his music, there were people who wouldn't let him sing the music in church because they felt the Devil had actually walked into the church through Dorsey. He talked many times about his struggle.

He coined the term *gospel* to be applied to these songs, but at one point during the thirties, his new songs were so popular that they were called "dorseys." Any new gospel song was called a dorsey. Your first gospel audiences, newly arrived black people trying to figure out how to make a life in the city, found in these songs that people call gospel the musical voice that named where they were. And they responded. They had to have the music. They flowed into the churches to get to the music.

WERTHEIMER: Let's close the circle and ask you to tell me where women fit into this, and where a group of women who sing sacred music fit into this continuum that you see?

REAGON: In the black community, women really are the carriers of the culture. Some of the earliest things I learned, I learned from my mother, from my teachers, and from watching other women. What better voice do you have to pass on a tradition than a group of women? There is, in Sweet Honey in the Rock, a way in which we erase boundaries. In a Sweet Honey concert, you will hear sacred songs next to love songs next to political commentary next to ritual, stages-of-life songs. Because we don't think that human beings have their lives split in compartments. We think that these are false divisions, and in that way we're closer to the African traditional style, where you don't have such sharp divisions. We're an appropriate voice for contemporary times. That such a voice belongs to a group of black women should not be a surprise.

Professor WILLIAM LaFLEUR, a Japan scholar at the University of Pennsylvania, was in Japan when he learned of certain Buddhist temples where rows of small Buddhas stand as memorials to aborted fetuses. The practices surrounding these temples led LaFleur to write *Liquid Life: Abortion and Buddhism in Japan,* a study of how another religion answers the psychological and spiritual questions surrounding abortion. He describes the memorial shrines in an interview with Robert Siegel. September 7, 1994

LAFLEUR: There are row upon row of small images of the Buddhist bodhisattva, who is called Jizō. He is the special protector of children, particularly deceased children, and people can go to these cemeteries for a while, and after they feel they have done enough of it, they let it pass from their own memory.

SIEGEL: People will go to those memorial sites and pay homage at the sculpture that recalls the fetus?

LAFLEUR: That's right. It's actually a rather emotional event to see. People feel some degree of guilt, but at the same time, because they are Buddhists, they feel that the fetus actually has another chance, maybe more than one chance, to return to the world at a time when it might be more wanted than it was on its most recent entry into a womb.

SIEGEL: Does this reflect the mainstream Buddhist view of abortion in Japan or, more broadly, throughout the East?

LAFLEUR: It does in Japan, though it's important to take account of the fact that the Buddhist countries of Southeast Asia have generally been more tolerant of the situation than some of the other major religions of the world. As they say in Japan, "We return the fetus to the realm of the gods and the Buddhas, but it can come back again."

SIEGEL: Do you know the comparative abortion rates for the U.S. and Japan?

LAFLEUR: It's higher in Japan than it is in the United States but lower than it is in eastern Europe and the former Soviet Union. I think the major point is that we have often heard and told ourselves that somehow our rather high abortion rate is destructive of family values, whereas Japan actually has a higher abortion rate, and yet we recognize that the family, education, all these things, are prized and actually reach a comparatively high level within Japan. There's no indication, from my perspective at least, and from that of most Japanese that I've talked with, that abortion is automatically destructive of family values. In fact, it's probably better not to have too many children who are not wanted in the world.

SIEGEL: Yet the institutions that you wrote about, these memorial parks to aborted fetuses, suggest that there's a certain amount of parental involvement with the aborted fetus that might be closely related to that strong family value.

LAFLEUR: That's right. I have even noticed that, at some of these memorial parks, siblings of the fetus are brought and informed that there were others in the family who are, in a sense, not there, and that what they have in terms of education, in terms of the love from their parents and so forth, is something that some other has paid a price for.

SIEGEL: Did you speak to many women who had had abortions and who had followed this ritual after?

LAFLEUR: I spoke to some. They feel that this is a good thing to do, that it's not right simply to forget, to think that this was what we call an "unwanted pregnancy." There was some kind of life there, and it's a good idea to pay attention to it. There are some Roman Catholics, for instance, who say that maybe this is the way to do it. I've recently become very interested in some American theologians who are noticing this and wondering whether it might be a better way for the Roman Catholic Church to go.

THE STORY OF THE YEAR: ELECTION '94

Members of the 103d Congress left Washington at the end of August 1994 to campaign for reelection. They left behind a record of some achievement and much frustration. In 1993, the Congress passed the Clinton administration's deficit reduction package. The next summer, the Congress passed a crime bill that included a ban on assault weapons. Nothing was accomplished on health care reform, which Bill Clinton had chosen as the defining issue of his presidency. As Clinton's approval ratings sagged, Republican members of the House sensed the possibility of victory. Relations between the parties and debates in the Congress were particularly acrimonious. The political scientist JOHN PITNEY describes for Jacki Lyden the forty-year legacy of House Republicans. Pitney is the author of *Congress' Permanent Minority? The Republicans in the U.S. House.* August 27, 1994

LYDEN: Why have Republicans been so good at getting their guy elected to the White House for the last forty years and so bad at getting seats in the House?

PITNEY: Here are a couple of reasons. One is what I call the structural explanation. Things like gerrymandering, incumbency advantage, and campaign finance have tended to advantage the Democrats. There's also the political reason, namely that the Democrats have a stronger base at the grass roots. There is hardly a district in the country where the Democratic party isn't well organized and couldn't potentially win a congressional election. On the other hand, there are many districts where the Republican party does not even exist. Therefore, the

Republicans have to do better in a smaller number of districts than the Democrats do. The combination of these factors has denied the Republicans a majority for forty years.

LYDEN: What do you think the impact of forty years of a Republican minority in the House has been on American government? What does it mean for us?

PITNEY: It means that the House has become increasingly rancorous. It's become increasingly difficult to achieve bipartisanship in the House of Representatives, and we've seen the fruits of that, particularly in the past year and a half. It's very difficult for Republicans and Democrats to come together on contentious issues such as health care. It's true in both chambers, but it is particularly true in the House of Representatives. It's a divisive atmosphere, in some cases even a poisonous atmosphere. It's fundamentally unhealthy for the country to have a single party in control of a branch of Congress for that long. The Republicans accuse the Democrats of becoming arrogant. The Democrats accuse the Republicans of becoming irresponsible. They have very little common ground to share, and the country suffers as a result.

LYDEN: In your book, you look a lot at the Republican leadership and you compare the style of an old-line Republican leader like Bob Michel, who is the minority leader — he calls himself the Republican leader just to get away from that tag — to that of Newt Gingrich, who was elected as a Republican whip in 1989. What's the difference between the two?

PITNEY: The major difference is that Bob Michel has tended to work in a more traditional style inside the Capitol, trying to seek accommodation wherever possible with the Democrats. Newt Gingrich plays the outside game. He's more confrontational, more immediate-oriented. But an important caveat: there have been many occasions when Bob Michel has been a partisan fighter, and there have been some occasions when Newt Gingrich has engaged in serious bipartisanship, most recently over the North American Free Trade Agreement. They have very different styles, but they're not as radically different as they sometimes appear.

LYDEN: Part of what's fueling the divisive atmosphere is the fact that an election is coming up, big stakes for both sides. How do you think the Republicans are going to do?

PITNEY: This will be a historic election. The Republicans currently have 178 seats in the House of Representatives. It's a near certainty that they'll pick up at least 15 seats. That will bring them to at least 193 seats, which will be the greatest number of seats they will have had since the election of 1958. It will break their so-called glass ceiling. That will be tremendously important for a couple of reasons. One, it will make it far more difficult for President Clinton to get his legislative agenda through the next Congress. Also, it will increase the morale of the House Republicans. For the first time, a majority will be in sight. In recent years it seemed almost like science fiction. That will enable them to better get campaign support, contributions, and it will go a long way toward erasing the self-fulfilling prophecy of the House Republicans as a permanent minority.

In mid-October a Times-Mirror poll concluded that a majority of Americans were likely to vote Republican in the November congressional elections: fifty percent of registered voters said the GOP would get their vote, as opposed to forty percent who said they would support a Democratic candidate. And the percentage of voters expressing support for the Republicans increased steadily over the next three months. ANDREW KOHUT, the director of the Times-Mirror Center for the People and the Press, tells Lynn Neary that this trend marks a break with years of surveys in which most voters preferred Democrats running for Congress. October 13, 1994

KOHUT: Democrats have carried the popular vote in every off-year election since 1950. If people act out these intentions, it will be the first time since 1950 that the Republicans have carried the popular vote. Actually, in 1950 it was a tie, according to the figures that I've seen most recently. But there is a lot of anger out there and this may be an expression of anger. As we get closer to the election, the incumbents may have had more time to work their constituencies and bring people back to their Democratic roots, but still, we don't typically see these expressions of support for Republican congressional candidates.

NEARY: You said people are angry. Are they angry at the Clinton administration? Is that what this is reflecting?

KOHUT: It reflects the three antis — anti-incumbent, anti-Washington, anti-Clinton — and it's hard to disentangle those three. We've seen for years the public saying that they don't like Congress. In fact, when we asked people, "Would you like to see most members of Congress reelected?" only twenty-eight percent said yes. Generally, there's a disjuncture because they then go on to say, "Well, my congressional representative, I'd like to see him or her reelected." In this survey, only forty-nine percent said that, compared to sixty-two percent four years ago.

NEARY: To assess the effect of the Clinton administration on the congressional elections, I think one of the really startling results of this survey, one I would think very disheartening for Democrats, is that only about half of the people you surveyed could come up with an achievement of the Clinton administration.

KOHUT: Pretty early in the interview we asked respondents to cite a Clinton achievement, and fifty percent said, "I can't." Now, when we asked this question in December, right after NAFTA, right after the Brady Bill victories, that percentage was as low as forty percent, but confidence in the administration and the sense that it's achieved something is at a really low ebb. The president's approval ratings started out at a high in our poll this year, fifty-one percent. They're now down to thirty-eight percent. People don't feel good about Bill Clinton and what his administration has achieved.

NEARY: The fifty percent that came up with an achievement — what were they giving Clinton credit for?

KOHUT: The most frequent mentions were — I think eighteen percent said health care, which is to say the Clintons put it on the agenda but didn't get it done, and then all other mentions were five percent or six percent: mentions of NAFTA, mentions of the crime bill, and the economy. I think one of the shockers is only five percent or six percent said the economy, and the economy is certainly a lot better today than when Bill Clinton took office, if you read the economic reports. Of course, the problem is that when people look at their paychecks, they get a different trend view than the economic reports and their paychecks haven't recovered the way the national economy has and profits have.

NEARY: And is there still some underlying fear? People just don't feel secure in the same way that they did, say five, ten years ago. The economy has just changed so much that even if it seems to be better at the moment, the security that people used to have isn't there.

KOHUT: There's a great anxiety in the middle of the economy, and also in the middle of the electorate, of people whose wages really haven't gone up, and they worry that they're never going to go up and that their children are going to have jobs that are as dead-end as their jobs. These people are typically Democrats, people that we call the New Economy Independents, and they're middle-aged people, largely, high school graduates, people under fifty years of age. But what we find today is that they're unanchored politically. They don't have a traditional view of the parties. They don't have a traditional ideology, and they keep drifting back and forth, and if the Republicans win big and the country has the sense that it's up to the Republicans to achieve things and they don't deliver, this group will turn on them.

The Voters Speak I

"It's all lies, so there's no point in listening to 'em [politicians] anyway." — *Casey Jarman, retail operations trainer, Chicago, Illinois, August 20, 1994*

"We live on Long Island, and our taxes are very, very high, and a lot of homes are for sale and it's time for us to change, you know? You know what bothers me about politicians? What they say is not what they do, and they have to realize — it's time. If you say you're going to do it, do it. Otherwise, you turn out to be a zero." — *Patricia Ram, New York voter, Flushing, New York, October 27, 1994*

"I think people are really getting fed up. Nothing's getting done, you know? They're not working together at all. I don't care if they're Republican, I don't care if they're Democrat, but it's ridiculous, some of the things that they're coming up with, and they're just not working together. This health plan: you can't do something that's half what it should be. It's either going to be a good plan, or don't do it at all. We don't go buying equipment here if we don't think it's going to do the job we need. If you're not sure the thing's going to do it, you just can't do it." — *Lon Shapiro, owner of Lon's Country Foods, Cambridge, Wisconsin, September 9, 1994*

The Republican congressional campaign of 1994 was unlike any in recent decades. Credible candidates were recruited to contest districts that in previous years had been virtually conceded to Democrats. More than three hundred Republican candidates signed the Contract with America, a national platform committing a GOP majority to bring to a vote, if not to pass, ten key pieces of legislation. The architect of the contract, Georgia Congressman NEWT GINGRICH, tells Linda Wertheimer how the Congress would differ under Republican leadership. October 21, 1994

WERTHEIMER: What do you think would be the biggest single change if you were Speaker of the House?

GINGRICH: I think we would be a dramatically more open institution. We're already committed in the contract that is printed in this coming week's *TV Guide*. There's a full-page ad. We're already committed to open rules. We're committed to changing the rules of the House so that when we report a document in writing we also report it electronically so that, for example, a conference report coming back would have to be available at that instant for every citizen in the whole country who wants to access it on their home computer or their business or library computer. I think you'd see a dramatically more open House and a more accountable House. I think that would be a major change.

WERTHEIMER: You would make it possible for any one of 435 members of the House of Representatives to present their version of a particular bill, instead of having it funneled through the Rules Committee, as it is now?

GINGRICH: Yes, we're committed for the first hundred days

to going back to the model that existed up through Sam Rayburn's time and having open rules on all of our bills. Now, you must admit it's fairly remarkable for the opposition party to be saying in advance that it would be willing to give the party which has dominated for forty years a much fairer chance to offer amendments. We would not apply to the Democrats the kind of machinelike, closed rules that they have used increasingly over the last fifteen years to stifle debate.

WERTHEIMER: You had a meeting with a couple dozen lobbyists recently in which you talked about some of the changes that you were considering. You talked about using the subpoena to conduct investigations that Republicans wanted to conduct and couldn't because the Democrats were in power.

GINGRICH: I was not trying to threaten anybody. I was just saying in the normal process of American history, if you have Secretary [of Agriculture] Espy resigning because of his ties to the largest chicken company in the United States, or if you have Secretary [of Housing and Urban Development] Cisneros accused of lying to the FBI, or you have the health task force in a lawsuit in federal court with all of its documents being subpoenaed by the court, not by the Congress — that normally in a normal legislative branch, you would in fact look into these things and you wouldn't just turn a blind eye and walk away. That wasn't a threat. That was just a comment that struck me as self-evident and one that normally the news media would have been enthusiastically supportive of.

WERTHEIMER: Do you think that if you are Speaker there'll be many such investigations?

GINGRICH: I don't think there'll be a single investigation that's political. There will be when there are clear allegations of illegality. I think the Congress has an obligation to look. I would simply say, if you'll tell me how many allegations of illegality you think there'll be about the Clinton administration, I can tell you probably how many investigations there'll be.

WERTHEIMER: Some of the people that the Democratic party

is having a very tough time supporting in this election — people who are close to losing — are freshmen, people who campaigned by saying that they would go to Congress and they would change things and that because they were there it would be different. The American people seem to be taking offense at the fact that they did and it wasn't. Do you think you're kind of asking for it here, Mr. Gingrich?

GINGRICH: Just the opposite, I think, Linda. The fact is the Democratic freshmen, as a class, are a total failure. To be a Democratic reform freshman is an oxymoron.

WERTHEIMER: Do you think that Republican reform freshmen will fare better?

GINGRICH: Republican reform freshmen are campaigning, saying, "If you elect us, we'll get a vote on term limits in the first hundred days." Democratic freshmen say, "Well, I might like term limits, but, after all, Tom Foley's filed a lawsuit against the people of Washington State to block term limits, so maybe I better not make too much noise."

WERTHEIMER: What happens if you have a vote on term limits and it doesn't pass? You can certainly say that you did your best and you only promised to get the vote, but if it doesn't pass don't you think the American people may feel that you did not keep your promise?

GINGRICH: I think first of all we've been very clear, saying over and over that we guarantee a vote. We can't guarantee passage. A term limit's a constitutional amendment. I think the Democratic leadership will fight it all out. I think the president will fight it all out. We may not be able to get it passed, but I think the American people recognize the difference between a Republican Speaker who brings term limits to a vote and a Democratic Speaker who files a lawsuit to stop term limits from going into effect, even when the people of his own state have passed them by a substantial margin.

WERTHEIMER: How's it going to be for you? If you were Speaker, you would be responsible for the House. Would you have to reform yourself? Dan Balz, the *Washington Post* reporter, called you a bomb-throwing back-bencher. Would you have to become a new Newt?

GINGRICH: No, you obviously have to grow with each assignment. I think that it would be an enormous responsibility and burden to both become the first Republican Speaker in forty years and to try to help lead a transformation of the system that we built in Washington. I think working with Senator Dole, who, I believe, in that setting would be the majority leader, and as he and I indicated together on *MacNeil/Lehrer* yesterday, we would hope that within a week or ten days that the president would invite us down to sit down and talk honestly and directly about how we could collaborate over the next two years and work together on what will have been a victory for the American people. I think we should say, "What are the lessons out of this election? And what does that say we should try to pass together, rather than just assume we're going to go into some kind of automatic partisan warfare."

The Voters Speak II

"People should be mad as hell and should take back their governments and take back the country and realize that we can run this country ourselves and not leave it to a bunch of boobs up there getting paid off by lobbyists and getting told what to do because they got to run again. We need fresh blood and fresh ideas, and that's certainly nowhere more evident than here in Oklahoma, where we've had representatives that couldn't be any further from the feelings of the people, such as Mike Synar and others. You have a situation in which they're up there voting their own beliefs, their own ideas, instead of the beliefs and the ideas that the people want." — *Harrison Brace, investor in real estate, oil, and gas, Okmulgee, Oklahoma, November 4, 1994*

"Whatever your political philosophy, it's time to throw the rascals out and get a new set of rascals. And I think that's what we'll get." — *David Hadden, assistant county coroner and Rotarian, Fresno, California, October 31, 1994*

"I just got to the point where, you know, it's kind of like eeny-meeny-miny-mo. Either way, I'm losing out it seems." — *Charles Murray, tennis coach at Northwestern University, Chicago, Illinois, August 20, 1994*

"Got the ad on TV with Pinocchio's nose, "That's Dave McCurdy 'cause he's lying all the time," by Inhofe. You got McCurdy running ads that Inhofe lied about when he graduated from college twenty some years ago. What in the world has that got to do with anything today? You know, and that's all we're gettin' out of this." — *Charlie Morgan, insurance company marketing manager, Tulsa, Oklahoma, November 4, 1994*

KATHLEEN HALL JAMIESON of the Annenberg School of Communications at the University of Pennsylvania describes to Liane Hansen how presidents — past and sitting — are being depicted in political advertisements on television. October 23, 1994

HANSEN: Let's start with an ad that's being run by the Democratic National Committee. This is an ad that runs against Reaganomics but not against Ronald Reagan, per se. Kathleen, what can you tell us about this ad?

JAMIESON: This is what is called a generic ad. It's an ad that is intended to air in many different places, and it is responding to the Republicans' Contract with America, which is a very important move on the part of the Republicans because it sets an alternative legislative agenda. The danger in a year in which you're running basically against the incumbent president, which is the Republican strategy, is that the Republicans won't take the burden of telling you what they would do if, in fact, they got power. The contract tells you that. The Democrats have responded to the contract with this ad, and they're responding as a party, not as individual candidates, so its sponsor is the Democratic National Committee. What they're arguing is that this is more of the same, but the same is Reaganomics. This is high deficits. This is the country that's on the skids. It also suggests that the Republicans who are being elected are not individuals, they're little robots. And so you see in the ad the Republicans, one after another, bending down to sign the statement. The ad is edited in such a way that it suggests that there's not much humanity left in those Republicans, that this is just an unthinking response by little robots.

HANSEN: There have been many stories about how some of these candidates are distancing themselves from the incumbent president. Are there any examples, actually, of ads that are using the president as a vehicle to kind of assault the opponent?

JAMIESON: Poor Bill Clinton. He's very popular this year, but unfortunately for him he's popular in Republican ads. The Republicans are taking, as a very important theme, that the problem with the country is Bill Clinton and the Democrats who have supported him, and so the first thing that you're seeing in the ads is visual. You're seeing one of two visual moves. The first shows a gigantic picture of Bill Clinton and a tiny, little picture of the Democratic candidate, suggesting that Bill Clinton dominates the candidate. The second, which is visually more interesting, transforms the candidate into Bill Clinton by a process called morphing that basically takes little tiny elements of the candidate's face and transforms them digitally into Bill Clinton's face. This was used for the first time in the 1990 race against [Senator John] Kerry in Massachusetts in what was one of the most involving and effective ads of this year. It's almost becoming commonplace in the advertising against Democrats. Now, the irony of course is many of these Democrats were not Bill Clinton's major allies in the Congress. You know, the support for Clinton by Democrats was not all that high through much of the last two years. The second thing that you're seeing in the ads is the percent going up on the screen of the number of times this specific Democrat supported Bill Clinton. So you see, for example, in the ad against [Senator Frank] Lautenberg in New Jersey, the percent of times that he supported Bill Clinton coming up on the screen.

HANSEN: Do you think this ad is going to be effective?

JAMIESON: Clinton is very unpopular right now, and identifying Democrats with Clinton suggests that if you put this Democrat back in Congress you are going to get more Clintonesque policies in the coming years. Yes, I think it's highly effective.

HANSEN: Health care, as an issue, sort of went down the drain at the end of the last congressional session. Is it showing up in any of the campaign ads this fall?

JAMIESON: No. One of the interesting things about this election cycle, to this point, is that someone appears to have died and no one noticed. We spent a year debating health care reform, and it is not a dominant theme in the races right now by the very people who put forward serious alternatives to the Clinton plan. The only place that we're seeing strong argument on health care reform right now is with Proposition 186 in California, and that's not about a candidate. That's about the single-payer proposition there.

HANSEN: Given that we are at midterm elections, and there will be a general election in two years, do you think some of the ads that we're seeing this time around might actually be providing a template for the ads we may see during the next presidential election?

JAMIESON: The crime rate is down, comparatively, and as the population ages. That was to be expected. One of the things that's interesting about crime is that we hold politicians accountable or give them credit for something that they really don't have a great deal to do with. It's very difficult to sustain crime as an issue over long periods of time. It tends to burn out as an issue. The airwaves are flooded right now with ads that show victims either indicating that the person that they support — Cuomo, Swett in New Hampshire, Kyl in Arizona — did something about crime or, alternatively, that a candidate in power did something that was terrible and increased the probability of crime, but that type of very highly emotional appeal doesn't sustain itself very well. I would be surprised if we continue to see that in 1996.

The Voters Speak III

"Crime has gotten worse. The number-one concern we get when we are talking to potential buyers up north, or prospects for our communities, their number-one concern is security. It used to be go do a seminar up north, which is what I do, and they'd ask you a question, 'Well, what about the bugs in Florida?' and all this other stuff, or 'What's the weather like?' or 'What kind of terrain do you have,' et cetera, et cetera, 'in your area of Florida?' First question I get today is 'What's the crime like in your area? Is it as bad as they say it is on television?' " — *Jerry Schwartzwelder, retirement community developer, near Tampa, Florida, October 17, 1994*

"We have it made here. I don't take the keys out of my vehicles. We don't lock our house. I was in Denver this summer and so happy to get back here, I couldn't imagine it. Assault weapons — I don't know how many crimes are committed by assault weapons. Maybe there's a lot, I don't think there is. I could be wrong, but this seems to cost a lot of money. Seems to me we don't have much money to spend anymore." — *Jim Morris, farmer, Cassville, Wisconsin, September 9, 1994*

"My neighborhood has gone from a pretty nice place to live to where you wouldn't want to drive down it in the morning. I mean, if you even drive down there with a vehicle, you have twenty to thirty guys that will literally bum-rush your car if you stop or not. They sit out there and drink most of the time if they don't get picked up. They've caused criminal elements to come in, such as hookers, drug dealers. Right now if I was to move to my neighborhood today, I wouldn't buy a place. I'd turn around and walk out." — *John Richardson, auto mechanic whose block is the site of a hiring line for Latino day laborers, San Mateo, California, October 13, 1994*

NPR asked three political campaign hands to design the ideal candidate to run in the mythical 436th Congressional District. We defined *ideal* in cynical, 1994 political terms: Who would win? Who was the campaign consultant's dream? The designers: SUSAN ESTRICH, a law professor and newspaper columnist who managed Michael Dukakis's 1988 campaign for president; FRANK LUNTZ, a Republican pollster; and JOE TRIPPI, a Democratic media consultant. Their assignment inspires Robert Siegel to write a political commercial for the synthetic candidate. November 3, 1994

ESTRICH: I think in 1994 it's a lot easier if the candidate's a Republican.

LUNTZ: I think a Republican would be the way to go for this election cycle.

TRIPPI: The Republican candidates would definitely have the edge, but I also think incumbency matters and that probably the most important thing this year is to be a challenger.

ESTRICH: Well, yes, in theory, as long as you've got Michael Huffington's money. It's still easier to raise money if you're an incumbent. So if you're going to be a challenger, let's make this Republican a multigazillionaire.

SIEGEL: Frank Luntz, do you like that?

LUNTZ: No. I'd rather make the incumbent mildly wealthy, above upper middle class, but someplace below rich, someone who could put about two hundred thousand dollars into their own campaign.

SIEGEL: We're going to have to compromise here on the money issue.

TRIPPI: How about the owner of a small business that has, say, forty employees?

ESTRICH: Built from scratch.

TRIPPI: You got it.

SIEGEL: Male? Female?

ESTRICH: I always like to see women run, and I think a woman Republican, particularly if she's built her business after successfully, you know, prosecuting murderers and rapists for a few years, would be in very good shape. I think she would have the potential, particularly if she's kind of liberal on the social issues, dare we say pro-choice, and doesn't get herself in trouble there. Very conservative fiscally, might be able to pull some Democratic and Independent women. I'll make her a woman because it's more fun.

LUNTZ: All I would add is that I would want her to be married and have a couple of kids that are at least high school age.

ESTRICH: Absolutely.

SIEGEL: And who cared for these children when they were younger?

ESTRICH: No illegal immigrants.

SIEGEL: And the husband had best be a man with no cults in his background, no real estate speculation, no business with regulatory problems. A smiling surgeon perhaps. How old should our candidate be?

ESTRICH: Forty-six, forty-eight, somewhere in there. Old enough to seem like she's a grown-up. She's not looking for a career in politics. She has raised her children. Young enough to be vigorous and energetic.

TRIPPI: I'd say early forties. In a year where you're trying to reflect that the old way's not working, you don't want to get too up there in the forties. I think it's better to be around early forties.

LUNTZ: I'll give her forty-five.

SIEGEL: You'll give her forty-five? You win. She's going to be in public all the time. She's going to be on television all the time. What does she wear? What's the image you're trying to convey about her? Susan?

ESTRICH: I think she can dress like Christy Whitman and

Kathleen Brown, which is to say, nice suits, not Armani. American made, a little more expensive than the average woman buys. But stay away from the five-hundred-dollar suits.

SIEGEL: That still leaves the question, What message does she run on?

ESTRICH: I think she runs against Washington, runs against the incumbent, says I'm not a career politician. This is not going to be a career for me. I built my business. I'm mad as hell at what I see going on in Washington, and I'm mad as hell at what I see going on here in the 436th District. I'm concerned about my children's future and that's why I want to go to Washington and shake things up. And then I'll be coming home.

TRIPPI: You've got to make it clear that she's tough on crime, that she supports the death penalty, and I think you've got to lead out of the box, because women are perceived or stereotyped by voters as weak on those issues.

LUNTZ: Well, one of the things to add to what Joe just said is, I'd like to have my candidate out on the air as much as possible. That is, that I would not do these ads with an announcer and show her doing things, all these quick cuts. I would actually have her talking straight to the camera.

SIEGEL: What does she say when she talks straight at the camera?

LUNTZ: She's talking about what's wrong with the system. I would spend about twenty seconds of the thirty-second ad attacking the system and only ten seconds offering alternatives.

ESTRICH: Ten? Maybe six seconds?

LUNTZ: Four or two?

ESTRICH: A big ten-second platform we're going to have here. But that's the point, Robert. I mean, the ideal candidate in 1994 doesn't have to be for very much. It's a question of what he or she is against.

SIEGEL: After Susan Estrich, Frank Luntz, and Joe Trippi designed the candidate of the year for us, her commercial pretty much wrote itself.

FEMALE VOICE: I'm Christine Mason-Dixon. After Don finished med school, I had a chance to pursue my own career. I went to law school and became an assistant district attorney. I put a lot of people behind bars. I have seen the worst. I've also seen the best. When I was home raising Timmy and Meredith, I started my own business. I met a payroll. I even provided health insurance. And when there was a problem at home or on the job, I figured it was up to me to fix it. That's why I want to go to Washington, to fix the mess, to make our government work for us, to put criminals in jail, to put the special interests and the Washington insiders on the outside.

MALE VOICE: Vote for Christine Mason-Dixon in the 436th Congressional District. Paid for by Citizens Who Are Mad as Hell, Just Like You.

The Voters Speak IV

"I do not believe that there is really an economic recovery because most of us had to tighten our belts so much, most all of us cut back in our business with employees. Maybe we didn't let anybody go, but as people left, we didn't replace them. I think that is the trend. And all you have to do is listen to the news and you hear how many big companies are still cutting back." — *Sue Wilson, florist, Rocky Mount, North Carolina, October 28, 1994*

"I think when you get to a lower-class scale of people such as myself — I mean, I have a job that's paying me twenty thousand dollars, but it's still lower class — I think we all vote together, democratically, and we try to help amongst ourselves. But when you get to the Republicans, we're considered lowlifes. It's just getting to the point where everybody is saying 'Lock everybody up, put 'em in jail.' I mean, we need some more people who care inside." — *Larry Chisholm, truck driver, Flushing, New York, October 27, 1994*

"The federal government needs to back off from the state, and the state needs to back off from local, and then the localities need to be a little bit more open to allow parents to get better involved in their school systems, and in how we want to spend our tax dollars." — *Mary Alicia, businesswoman, Norfolk, Virginia, August 26, 1994*

"I have a permit from the government to have a cabin on national forest land, and we've grown up on a mountain. We're there all the time, and if I'm told because somebody in New York thinks I shouldn't have access to that more so than them, I'm gone. And that's a concern." — *John Coyne, CEO of Big Horn Federal Bank, Greybull, Wyoming, November 4, 1994*

"When I was a boy, all the public land was open, and the sheepmen would have come right back to our doors with their herds, but now the Taylor Grazing Act, and that came in the thirties, saved the West, really saved the West for everybody." — *John Black, eighty-four-year-old rancher, Greybull, Wyoming, November 4, 1994*

"[Mayoral candidate Marion Barry] may have hurt himself by using drugs, but he's never hurt me. Sharon [Mayor Sharon Pratt Kelly] hurt me by taking my job. She hurt my family by taking my job. You see where I'm at? And I ain't got nothin' to do for the whole day. She cannot stop the violence. Give a person a job and the violence will stop itself." — *Derrick Stewart, living in a shelter with his family after being laid off, Washington, D.C., September 14, 1994*

Two days before election day, CHARLES COOK,
the editor of the *Cook Political Report*, tells Jacki
Lyden what he expects the outcome to be.
November 6, 1994

LYDEN: Charles, give us a little bit of history here, if you
would please. Tell us what the context is in terms of Republican
strength right now.

COOK: You know, the interesting thing is everyone's focused
on the Senate and Oliver North and Michael Huffington and
races like that, but the House is what really interests me. Newt
Gingrich likes to say that the Republicans last controlled the
House of Representatives five years before Fidel Castro took
over in Cuba. Nineteen fifty-four is when Republicans lost the
House. I was one year old. I mean, that's amazing. And the
Senate can change. It's a more volatile institution, but we are
looking at maybe a forty percent chance of something happening that happens once every other generation.

LYDEN: A seismic shift. When you take a look at this, are the
Republicans, in fact, beginning to downplay a little bit this
historical corner?

COOK: I think some of them are just pinching themselves.
It's like they can't believe that this is happening so soon after
having been evicted from the White House that they used to
own. What's happening with particularly a lot of Senate Republicans is, they see it happening, they see the evidence, but
there's this feeling of disbelief that it's real.

LYDEN: Let's get outside the Beltway. Give us a guide. What
should people look for if they want to feel that they're taking
the pulse as the numbers begin to come in, as elections are
decided?

COOK: I think the thing to watch is around six eastern time
when the polls close for most of Indiana and Kentucky. Within

the next hour, hour and a half, we can watch three very competitive races in Indiana. In the open seat where Phil Sharp is retiring, you have a race between Democrat Joe Hogsett and Republican David McIntosh, and you've got two Democratic incumbents that are in tough races, Frank McCloskey and Jill Long. And then in Kentucky there's Tom Barlow, who is a Democratic freshman who's in a tossup race in an open seat there. Those are going to be the first five races that I'm going to watch to see what kind of night it is going to be. I think we'll have a good idea by ten-thirty or so whether it's going to be a real long night for Democrats or whether it may not be so bad.

What polls are showing is, if you look at a sample of all adults, or of just registered voters, you'll find that Democrats are in some trouble, but when you look underneath the surface at likely voters and who is really likely to turn out, I have never seen conservatives as energized and galvanized as they are today, and they are going to turn out in huge numbers and I think that's what this election's all about.

LYDEN: Single-issue voters.

COOK: Single issue. People who, whether they listen to Rush Limbaugh or whatever, are motivated. I tell people, "Don't jaywalk on November 8 in front of a conservative on the way to the polls because they'll run over you."

LYDEN: You've been talking about a tidal wave in various forms. How much do you think it's a function of some sort of ideological shift in the country, or is it a function of the number of seats that are open, and of frustration? Is there going to be a mandate for Republicans?

COOK: You know, it's funny. I think Democrats are going to get absolutely hammered, but I don't see this as an ideological election. This is to a certain extent a continuation of 1992. People are so frustrated with government that I think they're going to vote the ins out, and it just happens to be that there are a lot more Democratic ins than not. I think because Democrats are seen as controlling the House, the Senate, the presidency, they're going to bear the full weight of this election, but I don't

think it's ideological. In fact, I would argue that voters are moving to the middle. I think we're seeing fewer extremist voters
than ever before, but at the same time I think we're seeing the
Congress moving out into the wings with the Democratic caucus increasingly more liberal and the Republican caucus increasingly more conservative and very few people in the middle
that are willing to move legislation. I think that's the problem,
a major cause for gridlock.

LYDEN: What are the consequences for President Clinton in
1996?

COOK: There's a theory that maybe now the president can
run against a Republican Congress. The problem is, I think
giving subpoena power to Republicans either in the Senate or
both the Senate and the House gives a whole new dimension to
Whitewater that we haven't seen before and can be real problems for this administration.

The Voters Speak V

"What's really spurred me though is the fact that I feel like
the government is disapproving of me, turned against me, that
I've been almost labeled a criminal. But, I mean, just voicing
your opinion I feel that I've been squelched, and my opinions
have been squelched, not only by the government, certainly in
the media, in our culture, and it's about time us on the religious right start raising our voices and allowing ourselves to be
heard." — Steve Kaminsky, analyst for Media Research Center, Alexandria, Virginia, August 26, 1994

"All we ask is for a fair chance for our long-proven values to be
given the proper reading, the proper air, in the media, in the
schools, in the libraries, in the government, and that's not happening today. That's why all the moms and dads and good single
people have risen up and said enough's enough. It's not because

we want people to go on to some radical ideas we have. What we want is to return to reasonable standards upon which this country was founded, and under which it flourished. We have not moved to the right; government has moved to the left. Why is the other side afraid of us? We don't break windows; we don't lie; we don't abuse our families. We vote. Is that what they're afraid of? That we're finally voting in greater numbers? We're good neighbors. We take care of the community. Why are they afraid of us? Maybe they're really afraid of what they've become, and they don't want to face up to it." — *Karen Jo Gounaud, housewife and Christian activist, Springfield, Virginia, August 26, 1994*

The election of 1994 lived up to the predictions of historic change. The Democrats were turned out of the House and Senate. In congressional and gubernatorial races across the country, not a single Republican officeholder lost a reelection race. Many Democrats did. Shortly after the election several pollsters and a historian tell Linda Wertheimer and Robert Siegel what they understand to be the message of the election. November 10, 1994

ANDREW KOHUT *(Director of the Times-Mirror Center for the People and the Press):* There were three messages. Republicans were voting their cause; they were voting conservatively; they were voting ideologically. Independents were voting frustration, and Democrats were voting despondently, diffidently, without the same purpose that Republicans had. Republicans were galvanized around second-tier issues, family values, taxes. They weren't the most important issues that the average voter cited, but they were the issues that gave the Republican party great margins of support. Democrats, when they felt something was at stake, for example, in the Senate races in California or Virginia, rallied and provided cohesive support to their candidates, but all around the country, Democrats tended to not be unified to the extent that Republicans were in the way they were voting.

WERTHEIMER: So the voters are saying to the leaders of the country in this election, "I'm not sure what you ought to be doing, but I do know that you haven't done it, or whatever it is you did do it wasn't the right thing, so do something else."

KOHUT: They're saying, "Deliver or else" and "We've shown you 'or else,' and we're prepared to show you 'or else' again."

siegel: Robert Teeter is back in the political consulting business after serving in the administration of President George Bush. He sees the election as ideological.

ROBERT TEETER *(Republican political consultant and pollster):* I think the election on Tuesday was focused on just one subject almost entirely, and that was the role of government. In that sense it was the most ideological election we've had in a long time, in fact, maybe ever, at least in modern time. This was not clouded by any specific issue. When you look at the exit polls or when you look at the poll that we did for the *Wall Street Journal* and NBC last night, what we found was that there was no overriding issue. What was really left was in almost a pure sense an election where the role of government really was the issue and people had just become increasingly unhappy, both with the size and the government's performance.

siegel: Do you believe that the mood that motivated voters in the 1994 election season was a direct continuation of the mood that voters experienced in 1992 when Bill Clinton was elected, or has the mood shifted radically in the past couple of years?

teeter: No, the mood certainly has not shifted. It was an amplification of the same. As we look at our polling data today what we see is that antagonism toward President Clinton was a greater part of this than even I thought it was three or four days ago. What you see now is a feeling that the president understood this desire and this mood of the country in 1992, articulated it well in the campaign, but then totally went in the opposite direction once he got in office and so, in many ways, duped the public, which has made them even more unhappy.

siegel: This feeling that so many voters seemed to have that Bill Clinton was a New Democrat, a new kind of politician, in 1992 and then betrayed many of the people who voted for him, I hear this a lot, and the question I always have is, What do voters see as the critical evidence there? What was it that proved to them that he wasn't the kind of Democrat they thought he was in 1992?

TEETER: I think there are probably a large number of things, but I think there are two that are more significant than others. The first one probably was the whole handling of the gays-in-the-military issue. There's no question that had something to do with it, but I think the much bigger one was health care. After he talked about more limited government and limited government spending and understood the pressures on middle-class people, when it came to the one area where he made his biggest and grandest proposal he made one that was a huge government program that represented all the things in many ways that people think are wrong with government: huge government bureaucracy, more government spending, and more government intervention into people's decisions.

LINDA DIVALL (Republican pollster): Number one, people want to see a more effective government. They want to see a leaner government. There was certainly a more conservative face on the voters on Tuesday, in terms of those who cast their vote, but I think we as Republicans need to be somewhat careful that we don't read this as a total embracing of a strict conservative ideological agenda, that more of the people want to see things in Washington get fixed. They want to see a more efficient Congress and they want to see a Congress that pays attention to voters' problems.

WERTHEIMER: What if the Congress does set off on a very conservative agenda, as some members of Congress have said they will?

DIVALL: That depends on which issues we are talking about here. Clearly voters are concerned about crime. They're concerned about welfare reform. They're concerned about health care. But the bottom line of what they said to the politicians is "We want to see reform. We want to see you work together to solve problems that we're concerned about. We want to see a Congress that is responsive to our needs." Voters are saying "Solve the problems that we're concerned about and do it now." Their threshold is getting lower and lower. They want action now. They're not willing to give people four years or six years, and our party will now see if they'll even give us two years to try to accomplish those things that they said are important to them.

GEOFF GARIN *(Democratic pollster):* I think voters were saying that things aren't working, that they are disappointed and frustrated with government, that government is not helping them in the way they want it to, and sometimes they see government as being part of the problem. They want to move things back to the center, and they want to send a message to President Clinton that they want him to move back to the center. I do not think it was the final word to Bill Clinton. The Republicans are using the word *repudiation.* It is something a little softer than that, but clearly there was a message there for the president.

SIEGEL: The message here, as you say, was in large part to President Clinton, but the people who actually received the message — and it wasn't pleasant — were a lot of Democratic candidates for Congress and the Senate.

GARIN: Life isn't fair. The best predictor of people's votes on Tuesday was their rating of the president's performance in office. Of people who approved of the job he's doing, eighty-five percent voted for Democrats in congressional elections. Of people who disapproved, eighty-five percent voted for Republicans. It's pretty much this straight-line correlation. The other thing I think we learned on Tuesday is that this is an electorate that is not particularly generous in doling out the credit for things. I think this goes beyond politics, but clearly the case in politics where the voters are now conditioned to look for the worst in everyone and really to disbelieve that there's very much good in anyone. It's hard to be a politician under those circumstances, but, again, I think this mood of looking for the worst in everyone extends beyond the political world.

CELINDA LAKE *(Democratic pollster):* I think they were telling us that they were angry. I think they were telling us that they were voting for change and they meant it. I think there were two emotions that dominated the election. One was fear and one was loathing. I think the fear was two kinds of insecurities. I think voters are overwhelmingly clear they do not think the economy is in a recovery. Women in particular do not think the economy is in recovery. They're worried about their pocketbooks. Men are worried about taxes. Women are worried about the pay at a company's jobs. They believe their families are not keeping up, and they wanted to say, "Hey, this is not good enough. I don't think the economy is back." Voters are also very worried about crime, and they think that it verges on a cultural revolution in our country when five-year-olds can be thrown out of windows by eleven-year-olds. And they think that leadership is not responding to that. They were angry and really find politics as usual, particularly politics as usual in Washington, despicable. I think one of the reasons you saw such an incredible wave on Tuesday was that anti-incumbency, which has been alive and well for a long time and intensified in this election, became anti-Democrat as well. Voters knew in their minds that Democrats had been in charge and still didn't get anything done, still didn't listen to them, still didn't represent them, and they have said very loudly, "We want change."

WERTHEIMER: So what does the Congress do now? I mean, what's the response to that?

LAKE: I think it's a burden on both parties to perform, get things done. Many of us on the Democratic side are frustrated because we think that we got record amounts done, but the point of the matter is that the public doesn't feel that way. They don't think we've gotten nearly enough done. And so I think results are the number-one thing that both parties have to get done, and I think that Republicans will be held accountable. It isn't going to be good enough in 1995 to just oppose legislation like it was in 1993. They're going to have to produce results. The second thing is, I think that they're going to have to reform themselves. I think both parties in 1994 missed the boat by not getting behind reform. That was the most popular part of the contract and it tested very well for Democrats as well, and the party that becomes the party of reform will become the majority party, I think.

MICHAEL BESCHLOSS *(Historian):* I think three things can be said about the election. Number one, we know from polls that there is a very great dislike of Bill Clinton. Number two, I think people thought they were electing a New Democrat in 1992. By 1994, I think they had doubts. Number three is most important, and that is, I think that for a long time America has been growing more conservative. The Congress did not reflect those changes because there was an artificial tendency of incumbency to preserve Congress as it was. Now that people don't have much reverence for people with a lot of seniority in Congress and are really very anti-incumbent, you see all that swept away in a Congress that, in a way, mirrors the conservative changes in the country.

SIEGEL: Can you find any precedent in presidential politics for the kind of midterm vote so much against the incumbent president as what we saw this week?

BESCHLOSS: Nineteen forty-six was a big Republican victory. It was a big repudiation of Harry Truman. Bill Clinton is governing in a much more conservative country. He can't rely on the same thing that Truman did, which was that in two years Americans would definitely see the error of their ways.

THE WORLD

The months preceding South Africa's first democratic election were marked by outbreaks of political violence, including attacks by blacks, against blacks. AGGREY KLAASTE, the editor of *The Sowetan*, South Africa's largest black newspaper, tells Linda Wertheimer that the violence stems from years of repression and degradation. March 28, 1994

KLAASTE: I actually pick it up from the days when my father used to work on the mines. They used to call black men "boys" — "mine boys." And then other black males, including the same Zulu chaps we see today, were called "kitchen boys" and "garden boys." It's a whole psychological attack on the humanity of these people, and it happens kind of silently. And people absorbed this for many years, so when things begin to open, almost like a flower, it becomes a cancer. Because all of these evils which have been planted into the psyche of the people begin to manifest themselves.

WERTHEIMER: Is it possible that this could actually turn aside the progress toward the election?

KLAASTE: I don't think so. I think we have particularly superb leaders. We have people like Mr. Mandela. I was just telling my sons yesterday that I went to jail for six months for some political crime. Mr. Mandela went to jail for twenty-six years, and he comes back and he talks to the same people who jailed him. I mean, I haven't seen such saintlike behavior in all my life. He's the kind of leader I think we are very lucky to have. And those are the kind of people who are going to get this complex and very tense situation to a kind of normalcy, because it needs a larger-than-life person. I think, chances are, we are going to make it.

WERTHEIMER: What happens after the election? I mean, the election is an event, it happens on a day, things change.

KLAASTE: Yes.

WERTHEIMER: But perhaps things don't change.

KLAASTE: Yes, that's another problem. But let me explain about these people who are against the process. They, luckily for us, are in the minority. Even this coterie of Zulus who are causing all the problems are not the majority of the Zulus. The majority of the Zulus want to see the election and the new changes. Now, if we didn't have these bitter people, we still would have problems after the elections because apartheid has led to the damage of the people's social, family, economic, even spiritual life. Now, you have the vote, right? The expectation is that after the vote, things will all of a sudden turn better, and inevitably they do not. I don't care who it is who's in power, including the saintlike Mr. Mandela, there is no way he will be able to deliver on at least some of the expectations of the people.

So we'll still have a lot of unhappiness after the voting, after the elections, but it seems to me in a very tragically strange way, that some of the violence is making the people wiser than they were before because even wise people had rather unrealistic expectations of what might happen after the elections. They are not too sure, now, about the ability of leaders to deliver all these in good faith because they are not too sure as to the power, the strength, of the political leaders to manage even the change properly, let alone after the change.

In Bosnia, the leader of the Serbs, RADOVAN KARADZIC, claims that a shell that struck the central market of Sarajevo, killing many Muslim civilians, was, contrary to widely held belief, not fired by Serb guns. In a telephone interview from Bosnian Serb headquarters in Pale, Karadzic tells Noah Adams that the shell might actually have been a Muslim attack, engineered to win sympathy abroad. February 7, 1994

KARADZIC: There are some allegations that it came from neighboring buildings. It's quite obvious that it was not from the Serbian side. The United Nations has decided the direction but not distance and they could not say who did it. It's quite unusual to have so precise a hit in the middle of market, only one shell, and to have too many dead bodies and too many injured people. It has to be something different than one shell.

ADAMS: Are you saying it's terrorism, or do you accuse the Bosnian government of doing this?

KARADZIC: Certainly it is terrorism, and it would not be for the first time that they cause a terroristic act in order to gain international sympathies and to accuse Serbs.

ADAMS: You don't really believe, do you, that the Bosnian government side would somehow contrive to have a shell go off in this marketplace? To have people killed, more than two hundred wounded, simply to gain some sort of international support and sympathy?

KARADZIC: Absolutely. I am convinced absolutely that they did it. We know they have a tradition of terrorism. Serbs don't have this tradition, and, as you know, Islamic countries are very familiar with terrorism and the Muslim side is in favor of war, not peace. They are ready to do anything just to get international support.

ADAMS: If you are interested in a quiet Sarajevo and not interested in shelling, why have fifteen thousand people died in this city in twenty-two months?

KARADZIC: Because they have been attacking Serbian parts of city. We have our own parts of city, and Muslims have their parts. This is like Beirut. We are protecting our parts of city against those who attack us.

In November, as Bosnian Serb forces advanced on the government-controlled pocket at Bihac, the United States abandoned its prior insistence on ordering airstrikes against Serb forces in response to cease-fire violations. The change of policy dashed the Muslim-led Bosnian government's hopes of American military support. It also brought Washington into closer agreement with Britain and France, which had ground forces assigned to Bosnia for peacekeeping, forces seen as vulnerable to Serb retaliation. WARREN ZIMMERMAN, a former U.S. ambassador to Yugoslavia, tells Robert Siegel that U.S. policy, whatever its course, must take into account the question of Sarajevo.
November 29, 1994

ZIMMERMAN: Sarajevo is not only the capital of Bosnia, but it's a city that has been symbolic for centuries because people who live there want to live as a multiethnic community, in harmony. Are we going to treat Sarajevo the way we treat Bihac? I think that is the big question.

SIEGEL: What you're saying is that the siege of Bihac and the assault on Bihac need not be the end of the Bosnian Serb's campaign? They might press the attack on the capital as well?

ZIMMERMAN: I don't have any doubt about it. When I was ambassador to Yugoslavia, almost three years ago, I had a long talk with Radovan Karadzic, and I said, "What do you want?" He said, "Well, one of the things we want is Sarajevo. That's going to be our capital." I showed a little bit of surprise at that since it was a city much more Muslim than Serbian. I said, "How are you going to make it your capital?" "Well," he said, "we're going to build some walls and divide the city so that no member of a single ethnic group has to live with any members of another ethnic group." I remember at the time thinking, How could this be, a year, as it was then, after the fall of the wall in Berlin, I'm talking to somebody who is speaking with great relish at the thought of building walls with barbed wire and checkpoints and all the rest? I think that's what awaits Sarajevo if the West continues to do nothing.

SIEGEL: What seems to have happened this season is that the differences between the United States on the one hand and the British and the French on the other have become irreconcilable over Bosnia, and we evidently have placed their objections over ours and decided it's more important to get back in line with the Europeans than to do something for the Bosnians. Do I have that right?

ZIMMERMAN: I think you have it right. I hope it's not a permanent situation, but it doesn't look very good. It's quite shortsighted on our part because, in effect, for better relations with the British and French, for the sake of NATO, we have taken an action which I think is going to weaken NATO immeasurably.

SIEGEL: How so? What we've been seeing for the past year hasn't done wonders for NATO's credibility. We've seen it reduced to a wing of the United Nations making what seemed to be rather halfhearted airstrikes at not even Bosnian Serb, but Krajina–Croatian Serb targets, with the United Nations almost instantly apologizing for the scope of those attacks. Hasn't NATO suffered enough?

ZIMMERMAN: NATO has suffered enough, but it will suffer an awful lot more if Sarajevo falls. I think that will be such a crystallizing event that it's going to be very hard for NATO to function as an alliance and certainly very hard for NATO to enlarge itself and its scope of commitments after such a defeat.

SIEGEL: Is there a case to be made, though, that Bosnia has been defeated, that the idea of a multinational Bosnia, as admirable as it may have been, has been destroyed? It has been beaten by the Serbs, and the next objective should be to figure out how to make life as not bad as possible for the residents of that area?

ZIMMERMAN: Well, if you assume it has been destroyed, then there's nothing you're prepared to do to help out the Bosnian people. You're prepared to witness without any participation the fall of Sarajevo. If you're prepared to do that, then you're not going to be able to do anything for the Bosnian people. They will be completely at the mercy of the victors, the Bosnian Serbs. If you are prepared to do the minimum for the Bosnian people, which is to defend their capital, then I think at least there is the possibility, a slim one, I admit, of some kind of a multinational entity remaining in the city and possibly even in some of the countryside.

Sᴏ́᷈...

SHERYL WUDUNN and NICHOLAS KRISTOF, a
husband-and-wife team of *New York Times* correspon-
dents, won a Pulitzer Prize for their reporting from
Beijing. They arrived in China seven months before the
Tiananmen Square massacre. Both are fluent in Chinese
(WuDunn is Chinese American) and were able to evade
the attentions of Chinese authorities sufficiently to
learn and write about the impact of Communist party
rule and reform on the lives of the Chinese at the end
of the twentieth century. They discuss their book,
China Wakes, with Jacki Lyden and tell how they
thwarted official controls to write the story of China's
nine hundred million peasants, whose poverty is partly
caused by exorbitant and arbitrary taxation.
September 24, 1994

WUDUNN: One man had four kids, and one of them was
handicapped, and his two older kids had no clothes on, just
T-shirts, nothing else. They had a pig, and on one side of their
little hut was a dugout pit where the pig lived. He slept on a pile
of straw, and in another corner there was another pile of straw
where his kids slept — man and beast living under the same
roof. I've no idea how many peasants live like this in China.

LYDEN: You say the system of taxation is not fair; a tax can
be imposed at the whim of a local petty official. Wasn't there
someone who decided not to pay these taxes as a protest, and
they came and bulldozed the house?

WUDUNN: They knock down houses when people violate
the one-child policy, and I met a family who had that experience. The woman — you're allowed to have two children in

some areas if you follow certain rules, and she had her second child three or four months before she was allowed to have it. So while she was still in the hospital, a SWAT team came to the house and knocked it down. There wasn't much furniture there, so they took the family cow. The grandfather of the baby was just horrified. He followed the cow — he didn't want to let it out of his sight — followed it all the way to the county. After she got out of the hospital with the baby, they came back a few days later and traipsed her off to the hospital and sterilized her.

LYDEN: Nick, you've seen these kinds of stories. What sort of future is China going to have? You write about the fall of Communism, something that even some Communist leaders were acknowledging to you is likely to happen because the system lacks credibility. But what will take its place?

KRISTOF: Well, already I think it has taken its place. I don't really think it's fair to think of China as a Communist country. It's run by a Communist party, but their bottom line is that they're going to remain in power and everything else is negotiable. None of the Communist leaders really believe in Communism, as far as we could work out, and I think that what we're going to see is something a lot like South Korea or Taiwan, where you've got a really very hard-line, military-backed, repressive regime that shoots students on occasion, that tosses political prisoners in jail, but presides over this economic boom that creates a middle class and creates more aspirations for political involvement. Eventually the tensions lead to either some kind of explosion, which I hope isn't going to happen in China, or more likely, to a gradual subversion of party control and a more open system. Already we're beginning to see that a little bit in China.

LYDEN: Do you think anything will change in the area of human rights? Many of the dissidents who talked with you later suffered for talking to you, and some of the stories that you tell of people in prison are among the most horrifying in this book — people put on tuberculosis wards so they would catch the disease, for example.

KRISTOF: I think that it's getting better only in the sense that now you have thousands of political prisoners, while you used to have 1.2 billion of them. These people are still going to be tortured. You know, the Chinese just have a brutal collection of torture instruments. They have something called the shackle board. There was a famous professor from Hunan University who offended the authorities and was attached to this shackle board. It's a board, and each of your arms are handcuffed to an end and then your legs are shackled to the bottom so you're spread-eagle. You're tied to this board and left there, perhaps for a month at a time and just hosed off occasionally. It's hard to imagine anything more brutal, and yet these things go on at the same time that you have this economic explosion.

LYDEN: You say there are a lot more success stories for each brutal story like that?

KRISTOF: Yes, for example, since 1980, China has lowered its infant mortality rates such that an extra 378,000 babies survive each year. So there you have a huge success story. If you go out to the countryside and talk to these peasants who now have babies who live through their first year, they're delighted by this, and they're living much better, and their kids are going to school in a way that was never possible before.

LYDEN: Sheryl, as the octogenarian clique around Deng Xiaoping starts to die off, what do you think the next leadership will look like in China? What will happen after those people are gone?

WUDUNN: The key thing will be Deng Xiaoping's death. He's ninety years old now, and the only official title he has is honorary chairman of the Bridge Association, but of course everybody knows he's the emperor, and in China an emperor rules until he dies. I think that his death will mean far-reaching changes for China. We may not see it immediately if he died tomorrow. Next month we still might not see anything. In the same way, however, that Brezhnev's death laid the groundwork for far-reaching change, I think the same will also happen in China. Deng's death, the death of an emperor, the death of a man who is the foremost and the last of the Chinese leaders, who made his fame before 1949, will mean the death of a dynasty, perhaps the Communist dynasty. It may be the end of Communism in China.

LYDEN: It'll look more democratic.

WUDUNN: We won't see that right away. I think it will be an evolution, but it can be an evolution in the same way that we saw South Korea change, and Taiwan change, and Mexico. Mexico is a flawed democracy, but if in China they had multiparty elections to rig, that would be great. If it had an independent labor movement to crush, that would be wonderful. China doesn't want Jeffersonian democracy or town hall democracy, but if they had a little bit more justice, the peasants would be a lot happier.

The case of eighteen-year-old Michael Fay drew
worldwide attention to Singapore's practice of corporal
punishment. Fay pleaded guilty to vandalism and
criminal mischief for spray-painting eighteen cars.
His sentence included six lashes with a rattan cane.
Despite appeals from American officials, including
President Clinton, the sentence was carried out. The
practice of caning is explained by FRANCIS SEOW,
a Singaporean exile, former solicitor general, and critic
of Singapore's dominant political leader, Lee Kuan Yew.
Seow tells Robert Siegel that the cane is about four feet
long and is wielded by a prison employee who practices
his stroke on sandbags. April 4, 1994

SEOW: The person is strapped to a trestle. Then his kidney
area is covered to ensure that no strokes land in the kidney area.
SIEGEL: You mean so as not to inflict permanent organ damage there?
SEOW: That's right. Correct. So it is aimed at the buttocks,
you see. Now, for the cane to inflict maximum pain and punishment, it is dipped in a brine solution. It serves two purposes.
One is to keep the cane flexible; the other is it also has a kind
of antiseptic effect. You see, the salt —
SIEGEL: It's an antiseptic. Tell me something, Mr. Seow, let's
not address the issue yet of whether this is peculiarly fit or unfit
punishment for an American admitted vandal. Do you regard
this as particularly fit punishment for any kind of vandal in
Singapore?
SEOW: Personally, I am not in favor of caning as a general
proposition. I think caning, if at all, should be confined to
crimes of violence like rape and robbery violence.

SIEGEL: Is there any capital punishment in Singapore?

SEOW: Yes, yes, yes.

SIEGEL: So that there are executions, but there also are these corporal punishments that are administered for various crimes?

SEOW: Oh, if you are sentenced to death, OK, then they wouldn't administer corporal punishment in addition to it.

SIEGEL: No, I understand that. But when you say that a rapist, for example, a convicted rapist, might be caned —

SEOW: A rapist, yes.

SIEGEL: Would that be in addition to imprisonment?

SEOW: Oh, yes.

SIEGEL: Yes, I see.

SEOW: Of course, of course. He's liable to a maximum of twenty-four strokes. And let me tell you this much. I know personally of people who prefer to serve a longer term of imprisonment than to undergo the sentence of caning.

SIEGEL: You mean, so painful is the caning —

SEOW: Oh, yes, yes, they know it, you know?

SIEGEL: Let me introduce one more factor into this story, which is that the eighteen-year-old who was sentenced to the six strokes of the cane is an American and he could easily be deported. You could just send him out and that would end what seems to be a piece of tension between Washington and Singapore. How does that alter, if in any way, your view of this sentence of caning?

SEOW: No, you see he has to undergo his punishment first. He will definitely be deported. That I promise you.

SIEGEL: You mean after the caning?

SEOW: Oh, he will be deported for sure.

SIEGEL: What do you make, Mr. Seow, of all of the articles and letters to the editor that have been written over the past couple of weeks and the appeal of the U.S. government, for that matter, many of which note that there is a cultural gap here between the kind of punishment that Singaporeans have come to accept as normal and suitable for certain offenses and something that strikes an American as cruel and unusual?

SEOW: Well, you see, the proof of the pudding lies in the eating. This is exactly what Lee Kuan Yew would say. Look at Singapore today. You can walk the streets quite happily without fear of being mugged, assaulted, raped, or robbed, and look what's going on in America.

A week after the Irish Republican Army declared a
cease-fire and Gerry Adams, the leader of the IRA
political ally Sinn Fein was received by the Irish prime
minister in Dublin, Noah Adams hears from Protestant
militants in East Belfast, Northern Ireland, about
why they mistrust the IRA's peace initiative. VIOLET
MASSEY, GARY ANDREWS, ENID KING, and JAMES
REED are members of the Orange Order, a Protestant
society committed to maintaining British rule in
the North. September 8, 1994

ADAMS: What is the threat to your community from the
cease-fire last week? What's the thing that concerns you?

MASSEY: There's not a cease-fire. The media, your country,
where you come from, America, cannot see the deception of a
murderer. Would you have a murderer governing your state?

ADAMS: Who are we talking about?

MASSEY: I'm talking about Gerry Adams. Would you have a
murderer to take any part in the affairs of your country?

ADAMS: That's Gerry Adams, president of Sinn Fein. You're
saying he's a murderer?

ANDREWS: Yes, he is.

REED: He is IRA.

ANDREWS: There's more blood on his hands than some other
hands.

MASSEY: Well, let's say this here, then: There was a bombing
in the Shankhill Road, and it went all over the world. And there
was a child blew up in that.

ADAMS: Is this at the fish and chips shop?

REED: That's right.

ADAMS: Last October?

REED: Yes.

MASSEY: And the next week, the peaceful Gerry Adams had the coffin of the man that blew up those people —

KING: Carried the coffin.

ADAMS: He carried the coffin at the funeral?

KING: On his shoulders.

ANDREWS: On his shoulders!

MASSEY: Would you, in your country, or any country, have a murderer sympathizer to govern the affairs of your country? Because, if you would, we certainly won't have him.

ADAMS: Well, tell me what you think is going on with the cease-fire?

ANDREWS: The cease-fire, all it is is just another ploy to suck the Protestants into something.

MASSEY: They want a united Ireland. If you go to any Catholic person — any nationalist person — ask them yourself, "What price is peace?" What really do they want? And it's Ireland united. And when Dublin is governed, and united Ireland — their law is taken from the Vatican, which is wrong, and there's absolutely no way will we be governed by the Vatican.

REED: That Church has done this in every country it ever was in. It's never done anything different.

KING: And from where it began, Rome always wanted to be an empire, and it will continue on.

ADAMS: Well, what about the United States? What about John Fitzgerald Kennedy? Good Irish Catholic president —

MASSEY: Pih!

ADAMS: What did Kennedy do to contribute to your fear about the Catholic Church taking over a government?

REED: Didn't he go, not long after he was installed as president, to see the Pope?

ANDREWS: Aye.

REED: To receive his blessing?

ADAMS: The people who have, in London and in Dublin and here, who have been working, trying to negotiate a cease-fire, have been, to a large extent, motivated by trying to stop the killings. You must agree with that.

REED: No, that's wrong. They're motivated by trying to get a united Ireland. I'm sorry you're confused. They have never once taken on the IRA. No one has. The only way you can defeat animals is —

ADAMS: You say, if they wanted to, the British troops could come in and wipe out the IRA?

REED: Yes, yes, they could do. Unfortunately, they're not going to be allowed to do it. They never have been allowed to do it. That's why we tell you, at the end of the day, in all probability what will happen here, the referee will get out of the road and then we'll see how good they are after that.

ADAMS: Get the referee out of the middle of the road? You're suggesting that the militias, the paramilitaries, would start fighting one another?

REED: That's right.

ADAMS: That's civil war.

REED: That's right.

ANDREWS: You're going to have civil war here sooner or later.

REED: We have had civil war here with our hands tied behind our backs.

ADAMS: When I talk to people here in town, and out in the country, they say, "The answer is that the two communities must know one another better; the answer is integrated schooling; the answer is churches that come together; we can all work for peace." Are these people just hopelessly naive about the real situation?

REED: I think they are.

MASSEY: Well, we did live together. I mean, no one had any bigotry in their heart toward a Roman Catholic person.

REED: Protestantism teaches protestation. That's where the word comes from, *protestation*, and it's protestation against the domination of any man's mind by any church, where you're allowed to believe, and should be allowed to believe, as you see fit.

ADAMS: OK, I would guess that in the United States, Presbyterians, Methodists, hearing this would be devout Christians but still not understand why people have to die in Belfast and Northern Ireland in the name of God?

KING: But it isn't in the name of God.

REED: We have a faction, I told you, a conspiracy. You see, you choose to ignore these things. We have all been consistent in saying that this is a conspiracy to bring about a united Ireland under the auspices of that church.

KING: Yes.

ADAMS: When people talk about what could happen beyond the cease-fire, nobody ever talks about denying the majority of the vote in the decision about the future.

REED: What do you mean? Don't listen to what they say. Look at the facts. Look at their past record. And that's exactly what they've done.

MASSEY: Well, we hope that when you go back to your Americans that you feel that the voice of the Protestant people — we are levelheaded people.

KING: We all want peace. There is nobody doesn't want peace.

MASSEY: We want peace. We never wanted anything else other than peace. We were quite livable with our neighbors. But we will still stand up. We will stand up.

....

In Rwanda, a rebel army led by the country's Tutsi
ethnic minority took control of the capital city of Kigali
from a regime dominated by the majority Hutu group.
Vast numbers of Rwandans, depending largely on
ethnicity, either returned to the country following the
rebel victory or fled with the defeated Rwandan army.
In the midst of these massive movements of people,
the new leaders in Kigali tried to rebuild a government.
MICHEL MOUSSALLI, the United Nations special
envoy in Kigali, describes that effort to Daniel
Zwerdling. July 24, 1994

ZWERDLING: I take it that the new rebel government has a
giant task ahead of them. What resources do they have to work
with?

MOUSSALLI: Resources? They have practically no resources
whatsoever, and that is one of the major tasks that they have.
They have to find resources, and this is why they count very
much on assistance from outside.

ZWERDLING: When you say "no resources whatsoever," do
you mean vehicles, telephones, desks? What?

MOUSSALLI: In Kigali, where I've been now for the past two
weeks, there is no electricity. There is no running water. Shops
are all closed, houses are empty. You can do no shopping whatsoever. Fortunately, I've been able to spend this time at the
building of the United Nations forces, and there I am sleeping
on the floor. I'm eating tinned foods, no hot food. It's a bit rough,
but it shows the situation.

ZWERDLING: I understand that the prime minister himself
is holed up in a former hotel, which has been trashed. Describe,
please, these makeshift government headquarters.

MOUSSALLI: There is no running water. There is no telephone. I cannot say that it smells good. Communications are out of order. There's no telephone, and this is a serious problem for the government.

ZWERDLING: Michel Moussalli, at the Zaire border, refugees are nervously starting to walk home. What are they going to find?

MOUSSALLI: Well, you see, the refugees who left are rural refugees. They left their hills, their huts, their land too, and now it's the harvest. Most of them would find their places still there. This is why we would very much hope that in spite of the fear that they have, which proves now to be unfounded, they will be able to come back and live again in a normal life in their land, in their huts with their families, rather than face the kinds of atrocious conditions that they are meeting in Goma at present.

ZWERDLING: But let's assume for a moment that when the refugees get home most of them do find, as you predict, that their houses are still there, their huts, their farms. Will their goats be there? Will their cattle be there?

MOUSSALLI: No, they will not find the situation similar to the one they left, far from that, but at least they will be on their piece of land and they'll be able to start cultivating or harvesting. In a few days from now it will be the harvest, and it will be a disaster if the people are not yet returning to the harvest. Of course, they took with them some goats, indeed, some cattle, and probably they have eaten them on the way. And, indeed, one could see lots of goats and cows dead and swollen on the streets. It was quite a dreadful sight.

ZWERDLING: As the refugees start returning home, how are the United Nations and other relief agencies going to help them? Are you going to have posts along the road?

MOUSSALLI: Exactly. We plan to, and we are also pleased that the United Nations force is also willing to have some military people on the road, a symbolic presence, just to inspire confidence and to reassure people. And we are going to have at various transit places where they can stop and have water, have food, have shelter if need be, and also medical facilities in case some of them are sick, and indeed we feel that some of them might be sick.

The world witnessed the plight of Rwandan refugees,
mostly Hutus, who fled across the border to Zaire, fearful
of reprisals for the massacres committed earlier in the
year (the Hutu-led Rwandan army had killed thousands
of minority Tutsis before being defeated by a Tutsi-led
rebel army). As the Rwandan exodus unfolded on
television, Americans watched unspeakable scenes
of death by starvation and disease. Professor KWAMI
ANTHONY APPIAH, a Harvard philosopher, British on
his mother's side, Ghanian on his father's, tells Robert
Siegel that the scenes of the Rwandans strike him as a
both a necessarily modern story — one that could only
happen in our time — and in other ways, the very
opposite of a modern story. July 21, 1994

APPIAH: On the antimodern side, it has been depressing to
see how the oldest weapons in the world, the cutlass, the knife,
can continue to be used to kill large numbers of people. I had
often thought that in the modern world, the scale of killing
derived from the fact that we had technologies that allowed you
to kill people at a distance. Now we see that people can go on
killing each other close up. They can kill children close up.
They can hack them to death. That's as old as the Iron Age. It's
as old as swords. On the modern side, it's so much the product
of the modern technology of the radio whipping up the feelings
that were released when the president was killed in that air-
plane crash.
SIEGEL: Rwandan radio?
APPIAH: By Rwandan radio, largely, by the Hutu-dominated
media against Tutsis. That makes it very modern because the

scale of the sentiment that you can whip up when you're talking to not just tens of thousands of people, but hundreds of
thousands, is a new thing. And then again, on the antimodern
side, the fact that most of these people are peasants, they're
people who work on the land, live at subsistence, have per
capita incomes that wouldn't pay one month's car payments for
most Americans. For them, their houses are easy to rebuild.
Their houses aren't worth much in terms of money, though
they're obviously worth a lot to them as they live in them. And
so, leaving, you don't leave behind so much in material terms.
What you take with you is most of what you value, namely, the
social capital tied up in your relationships with your friends and
your family and the knowledge that when you come back, you
can reestablish your relationship with the land. You can rebuild
a house in a single season and go back.

SIEGEL: Then there's the thoroughly modern phenomenon
of us —

APPIAH: Watching.

SIEGEL: Watching, listening, getting pictures, seeing video,
watching a cholera epidemic on worldwide television.

APPIAH: Yes. And it does give you an extraordinary sense, on
the one hand, of the power of our knowledge. Somebody can tell
you how many people will die next week. But it's a sort of
standing refutation of Bacon's notion that knowledge is power
because there's a sense of we have all this knowledge and in
theory, in some sense, we have the power to stop it, and for
reasons that are technical but also social and political, we don't.

In April 1994, the *Washington Post* reviewed State Department cables and memoranda suggesting that the U.S. knew that the head of the Salvadoran armed forces, Colonel Rene Emilio Ponce, was accused by credible sources of ordering the murder of six Jesuit priests, their housekeeper, and her daughter in the fall of 1989. At the time, U.S. officials did not help bring his name to light because they saw in Colonel Ponce the best hope for reforming the Salvadoran military. Scott Simon explores the implications of the U.S. attitude toward Ponce and others in an interview with Democratic Congressman JOE MOAKLEY of Massachusetts, a longtime monitor of U.S. policy in El Salvador. April 9, 1994

SIMON: What did you know, and when did you know it?

MOAKLEY: When the Jesuits were assassinated, Speaker Tom Foley set a task force up and named me to chair it. We made some trips down to El Salvador. We went around and got the picture pretty quick, and the thing that bothered me was that if we could get the picture that quick, three people, what the hell was the State Department doing? We found out that the State Department was trying to figure out what I was doing. They were trying to stonewall me, so I told Ambassador Walker, "Look, we've got this information, we've got that information, and we're going to drop it." He said, "Oh, don't do it now, we're right near peace." I felt all along that the State Department was coddling them maybe to bring the process of peace to a head.

SIMON: There are people who served in the State Department during that time who will tell you that what has since happened in El Salvador ratifies their policy, however uncomfortable it might be.

MOAKLEY: What else can they say? But look at the record. Nothing happened in the name of peace until the Jesuit case. We shut off their money and threatened total shutoff. That's when they started listening to us.

SIMON: Well, I remember running into a U.S. adviser in a supermarket in San Salvador ten years ago. His eyes just got very wide, and he said, in rather plain language, as I recall, "Well, you know these guys are a bunch of murderers, but the fact is if we weren't here, it would be far worse."

MOAKLEY: They've said that in Russia. They've said that in every foreign country. The problem was it was very hard to see where the El Salvadoran military left off and the United States military and embassy picked up.

SIMON: Well, Mr. Moakley, looking back on it, what would have been a better policy? Because when you guys got around to issuing your report in your statement, it's not as if you specifically mentioned Colonel Ponce either.

MOAKLEY: We had the same problems. People were saying, "You know you might be right with Ponce, but jeez, if you mention his name now, you know, he's a strong guy, he's in a powerful position, he may pull the military back, and you're going to blow everything that's been happening since you people got into this matter." We mentioned his name, and then we expanded upon it at a later time.

SIMON: Weren't you, in many ways, carrying out the same kind of policy the State Department was?

MOAKLEY: No, because we were forcing the State Department's hand. I think if we didn't get into the case, then the Jesuit case would not have been settled, Ponce would still be head of the military, and life would be wonderful. And that's the way the State Department wanted it. I thought peace was more important than anything else, and if naming or not naming a person directly is going to put that peace in jeopardy, I'd just as soon hold it back a little while.

SIMON: Does the practical extrapolation of what can now officially be confirmed as the role of many of the highest ranking officers of the Salvadoran military, and the fact that this stuff is coming to light after the fact, demonstrate to future allies that as long as they serve the specific national interests, that they feel they know what the U.S. wants out of them, they can do as they please on the issue of human rights?

MOAKLEY: Well, I think that's what was the case in El Salvador, but I think it's changing now. The thing that I hope that comes out of this whole investigation is the State Department reexamining their policies and how they arrive at their policies, and that they don't make political policies under the guise of some military gesture. The lesson is that truth is not the enemy of peace.

WASHINGTON

The author, political observer, and *Morning Edition* commentator KEVIN PHILLIPS takes aim at Washington's political class in his book *Arrogant Capital: Washington, Wall Street, and the Frustration of American Politics.* Phillips, a longtime observer of politics in the nation's capital, tells Bob Edwards that drastic measures are needed to reform the system. September 29, 1994

PHILLIPS: Twenty-five years ago I wrote a book called *The Emerging Republican Majority,* and one of my theses was that we have these waves in American political history of a new politics sweeping out this city. And of course, the Republicans, after 1968, dominated the presidency for twenty out of twenty-four years, but they could never sweep out this city. This city has become entrenched. Then Bill Clinton runs against Washington, comes in, talks about everything he's going to do against insiders and lobbies and special interests, and they just roll over him like a wave. So I've finally gotten to the point where I think the old election system of critical elections that come and sweep out Washington doesn't work anymore.

EDWARDS: How did things get that way?

PHILLIPS: If you look at the evolution of Washington from the early nineteenth century up to FDR and the New Deal in the 1930s, you see a city that's really growing, but it's still a small city relative to the centers of population. After World War II, growth was extraordinary. This city was not simply the center of the American political universe, but the center of the global universe, and everything came here. The explosion of staff and power and people here, not just to rule a city or a country, but to rule the world, that built the extraordinary city we have now. The statistic which blows my mind is the estimate of ninety-one thousand people in metropolitan Washington associated with lobbying. Ninety-one thousand.

EDWARDS: Now we've got lobbyists from the Right of Citizens to Petition the Government for Redress of Grievance.

PHILLIPS: In theory. What you get them from in reality is an outgrowth of lawyering. They have lawyers' ethics, which is to say, marginal ethics. "If you can afford me, you're entitled to have me."

EDWARDS: Hasn't some of the growth of Washington been a response to failure elsewhere? For example, if the states could have protected the rights of all of their citizens in the civil rights era, would Washington have been so powerful? Would Lyndon Johnson have built up this town as much as he did?

PHILLIPS: That's certainly true. Part of the federal growth has been a response to failure in the states, whether it be environmentally or in labor standards or in civil rights. What's happened here is that the failure of the states, which did happen, became an excuse for a feeding trough here. Each crisis, each wave of public policy, would create a buildup of experts here, and the crisis wouldn't be solved, but the buildup bore no relation to whether the crisis was solved. You could make money out of the crisis.

EDWARDS: You point out a relatively new development. Once upon a time the financial capital was in New York and the political capital here, and they were pretty much separate. But Wall Street is very much part of the Washington scene right now.

PHILLIPS: We used to have waves of politics in this country that would fight Wall Street, whether it was [Andrew] Jackson or William Jennings Bryan or FDR in the 1930s, even Harry Truman. In the last twenty, thirty years, that hasn't happened anymore, and there are several reasons for this. The first is the enormous growth of finance and its political role, and its ability to come in and offer a certain amount of monetary reward. The second thing that's happened is the enormous growth of debt in the United States. Wall Street purports not to like debt, but in fact, that's what they trade in. They don't invest so much now as they trade, and the volume of these trades, in terms of the dollars involved, is thirty or forty times the whole GNP of the United States each year and has created this enormous pile of money. It's extraordinary. The money that flows into Wall Street is so much now that politicians want to go there instead of prestigious law firms when they hang it up here.

EDWARDS: OK, the Phillips plan for making the world better: first you want to disperse power away from Washington. How do you do that?

PHILLIPS: That's absolutely critical and there are several things we can do. Some countries have tried to split capitals, some they've tried to move. We could move part of the government out of Washington. You could have Congress spend ten weeks each summer out west, and it would not only give them better temperature and humidity, but it would get them out of here. It would force the lobbyists to disperse too. Some of these fellows that operate in Washington would be out of luck if they couldn't clone themselves to be in several other places. There's something else they can do. It's been proposed that congressmen and senators be allowed to vote, in case of emergencies or illnesses, from their district or home state. I think it would be a good idea if they were allowed to do this, with a requisite formality that something would be set up in their district office which would allow them to do it. If they were spending all this time back home, not here with the lobbyists, they wouldn't be here in this enormous feeding trough, they'd be back talking to real people in real districts who have real problems. It would be a whole different climate. If you could disperse this power and presence back to the grass roots, I think it would have an enormous impact on Washington. This city's whole structure of influence-mongering would have to run scared if these people could actually represent their districts from their district.

EDWARDS: You're a man from New York City. You're not a native Washingtonian, but you came here. You got involved in this town. You're still here, Kevin. Aren't you part of the very structure that you're criticizing?

PHILLIPS: I'm sure some people would say that I am. I came and I still remember vividly, I was the first transition officer for the Republicans in the Justice Department after the 1968 election. The assistant attorney general for administration told me that the whole secret to coming into this city was just to get along with everybody, and there are all kinds of niches here, and this is an enormous opportunity. I thought to myself at the time, You don't understand. I came here to purge this city. I want to see it change, and if that forces me to leave because people want to hunt me down, I guess I'll leave.

After President Clinton's first State of the Union address this past week, the veteran broadcaster JOHN CHANCELLOR discusses Clinton's speech and his presidency with Jacki Lyden. January 29, 1994

LYDEN: Bill Clinton came into the office with pictures of him shaking John F. Kennedy's hand. How far can we draw this analogy?

CHANCELLOR: Bill Clinton lives a kind of an exciting, Harry Houdini kind of life. I liken him to Indiana Jones, who gets into and out of scrapes about every fifteen minutes. But I think it was an extraordinarily good year for any president. In terms of his legislative successes, Clinton did better than any president since Eisenhower's first year in 1953. That's forty years. Clinton got a higher percentage of his proposals through the Congress than John F. Kennedy, Lyndon Johnson, Jimmy Carter, and a number of Republican presidents. So you have to go back to Ike to get a success record this good.

LYDEN: There have been moments during the president's first year which were difficult. You mentioned he teetered toward the cliff sometimes, à la Indiana Jones. Is that kind of behavior a predictor of difficult times ahead?

CHANCELLOR: I think that the president's first year in office is not a good predictor of what is likely to come after, good or bad. For example, in 1961, John F. Kennedy's first year in office, in April, he had the Bay of Pigs Invasion, a great American foreign policy disaster involving Cuba. In the middle of the year, he went off to Vienna to meet Nikita Khrushchev, who was the head of the Soviet Union, and got verbally beat up there, and the Berlin Wall went up about two months after that. The Russians had the first man in space that year, and it was a terrible year. But Kennedy had a good year and a half or year and three quarters after that.

Contrast that, for example, with Richard Nixon, who came in as president in 1969 and had a really wonderful first year. The first moon landing. Americans were on the moon. Unemployment was at about a fifteen-year low. The economy was strong and Nixon looked very good. So the first year is not a good predictor.

LYDEN: John, when I think about Democratic presidents who have to push their way through the Congress, I think of Lyndon Johnson, also a southerner, a very different personal style, but also a president who wanted to craft a strong domestic agenda. Can you make comparisons between Mr. Clinton and Lyndon Johnson?

CHANCELLOR: I think Lyndon Johnson accomplished some very big things, the Voting Rights Act for one, that changed race relations in the United States while he was president. But Johnson and I used to talk about this, and I once asked him if he would believe the following premise, that his success was based on the fact that he succeeded a handsome, young president who'd been murdered, more or less in front of our eyes? That kind of stopped Johnson in his tracks, and I think he agreed with me, that part of his success was the fact that people were so upset by the death of Kennedy, that the legislative program that Johnson very skillfully put through was easier for him to get passed.

LYDEN: Bill Clinton has had to contend with a scrutiny that certainly neither Kennedy nor Johnson did. If you were in the White House today, say as a media adviser, what would you tell Mr. Clinton about how to deal with today's press? How would you tell him to proceed?

CHANCELLOR: One of the things I would tell him with a sense of real urgency is to try to get his personnel policies and his personnel techniques polished up a little bit. I don't think he does a very good job on that. We have more women and minorities in the administration than we did in the previous administration, but look at what happened to Kimba Wood and Zoe Baird and Bobby Inman. He had to fire his secretary of defense. He fired the number-two man in the State Department. The number-two man in the Justice Department quit last week. He lost his chief lobbyist, his deputy chief of staff. It just goes on and on. Bill Clinton is a man of extraordinary skill and determination, and I think he's going to be a good president, but he has a hopeless personnel policy, and I don't — that's the first thing I think he ought to change.

LYDEN: Do you recall that back in June the Clinton presidency was being almost written off, sort of dismissed?

CHANCELLOR: I think it was and I think that has something to do with the peaks and valleys in the president's own career, as president, as a candidate when he was running for president, and as governor of Arkansas. I think Bill Clinton loses his concentration sometimes after he has a success and goes into what we might call a drift mode, in which they send out for pizza and they congratulate each other and they talk about various government programs. And then suddenly they realize that they haven't been working on something — NAFTA was one example of this — and then you get this full-court press that the White House does, with everybody working day and night, especially the president, until he gets hoarse and can't speak and they squeeze it out by one vote, like the deficit reduction bill and some of the other things that they did. I think that characterizes this president and makes him terribly unlike certain other presidents. Nixon again comes to mind, who wore his coat in the office almost all the time and had a very tightly run staff system, and the Clinton people look as though they're in a fraternity house some days.

LYDEN: What do you make of the changing role of first ladies?

CHANCELLOR: That's really one of the accomplishments of this administration, I think, and I credit Mrs. Clinton with it more than Mr. Clinton. I think she has established a new job. I call her not the first lady but the first mate. I think she's in on everything, and she is, I think, the tougher, smarter, more disciplined partner in that marriage. All marriages have one. You can ask Mrs. Chancellor. But I think that she is doing a very good job without being too abrasive, and I think she has made it possible for future first mates or first ladies to be a lot more important than they have been in the past and I think that's something that the historians will write about.

CALVIN TRILLIN, best known for writing about food and for his column in *The Nation*, explains and illustrates to Alex Chadwick the craft of topical verse. Trillin published a collection of his work in the book *Deadline Poet*. April 11, 1994

CHADWICK: Explain if you can for us how John Sununu, the former chief of staff to President Bush, inspired you to begin a regular on-deadline poetry column.

TRILLIN: It wasn't because he was the best target of that administration, although we always look for people who think they're very smart and tell you how smart they are, but, oddly enough, it wasn't that which drew me, it was his name, which is a beautiful name, Sununu. It kept running through my mind, and finally one day, I thought, If you knew what Sununu. It just sounded like a poem to me.

CHADWICK: And that was it? That's what tipped you over?

TRILLIN: That was it. I didn't say "Eureka," but I felt eureka. He was always, in a way, the favorite punching bag of that administration for the rest of us. Quayle, as you know, was of virtually no use since he had become a knock-knock joke by the end of the campaign. And I had been laboring under the handicap, for someone in my line of work, of rather liking Mrs. Bush. We jackals in the press usually try to get at people through their families. That seems to me the most underhanded way to do it. And, of course, she was often compared to her predecessor, and I think there's a couplet in there somewhere where I admit that I like her, saying, "Her visits to her kids and to her spaniel/ Seemed more than show and more than semiannual."

CHADWICK: You had been writing a regular column for *The Nation*, and you turned it into a regular poem. The title of your book is *Deadline Poet*, but aren't deadlines and poetry sort of at odds?

TRILLIN: I think they have been traditionally. From what I understand, Wordsworth had no deadline, and poetry was written in a way in response, I suppose, to inspiration, but I think that poets that are down on the poetry chain a bit, such as myself, are more easily inspired than what my wife has the unfortunate habit of calling "grown-up poets."

CHADWICK: You wrote a very nice piece saying good-bye to President Bush when he left office. I wonder if you could read that for us?

TRILLIN: Sure, it's called "Adieu, George Bush."

> Farewell to you, George Herbert Walker.
> Though never treasured as a talker —
> Your predicates were often prone
> To wander nounless, off alone —
> You did your best in your own way,
> The way of Greenwich Country Day.
> We wish you well. Just take your ease,
> And never order Japanese.
> May your repose remain unblighted —
> Unless of course you get indicted.

CHADWICK: As a poet, and a guy who's been in the business now for what, three or four years —

TRILLIN: That's right. As a deadline poet, that's right.

CHADWICK: How important is rhyme to you?

TRILLIN: Rhyme is all. I don't know who said that. I think it was perhaps William Shakespeare.

CHADWICK: It could be, however, that you again are kind of running against the tide in your seeking greater recognition because hardly anyone's writing in rhyme anymore.

TRILLIN: Well, there are a few of us out there. I actually just did a reading for the Authors Guild Foundation, when we were — five or six of us were asked to write letters of rejection for noted works of literature. Garrison Keillor turned down

Walden at that time. He said, "It had a lot of good aphorisms, but the structure wasn't very good," so he suggested turning it into a calendar. And I rejected *The Waste Land* by T. S. Eliot. Of course, I did it in rhyme. The poem began, "Dear Tom, I'll be direct, we both hate fuss, / *The Waste Land*'s great, but sorry, not for us. / The language great, the scholarship sublime. / But, Tom, this poem simply doesn't rhyme." And I believe the end of that poem, the final couplet, is, "I know this is a blow, Tom. Not to worry, / You're still the greatest poet from Missouri."

I think there are a lot of rhymers out there, and many special-occasion poets are rhymers, the sort of poets you hear on weddings and big anniversaries and that sort of thing. And some people send me poetry in response to my poetry, and it's comforting to know that there is poetry out there worse than my poetry.

CHADWICK: And it arrives in the mail —

TRILLIN: It usually comes in the mail.

CHADWICK: With some regularity?

TRILLIN: That's right, that's right.

CHADWICK: Are you at all concerned about running out of topics for poetry, since this is not only deadline poetry but really topical poetry?

TRILLIN: Oh, I don't think so because I'm just standing watching these people go by. And actually, the last poem in this book says:

> The news presents a motley little band
> That I observe, tomato in my hand:
> The congressmen fine-tuned to every fax
> That indicates the wishes of their PACs;
> The White House staff, the President's defenders,
> All working late, and all in their suspenders;
> The tasseled lobbyists, may God forgive us,
> Who entertain with steaks washed down with Chivas;
> A President who always makes me feel
> The last one was attacked with too much zeal;
> A candidate who poses as our savior.

It helps if all are on their worst behavior.
The job of deadline poet is a calling
Dependent always on the most appalling
Behavior that our public figures show —
Supplies of which seem rarely to run low.
Rascality is what we need, plus greed
Overt enough to draw a blush from Tweed.
A fool is fine. A pompous fool's sublime.
It also helps if they have names that rhyme.

LANI GUINIER is the University of Pennsylvania law professor and civil rights litigator whose 1993 nomination to be assistant attorney general for civil rights was abandoned under fire by President Clinton. Branded "the quota queen" by her detractors, she never had a confirmation hearing at which to explain her views on such subjects as the politics of race and enforcement of the Voting Rights Act. So she wrote a book, *The Tyranny of the Majority*. As she tells Linda Wertheimer, Guinier finds that her little son's idea of playground democracy is not far from her own when he is posed with a problem of majority rule. What if a majority of the children want to play tag and a minority don't? March 18, 1994

GUINIER: He said first they'll play tag, but then they'll play hide-and-seek or whatever it is that the minority prefers, a solution of taking turns. He acknowledged that the majority would go first because they had more support, but he also was concerned that the minority feel that their preference was recognized. That's the nub of my idea of democratic fair play, that we should take turns. The majority should get a majority of the power but not necessarily all of the power, particularly not if the majority uses its power to exclude a minority, whether it be a racial minority or a gender minority or a minority based on ideas.

WERTHEIMER: You point out that a majority is tolerated and is not tyrannical in most situations because the majority shifts.

GUINIER: That's right, because the majority rules in part in recognition of the Golden Rule. That is, the majority rules knowing that it's not a permanent majority, that it has to worry about defectors, it has to worry about the minority becoming the next majority. Therefore, the majority doesn't normally tyrannize the minority because you do unto others as you would like others to do unto you. There's a mutually beneficial system of cooperation which breaks down if the majority is permanent, and if the majority operates without having to worry about defectors.

WERTHEIMER: And that's what you suggest happens on racial questions, that the majority is permanent?

GUINIER: I don't say it happens on all racial questions. I say it happens in some instances where race corrupts the bargaining process. It happens in many small county and municipal governing bodies in the South, where I've litigated cases.

WERTHEIMER: Examples would be what?

GUINIER: In Texas, the first Latino was elected to a school board, and as soon as she was elected they changed the rules. Before she was elected, any member of the school board could put an item on the agenda. As soon as she was elected, they said, "No, now you need two votes," just to get an item on the agenda. So she couldn't even get her constituents' issues discussed by the majority.

WERTHEIMER: You suggest that in efforts to solve this, the courts are leaning very heavily on the notion that if everyone has the right to vote, the right to elect, that this answers the difficulty, that they are then political participants. But you say no.

GUINIER: I say that we have to think more deeply about the relationship between minorities and majorities where there is a schism, a fault line which tends to separate the two permanently. We not only have to look at rules within collective decision-making bodies, but we also might want to reexamine the way in which we elect representatives to ensure that we're not reproducing the very polarization that created a permanent majority faction in the first place.

WERTHEIMER: How do you do that?

GUINIER: I don't think I have the answer, and I'm not proposing a grand plan for the United States. I don't have a crusade for a particular program, but I have some ideas, and one is moving away from solutions, such as race-conscious districting, where the solution simply isolates the minority into a district in which it controls that district, but in which the members of the majority are then isolated into their majority districts.

WERTHEIMER: So the solution of attempting to create a district which will elect a Latino or black or whatever is not good enough?

GUINIER: In some instances. I am not saying that it's a remedy without any use at all. I'm saying that it may be a remedy that has outlived its usefulness. On the other hand, I'm not saying there should be no remedy. One of the alternatives that I'm suggesting we look at is cumulative voting. Cumulative voting allows voters to district themselves by the way they cast their ballots. In a city council where there are four members of the council governing body, or in a school board with four school board members, every voter within that jurisdiction would get four votes and could cast those votes in any combination of the voter's preferences. It gives a politically cohesive minority — whether it's a racial minority, a gender minority, a group of Republicans — it gives that minority the opportunity to express the intensity of its preferences, but it also allows the majority to get a majority of the seats, but not all of the seats.

WERTHEIMER: Say, for example, you have a district that has a substantial black population, and everybody in that district casts all four votes for the black candidate and the black candidate is elected. Any passionate minority could do the same thing. What you might get then would be an array of minorities that isn't representative of the community.

GUINIER: Cumulative voting allows voters to district themselves each election, so they are not forced into assuming a minority identity forever. It says, "If this is an important issue for you at this election, you have the option of exercising your voting strength in a way that allows your viewpoint to be represented on that issue." Once people have that sense that their voice is being recognized, they then are more willing to move to consensus. Once people feel that their ideas are respected, that their views are represented, I think that you will find a move toward cooperation. People are much more conciliatory once they feel that they've been respected. That's the threshold that we need to get to: the idea of respecting different viewpoints.

WERTHEIMER: A critical mass achieving a level of respect?

GUINIER: A critical mass moving toward cooperation. I don't think that people are necessarily inclined to fight. I don't think people are necessarily inclined to view everything as an up or down situation, as a win-lose situation. I think we push people in that direction by our choice of election system, because if you don't win, you lose everything. If you don't get fifty-one percent, you get nothing, and therefore it polarizes people.

WERTHEIMER: But it isn't quite true, is it, that if you win, you win everything, and if you lose, you lose everything? There are Democrats sitting in Republican districts and Republicans in Democratic districts, and blacks who are represented by whites, and, as in the case of the District of Columbia, whites represented by blacks. You assume a level of goodwill on the part of your representative, that this person is going to take it into account that you're here.

GUINIER: That's right. But on the other hand, in terms of the choice that you made at the voting booth, you have lost. The person that you preferred is not anywhere in power. They are the loser. You are assuming that the winner is going to be respectful of your viewpoint and is going to represent all of his or her constituents.

WERTHEIMER: I think the whole system is based on that possibility.

GUINIER: And where it works, that's fine, but where it breaks down, there are alternative, equally democratic systems for electing representatives that will waste few votes, that will enable all voters to vote for someone who has a chance of getting elected.

WERTHEIMER: You say some strong things in the book about President Reagan and his tenure in office and the opposition to the progress that civil rights legislation and court decisions had made over the years. How do you feel about Bill Clinton?

GUINIER: I think that as a person Bill Clinton is committed to moving forward. I think he's committed to racial healing. I don't hear that personal voice right now. What I hear is the voice of a politician who feels constrained by political expediency, so I am concerned that the leadership that the country so desperately needs to move us beyond the polarization and the rhetoric of the last twelve years has been missing. In 1988, one of Reagan's appointees in the civil rights division, Brad Reynolds, wrote a memo in which he outlined the policy of that administration. He said that they were committed to polarization. He said, "We don't seek consensus. We must confront." Unfortunately, that was a policy that was both deliberate and effective. We are more polarized in many ways on race than we ever had been, and yet we can't talk about race. We're afraid to talk about race. We're in a state of denial about race. As a result, I don't think people know how to talk about race without shouting at each other. We are desperate for somebody to move into that middle ground, to show us that it is in our common destiny as a country to get beyond a politics of polarization.

MADELEINE KUNIN, a three-term governor of Vermont, went to Washington to be deputy secretary of education in the Clinton administration. Kunin describes her experiences of eighteen years in public life in a book called *Living a Political Life* and in an interview with Susan Stamberg. April 16, 1994

STAMBERG: This is an astoundingly honest book, astounding for a politician to have written, astounding for a woman to have written. Your first sentence, I think, tells everything. You are writing about the moment before you announced that you weren't going to go for a fourth term in Vermont. The sentence is —

KUNIN: "Don't cry."

STAMBERG: " 'Don't cry,' I told myself fiercely. 'Stay in control.' "

KUNIN: That's right. When I first wrote that sentence, I wasn't sure I could bare to keep it in there, frankly, because I felt maybe it made me too exposed. But part of political life is this tension between the inner self and the need to keep control.

STAMBERG: It's also a sentence that only a woman in politics would write. That notion of being a woman in politics — the two are so symbiotic you can't separate one from the other — is really what you're telling us about in this book. You can't risk showing emotion in public if you're a woman and in political office. You can't get away, however, from feeling vulnerable and the usual fears that successful women have: that they're frauds in some way, that they really don't deserve to be there. You had all of that.

KUNIN: Right. With each step, it's a new challenge, and it's a combination of excitement and exhilaration as well as trep-

idation. When you're going before a press conference, you cram
for it like you do for an exam, and I think women have been
taught always you've got to have all the right answers. It took
me a long time to get to the point where I said, Hey, it isn't only
having all the right answers. It's how you feel, how you project,
your conviction. Those things are just as important. You have
to free yourself from some of the old assumptions.

STAMBERG: You went into politics as the mother of four
children. These were young children, and that made for some
sleepless nights on your part, too.

KUNIN: Yes, I felt a lot of wrenching and pulling and tugging
at my skirts. The first time I officially left the house after I'd
been elected to the state legislature, I had to get to a meeting in
Montpelier, and all the kids gathered around me, and said,
"Mommy, don't go." I'm sure so many women have felt that,
but you know that you have to go.

STAMBERG: What do you say to yourself? "I have to do it
because I need to have that life"? "I have to do it to make the
future better for these little children"?

KUNIN: One, you tell yourself that the children will be fine
once you're out the door, and that's usually the case; they do
recover. The other is that you are needed, and that you have
something important to contribute. That's how you get through
it. And your children grow up and hopefully turn into pretty
good human beings.

STAMBERG: You write about the first day of being governor
and going into the executive bathroom for the very first time.
You put the toilet seat down.

KUNIN: That's right. The ultimate takeover by a woman of
a male space. Eventually, you know, we changed the soap and
the towels and the furniture in the office.

STAMBERG: You wanted to govern well, you write, and you
wanted to govern as a woman. Do women govern differently?

KUNIN: That's the toughest question of all, Susan, because
not all women, obviously, are going to govern alike, just as
they're not going to vote alike or cook alike or bring up their

children alike. Having said that, though, just because we're newcomers, I think there's a difference. You see things that other people may not see. You question things that other people may not question who've been there forever. More importantly, perhaps, you bring all the values that you've built up over a lifetime into the political arena. For women who have children, parenting is part of that experience. Concerns about child care are part of that experience. So there is a difference, but it is not a uniform difference, and it isn't there on every issue.

STAMBERG: As governor you obviously had a great deal of power in your state, and you write about it on the large scale, but also on the small. I wish you would read the section about the social implications of getting the kind of power that you had. Maybe set the scene a little here for us.

KUNIN: This was a party at the house of the president of the University of Vermont, people I'd known for quite a long time. At this particular point, I write, "Politics popped up in colorful bursts in the center of conversation, like sparklers on the Fourth of July, drawing a curious crowd.

"Eye contact was different. No one looked through or past me. Everyone looked at me. Neither men nor women allowed their eyes to stray toward someone more interesting, important or fun. It was me they wanted to talk to. And it was they who wanted to be heard.

"Remember this, I warned myself. It will evaporate like rain in dry heat."

STAMBERG: You write about how difficult it is living a political life and about the tradeoffs you have to make and the internal questions that you face all the time. Can you honestly turn to other women and tell them to embrace that life? Can you encourage them to do what you've done?

KUNIN: Yes, I can. I want to. Because I think the way politics is viewed today, many people think it's worse than what I've described, but that is not the case. I'm still an optimist about politics. With each new person that enters into the system, the dynamics of the system do change, and what I experienced, for example, as a freshman legislator in Vermont when there were just sixteen women in the legislature is very different from what women experience today when more than a third of the legislators are women. Each woman is not put under a spotlight in the same way. In addition, this critical number does affect the rules and does affect the whole climate. That's beginning to happen in the United States Congress, because you have some very courageous, outspoken women, and even if they're still a small percentage, they are changing the questions that are being asked. And they are very supportive of one another. This reaching out of mutual support overarches party and often real political differences.

In his book, *Dead Right*, the young conservative journal-
ist DAVID FRUM rejects the upbeat optimism of former
New York Congressman Jack Kemp and the moralizing
of former Education Secretary Bill Bennett. Frum
describes a different stream of conservativism, a new
form of nationalism that he discusses with Linda
Wertheimer. October 3, 1994

FRUM: I think that nationalism is the next big thing in American politics. What you're going to see among conservatives is
much more concern about immigration, much more concern
about black-white issues, and a much tougher line in defense of
issues of America's majority population, much stronger opposition to affirmative action. This can spill over into international affairs, too: much stronger assertion of America's rights
as a nation, not as a system of ideas. That's why there's so much
hostility to the Haiti intervention. That's too altruistic and not
good enough for America. And much less enthusiasm for the
old ideas of free trade.

WERTHEIMER: In some sense, it's a return to isolationism, to
America first.

FRUM: I don't like the term *isolationism* as much as I like
nationalism because, except for a few really flaky people, most
people understand that the world is there and isn't going to go
away. The question is, How do you meet the world? Do you
meet it in a kind of cooperative spirit, or do you meet it in a
more tough-minded spirit? I think this conservative nationalism is going to play a large part in forming the Republican party.
Certainly the speech that Pat Buchanan gave at the 1992 con-
vention was the most memorable speech given there, and it
expressed these views entirely.

WERTHEIMER: What about the theory that the Republican party doesn't really have, at this moment, a coherent enough thing to offer or a blinding enough candidate to actually break through in 1996? That 1996 is just not going to be a Republican year, no matter how unsuccessful President Clinton manages to be?

FRUM: It's true what you say about the candidate. I got involved in this kind of politics in the late 1970s, and maybe my memory is playing tricks on me, maybe I was just a younger and more romantic person in those days, but the way I remember it, we talked, among conservatives, a lot less about candidates and a lot more about ideas than we do now. We did not have the messiah complex that I sense among many Republicans, of, well, if we can get the right candidate, everything will be OK.

As for the core body of ideas, that's a little bit of what I'm trying to offer Republicans, and there has been some response to it. Which is to say, take aim at this big beast of government. What you find is much more skepticism among voters about it now than there was in 1980. That's not just my impression. We can document that in all kinds of ways. Surveys show it, this new Times-Mirror poll.

There is a latent, inchoate skepticism. No, it isn't partisan, it isn't ideological, it isn't necessarily even very sophisticated, but it's there and you can use it. What you can also say in order to hold the party together is, "Look, there are a lot of American social problems" — and again, when you do sophisticated polling, you find that these are the things that voters most worry about. Of course, they have profound and many and deep causes, most of which are beyond anybody's control, but one thing we can do is to say, "Look, if we get control of the size of government, eliminate a lot of the transfer programs, eliminate a lot of the welfare state, there's good reason to hope that a lot of America's social problems will cease to get worse and maybe even get better." I'm saying all of this with some caution because obviously, you can't make very confident statements about why people do what they do. They're not ball bearings.

They don't obey laws of physics. They think. But one of the things that has been the biggest factor in American social life since the early seventies has been the weakness of the family.

Families are breaking up, they're not being formed. There are many more children being raised outside of marriage or in re-combined families that have many of the same social problems that single-parent families do. Now, why is this happening? A lot of reasons, but one of them is that the whole point of activist government is to replace a lot of the economic functions that a family used to do. It used to be a family that paid for its kids to go to college. It used to be a family that took care of its members in sickness and old age. Now, it didn't do a great job, and that's why the whole modern welfare state was created, but the fact is, in solving those problems of the family's incompetence at a number of these things, you give rise to new problems.

And that is, in a nutshell, a simple version of the social history of the past twenty-five years. Conservatives, by talking about the government and its role in substituting for the family, can, in a way that doesn't invite the state to muck around in the private affairs of people, say something that is meaningful to both their economic and their social links.

WERTHEIMER: The thing that I'm curious about in your notion that you can put this forward as an idea that the Republican party, and then the American people, might find appealing is that the transfer payments that the government is dishing out are mostly going to the middle class.

FRUM: Oh, yes.

WERTHEIMER: The farm program, the Medicare program, Social Security, paid beyond the amounts that support them. I have seen nothing in the last twenty years to tell me that you can say to the American people, "I'm going to give you a dose of medicine here. I'm going to take away your benefits," that would cause anybody to vote for you. That doesn't sound to me like something that would work.

FRUM: Some of the more cynical Republicans I know say exactly what you have just said, and I suppose my reply to that is a question about what you think the function of political leadership is and how you think public opinion works. Do you think that there is a formed, coherent public opinion out there that has answers to the nineteen most important questions of the day and that your job is to go out and listen to it and figure out how to do what it wants? Or do you think that people have kind of aspirations and beliefs and values and principles that don't give specific answers, and that the job of political leadership is to take the convictions and express them in ways that maybe are meaningful to those people? I tend to think that just as people don't know that they need a fax machine before there is one, they don't know they need a lot of public policies before there is one.

It is true that what I'm calling on is for Republicans to take more risks politically. On the other hand a lot of Republicans, think — and this 1994 congressional election is a perfect example of this — that you can sort of sidle into power by keeping quiet and counting on the incompetence and unpopularity of your opponent, and then once there you can do what you want. I think the way political power works is like that old picture of Babe Ruth pointing into the stands to where he's going to hit the ball. In politics, a run only scores if you first point to where you're going to hit the ball, and if you don't point first the run doesn't count.

....

Can love triumph over politics? Evidently it can, according to MARY MATALIN and JAMES CARVILLE, newly-weds when they wrote *All's Fair: Love, War, and Running for President*. Matalin was the political director for the Bush reelection campaign. Carville was the top Clinton campaign strategist. They tell Linda Wertheimer that their differences do not overwhelm their life together. September 23, 1994

CARVILLE: The truth of the matter is, we get enough politics during the course of the day. I mean, both of us probably talk, eat, breathe, live, and work politics twelve, fourteen hours a day. It's almost a relief to go home and know that you shouldn't talk about that. Another thing is we just don't want to. I mean the only thing I can say is it must be like a professional football player goes home from practice in the afternoon, and the kid says, "Hey, Pop, you want to throw the ball around a little bit?" I'm sure the guy says, "No. I just want to sit by the fire and chill out."

MATALIN: We don't like to fight. Our convictions are such that when we transcend talking about the process of politics and about some economic issues and some role of government issues, we fight. Now, I don't really know very many people who go home and talk about the role of government, but this is true. We started having a discussion about the role of the judiciary in the choice issue. We had a huge fight, and I pouted for two days. We don't want to. That's not how a marriage works.

CARVILLE: Somehow or another, as a consequence to this, I have to give up talking about the role of the federal judiciary and the choice issue. That doesn't seem like a very big thing for me to give up in this world. I'm more than willing. That seems like a pretty small thing to do, to tell you the truth.

WERTHEIMER: But it does strike me that even though one of you is a Republican and one is a Democrat, there are a lot of things about you that are an awful lot alike. One of them is that you take what I guess you could kindly call an operational view about politics. On page 45, Mary, there's sort of a philosophical statement from you about what you will and will not do as a political professional. I wonder if you could just read that for us.

MATALIN: "Politics is about winning — there are no Pyrrhic victories or honorable defeats. Participating in a presidential campaign full-time, as a professional, is very emotional and very draining. You don't want to put that much effort into a race unless you have a real chance. Unless you're an ideological nut, which very few political professionals are, you don't want to run a race with a dog candidate just to prove a point. It takes too much out of you."

WERTHEIMER: And page 55, James, there's a similar part. This is part of the going back and forth that the book does. You both make statements about the same things in roughly the same places in the book.

CARVILLE: "I will work for a Democrat who I can get along with who is neither a bigot nor a crook.

"But let's say there's a smart, well-meaning person I agree with on the issues who is running for office and can pay me $5,000 a month. There is also a tough, sort of cynical but not dishonest Washington insider who has raised a lot of PAC money and can pay me $20,000 a month. I'm going to work for the second guy. I mean, this is what I do for a living."

WERTHEIMER: Don't you think that sounds a little cynical, when you kind of separate it out like that?

CARVILLE: I don't know whether it sounds cynical or not. What we tried to do is write an honest book. I couldn't have written an honest book without saying that. If I would have said, "No, gee, James Carville's the kind of guy who'd go look for sort of the most pristine person that could pass my own, personal ideological test before I worked for him," that would be a dishonest statement, and I think a reader would pick that up.

MATALIN: You know, it's usually intellectuals that find us in a cynical profession, which makes me want to laugh out loud because if you follow intellectuals throughout their career, you'll find that they shift quite easily. Their views are always shifting. Furthermore, a lot of intellectuals don't live in the real world and never have to be subjected to their policies played out. I mean you're sounding almost defensive about our profession. I'm very, very proud to be a political hack. It's a very honorable profession.

CARVILLE: Come back a minute. No, I'm not trying to sound defensive. What I'm trying to do is to sound honest about what it is that we do for a living. One of the things that we wanted to accomplish in this book was have people understand what exactly it is that we do for a living, how we operate with the culture of political campaign operatives, what kind of culture is it.

WERTHEIMER: You talk about the care and feeding of the press. You have five rules, and the first one is, "Don't lie to the press." Michael Kinsley in *The New Yorker* takes you on on that, both of you, on being spin doctors, on spinning, all of that. If spinning is good and lying is bad, what is the difference? he asks.

CARVILLE: First of all, let's back up. What I say in the book very clearly is that if, as I understand spin, it's that we go out and try to put our candidate in the most favorable light. I got one word to plead to that charge, *guilty*. Guilty, guilty, guilty. That is my job.

MATALIN: In fact, one of the more loathsome creatures on a campaign, and I suspect these are Michael Kinsley's favorite sources, are those who talk ill of their candidate, usually off the record or "on background" so the candidate won't know exactly who they are. Those are the lowest life form known to mankind in a campaign culture.

WERTHEIMER: You talk about when you were trying to cope with the problem of whether or not Dan Quayle should stay on the ticket, and there were lots of questions being raised about it. But you had polls that said that he was a drag on the ticket at that moment. You told the press that you had no data on that, but you did.

MATALIN: This is protecting the candidate. I never thought that was an issue of national security or something like that, that the whole world would fall. If we went out there and said that Dan Quayle's a drag on the ticket, that would have hurt the campaign. It desperately would have hurt the campaign. Furthermore, there was no circumstance under which Dan Quayle was going to be dropped from the ticket. Talk about spin: the reason I put that story in the book was as an example of George Bush's loyalty.

WERTHEIMER: One of the political aphorisms in this book that jumped out at me was something that you wrote about the Tsongas campaign. "There comes a time in a campaign when you want your opponent to catch the clap and die."

CARVILLE: Right, yes. It's a very, very, very competitive thing, and that just doesn't happen in presidential campaigns, it happens in campaigns for the school board even.

WERTHEIMER: How seriously do you mean that?

CARVILLE: Well, what you mean is, you don't want anything good politically to happen to your opponent. I don't want him to get a divorce, I don't want him to get sick, or anything like that. But I don't want him to have any good political days, of course. And I spend a good part of my day trying to figure out ways to do everything I can to assure that they have a bad political day.

WERTHEIMER: Do you imagine that people will come away from reading this book with a good feeling or a bad feeling about politics as it's practiced in America?

MATALIN: If people are any more cynical after reading this book, I don't think — you know they're already cynical. And you know what they're most cynical about? The media. There's twenty-one — only twenty-one percent of the people think they're getting real information from the media. So I think they will be — I think they'll be interested to see how these things work behind the scenes. Though if they're cynical, it's not going to be because of this book.

CARVILLE: Well, I really doubt if anybody is going to be surprised to find out that political campaigns do everything that they can to put their candidate in the most favorable light. Also, I think that political campaigns have evolved fairly well. It used to be that they spent all their time trying to get dead people to vote. We don't do that anymore. But if people are looking for political campaigns to be substitutes for civics lessons, they're not going to find that.

WERTHEIMER: You both talk about how you remember mistakes more clearly than you remember triumphs. What was it like to sort of put yourself in the other's place? I mean, here you were going through a campaign where you were not the only person with whom you were involved who had a major stake in this coming out, and one of you had to be miserable.

MATALIN: Guess which one was miserable, the loser or the winner? The loser, I'm embarrassed to say. I was a very, very bad loser, and I was sad for a long time and I still get, as you can see, I can still get worked up about it.

CARVILLE: Look, show me somebody who's worked on a lot of campaigns, and I'll show you a loser. I mean, it's just — only somebody who did what I did could know how she felt.

....

As the Congress approached a decision on reforming
health care (the decision was not to), many consulted
with Dr. C. EVERETT KOOP, the former surgeon general
who in 1994 was a one-man lobby for health care reform
and a supporter of the doomed Clinton plan. In an
interview with Robert Siegel, Dr. Koop says that he has
told several congressmen of the need for a provision in
that plan: an information infrastructure linking general
practitioners to colleagues, medical schools, and
hospitals. It is, he says, the sort of proposal that was
eclipsed by more controversial issues in the yearlong
national debate on health care. July 13, 1994

KOOP: This big debate has bothered me for a couple of reasons. First of all, I give the first lady enormous credit for having
put together a tremendous bill, which is an inventory of everything that is wrong with our present health care nonsystem.
Nobody objects to that. What they object to are some of the
remedies that she has suggested. Congress is now debating all
those little facets of the bill. I wish they would have begun with
page one, and said, "These are the things that are wrong. How
do we expect to address them?" If that had been done with
much more input from physicians than was the case, we would
have a medical profession behind the bill instead of opposing
the bill.

SIEGEL: How so? Who actually enjoyed the influence that
you think physicians didn't get?

KOOP: In the beginning, when there was a very large group of
people advising the first lady and the meetings were behind
closed doors, that met with the disapproval of a tremendous
number of people in science and medicine. My first conversa-

tion with the president after the bill was out was to say that he had alienated the medical profession by the manner in which the proposals had been made, and I think he knows that now.

SIEGEL: It's almost impossible to characterize the medical profession, but I guess you're saying at this moment it seems to be largely against the administration.

KOOP: The medical profession knows that they desperately need health care reform. Idealistically, they would like to see everybody covered. In so doing, they would also like to be sure that patients have a choice of physicians and that physicians have choice of the way that they practice. Some of the things that are being suggested would deprive both patient and physician of that liberty, and that is very distressing to both patient and physician alike.

Many physicians are justifiably frightened about two things that are keystones to all of the plans. One is managed care, which takes away the prerogative of physicians and puts a middle man, a bureaucrat — whether that's a government employee or an insurance clerk — between the patient and the physician's decision. The other thing they're scared to death of is managed competition, because they have never seen that work anyplace and they're not sure that it can.

SIEGEL: But there are many doctors, physicians, and surgeons in America today who've had the experience of saying, "I want to keep patient John Doe in the hospital for five days, even though this insurer says that's a four-day stay," and having to get on the phone and justify it. That's not from another planet. People know what that's like and generally don't like it.

KOOP: In general, physicians don't have trouble with four-day stays, but when they have somebody who has a four-day stay for a gallbladder and also has coronary heart disease and diabetes and has had a recent stroke, I don't think they should have to justify that extra day to a clerk who's never been to medical school and can't even pronounce or spell the words that they're trying to discuss.

SIEGEL: Do you share the fear of many of your colleagues,

that ultimately managed care is going to mean a national caste of employees who fit exactly that description?

KOOP: I fear the superimposition of another bureaucracy on an already overly large bureaucracy that takes care of health care. I wish that there were some provision for the removal of one before the imposition of the other.

SIEGEL: Let's assume that there is a bill passed by the Senate that doesn't lead to immediate, universal coverage and doesn't have employer mandates or has strange trigger mechanisms in it, perhaps, that defer to a later date the imposition of mandates. If you were to receive the big phone call for advice from the White House, and it were up to you to give advice to the president about whether you sign this very imperfect, by his standards and yours, health care reform bill, or not sign it and slug it out on another bill, what would your advice be?

KOOP: If you're asking me that question in the narrow confines of that, without any other things that we can take into consideration, I'd say I would go for a bill such as you have described it rather than no bill because I think no bill exposes the country to two serious problems. Remember that this president has accomplished a tremendous amount in the way of health care reform already just by threatening or promising health care reform, and so now we have all kinds of voluntary alliances and networks poised, under certain restraint, because they don't know what's going to happen, waiting for health care reform to be enacted. If you suddenly say we will not have a bill, then I think you will see unbridled competition, and you will have essentially private medicine run amok, and two things will happen: quality will go down and costs will soar. A bill that resembles the modification of the president's plan that has been proposed by moderates on the Senate Finance Committee — I think if that were the choice or nothing, I'd take it.

In the book *Turning Point: A Candidate, a State, and a
Nation Come of Age*, former president JIMMY CARTER
describes his first campaign for the Georgia State Senate
and the small-town corruption he encountered. In
1962, Jimmy Carter entered the race two weeks before
the election, after the U.S. Supreme Court issued its
landmark one-man–one-vote ruling. His opponent was a
two-term incumbent backed by the county's political
boss, Joe Hurst, who had a reputation for stuffing ballot
boxes. Although Carter's last-minute decision to file
for office changed his life, he tells Bob Edwards that he
did so without telling his wife. January 13, 1994

CARTER: It is inconceivable to me now, in retrospect, that I
did not consult Rosalynn about it, but I got up on October the
first, and instead of putting on my work clothes I put on some
kind of dress pants. She said, "Where in the world are you going? Is somebody dead? Are you going to a funeral?" And I said,
"No, I'm going over to the county courthouse and qualify to run
for the state senate." She was surprised, to say the least, and
somewhat disconcerted because we were in the midst of buying
peanuts and ginning cotton, and the burdens of the warehouse
business in the harvest months were very heavy, and I kind of
left it to her and my boys, who were not all that old at the time.

EDWARDS: The thing I found fascinating was the assump-
tion made by the powers that be in that county that though you
were a school board member and had the peanut business, you
were a nobody, and they could push you around. They could
have their way with you and you wouldn't be the wiser.

CARTER: Exactly. The people who controlled that county
also controlled the trial judge, the district attorney, and the

sheriff. The sheriff, as a matter of fact, was a partner with Hurst in the moonshine manufacturing and sales business. He thought he was totally impervious to any sort of outside interference, even from a candidate who saw him stealing the election.

EDWARDS: It's the classic case of the small-town power who's got the whole system locked up.

CARTER: Well, some people here in Chicago think it was not just small-town. When I was in Boston for Tip's funeral, they don't think it was just small towns either. But this particular character, whose name was Joe Hurst, also controlled the Democratic party apparatus, and his wife was a welfare director. Quitman County, by the way, was the only county in the nation where all the welfare checks came to just one post office box. So Joe Hurst and his wife hand-delivered the welfare checks to recipients each month. If they didn't vote the way he wanted, they lost their welfare. And he would stuff the ballot box to whatever extent it was required to win.

EDWARDS: Including literally stuffing. I mean, he had a lot of sophisticated ways to do this, but he literally put votes in.

CARTER: Yes, he did, even with me watching. I went over there that morning, not having any idea that this kind of thing could happen in the United States of America, and saw him depriving people of a secret ballot. The voting booths were not used. He told everyone who his candidate was — that was my opponent — and he watched them mark their ballot. He argued with them if they marked it in the wrong way, and then after they left he would reach into the box, which has a five-inch hole in the top, and take out their ballot and sometimes exchange it. When they counted the ballots that evening, although only 300 people had voted, there were 430 ballots in the box. One hundred eighteen of them voted alphabetically, down to the fourth letter in their name, and a number of those voters were dead, and had been dead for quite a while, and were in prison or were in a distant state and obviously hadn't come home to vote. So whatever was required, he wanted to have a big victory.

EDWARDS: And despite all that, and all the witnesses you had, you still had to go to court.

CARTER: I had to go to court. And then the law in Georgia was that no matter what the court ruled, the ultimate judge of who won or lost an election was a county democratic committee, and this was controlled by the same guy, Joe Hurst, who had his own lieutenants controlling the committee. It was only because I found one courageous reporter who worked for the *Atlanta Journal*, John Pennington, that this case ultimately got nationwide, certainly statewide, publicity. It was a strange thing to have numbers of voters alphabetical, and dead people voting, and it brought a lot of attention, and became such an embarrassment to the Democratic party that eventually I prevailed.

EDWARDS: Now, what if you had lost? Back to the peanut warehouse?

CARTER: I never would have run for another office. I was pretty interested in politics then. I was on the local county board of education. I was chairman, as a matter of fact, and the only reason I ran for office was because the one-man–one-vote ruling, I thought, brought a new era to Georgia politics, and also I wanted to protect the public school system because even the candidate who became governor won the election on the basis of a campaign promise, "No, not one." He would raise one finger, and say, "No, not one," and it would arouse great applause in the audience because it meant "No, not one black child in a white school classroom." He threatened to close down the entire public school system if it was integrated. When I got to the state senate, the only request I made was that I be put on the education committee, which I was, and then I became chairman of the university committee. And so that was the way I got into politics, the only reason. If I had lost this election I would have abandoned politics.

EDWARDS: It's incredible how close Gerald Ford and Ted Kennedy came to never hearing about you.

CARTER: Yes, that's true. We tried to reform, and did reform, the entire Georgia electoral system after I got into the senate. When we were debating this case, one of the senators, Bobby Rowan from a place called Enigma, Georgia, offered an amendment that was heavily debated, that no one in Georgia could vote in the general election or the primary election who had been dead more than three years. And this was quite a transforming amendment. A lot of debates took place, some tongue in cheek, of course, about how long could a person be dead and still have their families accurately predict how they would have voted had they lived? And so his amendment was that three years was the maximum.

EDWARDS: It gets into those theological debates, when the soul leaves the body and all of that.

CARTER: [*laughs*] Exactly. But, you know, if a husband does die, of course, there's a time after it when the wife and children might pretty well accurately predict how he would have voted. [*laughs*]

EDWARDS: Well, this makes you immensely qualified, I think, to be an election monitor, which you do in many elections around the world.

CARTER: Well, I've never run into election fraud anywhere in the world that would equal what happened to me in this first election, although we do conduct many of them. We were in Paraguay this past year, and before that in Guyana, and Zambia, and Nicaragua to end the contra war, and Haiti, and the Dominican Republic, and Ghana, and so forth, and so I think I know all the tricks that might be attempted in these foreign countries because I've experienced the tricks myself.

AMERICA TALKING

On the tenth anniversary of the invention of the Macintosh computer, STEVEN JOBS, who cofounded Apple with Stephen Wozniak in his parents' garage in California, recalls both the Mac's creation and his eventual separation from Apple. Jobs was forced out in 1985 after the company had grown to a two-billion-dollar enterprise. Speaking with Jacki Lyden, the thirty-eight-year-old computer guru explains that the birth of the Mac was a team effort. January 22, 1994

JOBS: A lot of people worked very hard at Apple, a lot of very talented people, and that certainly accounts for a lot of the success. Another part of it was that we were at the right place at the right time. I always used to think of the computer industry as this vector being drawn off into the future, and we were literally in the first inch of the vector. When you alter the course of a vector in the first inch, it doesn't look like much right at the beginning, but when you get out a mile, the whole course of history is changed. We felt like we were able to alter the progression of our industry and of this phenomenon called the personal computer.

LYDEN: Did you ever think, Gee, I could be the next Henry Ford or I could be like Orville Wright thinking about redesigning flight, or was that just too grandiose?

JOBS: We were really engaged with the technology itself. The reason we started Apple was because we wanted a personal computer for ourselves, and we could not afford to buy one of the very early kits, so we built one out of spare parts. My partner worked at Hewlett-Packard at the time, and I worked at Atari. I was nineteen and he was about twenty-four. We scrounged some parts and built computers for ourselves, and then our friends wanted them. Unfortunately, these computers were taking about a week for us to build manually, so I sold my Volkswagen van and Woz sold his HP calculator and we got about thirteen hundred dollars together and we paid a friend of ours to make what was called a printed circuit board so that we could cut the assembly time down to an afternoon. And that's how we got started.

LYDEN: I'd like to ask you about your personal use of language. You have such wonderful catch phrases. I have read that you said that you wanted to design a computer that was not merely great but "insanely great"; that in the creation of the Macintosh, you wanted to do it quickly, with "real artistship"; that you were going to put a "dent in the universe" with the machine. Do you always think in hyperbole?

JOBS: I don't know how to answer that. We were all in our mid- to late twenties, and we were working between fifteen and twenty hours a day for long stretches of time. This was a very difficult birth of this product. When you're working with a team of people, it's important to communicate in ways that people will remember, that what we're doing is larger than ourselves. Otherwise you get real tired. It's easy to look around at all the things you're sacrificing in your life for this computer that isn't even born yet. Part of the job of a leader is to keep everybody motivated and keep everybody heading in the same direction towards a goal. That was part of my job, and sometimes I would try to remind people of things that they felt in their gut anyway in a way that they'd remember.

LYDEN: I suppose it's a bit like being a football coach, only more than that if you think of yourselves as technology revolutionaries. I really like descriptions I've heard of Apple in the early days where people felt like rebels.

JOBS: One of the analogies I have always used is, I read this article in *Scientific American* when I was growing up, where they measured the efficiency of locomotion for the various species on the planet: how many kilocalories per kilometer they burned to move from point A to point B. And humans came out not so great. The condor won. It was the most efficient, and humans were about a third of the way down the list, except that someone there had the insight to test the efficiency of a human riding a bicycle, and it blew away the condor. It was all the way off the charts. I remember maybe when I was about twelve, that made a very big impression on me: that humans are tool builders; that's what separates us from most of the other species. One of the phrases that we coined in the Apple II days was that the personal computer was a bicycle for the mind.

LYDEN: Did you have a sense of your audience? I myself held on to low technology until the very end. We used to joke that they could put all the typewriters in my office and I'd be quite happy. How do you win over someone who is absolutely loath to think of computers as something useful for them?

JOBS: You know, this is going to sound a little harsh: we always felt that death was the best invention of life, that sooner or later people who were afraid of these things would all die off. We had a long history of working with education. During the Apple II days even, we put a lot of computers into schools, K through 12. We saw what these kids did with them and we knew that they were familiar with them and were going to use them for the rest of their lives. So it was just a matter of time. History was on our side. We didn't spend a lot of sleepless hours worrying about how to convert every last person. We figured we would get these things out there, there'd be a lot of early adopters that would love them, and history would take care of the rest. I think that has largely proved to be the case.

LYDEN: Do you see yourself as a creator, an inventor, or as a synthesizer of the ideas of others? Would you not see that as a criticism?

JOBS: I think it was Picasso who said that good artists copy, great artists steal. I have always encouraged everybody to steal good ideas wherever they could find them. There are plenty of things that need to be invented, so if somebody else has already done something, grab it and incorporate it into what you're doing. I guess I also try to surround myself with people who think of themselves as into technology and, of course, quite good at engineering, but also, if they weren't doing this they'd probably be an artist somewhere. I think that aesthetics in computer and software design are just as important as in many other fields, and we try to attract people like that.

LYDEN: Eventually you had to leave Apple in 1985 and were forced out of the company that you yourself had helped to found. Have you made peace with that?

JOBS: To the extent that one ever does, sure. When I left in 1985, I was mostly stunned for a while. After that I just decided, you know, you've got to get on with your life. Life is short, so it is not a good idea to spend too much time dwelling on these things.

LYDEN: Looking back, is there any way you would change the end of this story? Would you rewrite it in any way?

JOBS: Oh, sure. But I think we all feel pretty good about it. All of us think that the ending could have turned out better, that the Macintosh could have kept on going and been much more successful relative to Microsoft, but that's not the way the cards played out. I think the ending is just fine. You know, one of the nicest things is that at least a few times a month I still get letters from people, thanking me and, more importantly, Apple and the Mac team for the Macintosh. They relay, a lot of times, the story of the first day that they unpacked their Mac out of the box and they never thought that they could use a computer and they plugged it in and, lo and behold, they figured it out. They actually were driving this computer. To this day, I still get a few letters every month, and I try to send them to Apple to circulate around to the team back there.

LYDEN: Well, I confess to you that I only really got introduced to one quite recently. I thought it had a very pleasing, witty, and fun personality.

JOBS: You know, that's an amazing thing to think about. People do come away from the Macintosh thinking that it has a personality. I think it does have a personality. People who worked on the project put a lot of themselves into that product.

DON HAMILTON, a teacher and former student at the local high school in New Castle, Indiana, tells Bob Edwards about his state's particular obsession with basketball — and with gyms. New Castle Chrysler High is home to the largest high school gym in the country: it holds more than nine thousand fans. Hamilton, who has compiled a book of stories and photographs called *Hoosier Temples: A Pictorial History of Indiana's High School Basketball Gyms*, says folks in the Hoosier State have not always driven the lane in such spacious accommodations. March 25, 1994

EDWARDS: You had games played in barns? You had a gym in Burlington, in Carroll County, that was above a store?

HAMILTON: Yes, and there was a window right under the basket, so that if you'd go in on a fast break, there was some danger of going from the second floor to the first floor quickly.

EDWARDS: In Indiana you have the six biggest high school gyms in the country, sixteen of the seventeen biggest in the nation, and of the thirty-six biggest, twenty-eight are in Indiana. Why is this?

HAMILTON: Beginning in about the 1920s, there really wasn't much else to do in town. Basketball became the thing to do on Friday and Saturday nights during the winter. Then a series of sort of the medium-size towns in the state — Lafayette, Kokomo, Anderson — they got in a competition to see who could build the biggest and the best gym. In the nineteenth century, it was really important for a town to have a large school, or a large courthouse, or some type of public building. Well, in the 1920s, the gym joined that list of public buildings needed for a town to be first class.

EDWARDS: So that was your local identity, your high school basketball team.

HAMILTON: It really became that. If your team was playing well, you felt better about yourself.

EDWARDS: So if Muncie had a bigger gym than Kokomo, then Kokomo had to build a still bigger one.

HAMILTON: That's right. And that's exactly what happened for many, many years.

EDWARDS: So then you get up to New Castle, which has the biggest in the country.

HAMILTON: We had to go to Muncie for the regional, and year after year we'd lose, so we decided to build a gym much bigger than the Muncie field house, and we gained the regional. Then they had to come to New Castle from then on, which really bothered them. Of course, they won another four or five state championships after that, so I don't think it hurt them too much.

EDWARDS: New Castle holds 9,314 people. There are quite a few colleges that don't have gyms that big.

HAMILTON: That's right. This last year a film, *Blue Chips*, was done in Indiana, and I got a phone call from the state film board. They were looking for a site for the filming, and I suggested New Castle, and they said, "Well, no, it's too big. We need a gym that looks like a university arena but will only have about five thousand seats." They were afraid they wouldn't be able to fill the gym.

EDWARDS: I really love the architecture there, and that gets us into another aspect of this. Some of these really were temples.

HAMILTON: They really were. And you could tell that the people in the communities took a great pride in these buildings because they were very definitely impressive public buildings. I have pictures in the book of gargoyles being carved, griffins, winged lions, all types of things on the facades.

EDWARDS: Stained glass, Palladian arched windows?

HAMILTON: That's right. It's amazing how fast some of

these buildings went up too. Muncie won their state championship in March of 1928. They had an eight-thousand-seat gym built by the following November. Raised the money, constructed the thing, everything in less than six months.

EDWARDS: Priorities.

HAMILTON: [*laughs*] That's right.

EDWARDS: Attendance has fallen off, though. There's some indication that there's competition for the fans' attention.

HAMILTON: Absolutely. On any given Friday night, there are probably three or four college basketball games available on cable television, a couple of pro games, people can sit home and watch video, play video games, they can watch recorded films, there are all types of activities available.

EDWARDS: But the interest in Indiana is still out of proportion to the rest of the country, wouldn't you say?

HAMILTON: Well, to give an example, I talked to athletic directors out in California, and they said that last year they had a good state tournament. About two hundred fifty thousand attended, and that's out of a population of about thirty million. Indiana has less than six million, and we have over eight hundred thousand fans at our state tournament, and if you combine the boys' and girls' totals, we still have over a million Hoosiers attending the state tournament games every year.

Pictured on the cover of Eugene Richards's book of
photographs, *Cocaine True, Cocaine Blue*, a woman
whom Richards calls MARIELLA balances a syringe in
her rotting teeth, her soft brown eyes swelling out
of her sallow face. Scott Simon visited Mariella and her
companion, JOE, in the dingy, windowless apartment
they share in the East New York section of Brooklyn.
They describe their lives and their addiction.
October 1, 1994

MARIELLA: We don't have much more energy left. My teeth
are all out. I can't even get a job or nothing.

JOE: You don't have the desire or the get-up-and-go any
longer. You lose it. The only desire that you have is to go out
and score some more.

MARIELLA: We do it and we get nervous and we don't even
enjoy it anymore, but it's still like you want it. It's so sick, like.
There's so many things that could happen. It happened to me
already. I got beat up, I got my teeth knocked out, I got a gun put
to my head.

JOE: And then she'd be doing it just as much as I would and
she would still say, "We gotta get out of here, this is no good."

MARIELLA: And then I was like, I can't beat 'em, join 'em.
And that's what I did. People give up sex, they give up everything for this drug, so imagine how great it is. They give up their
families, their self-respect, their pride, their money, every dime
they have, their cars, their families, their kids. They give up
everything. So imagine what this thing is, you know what I
mean?

SIMON: Will you help us understand what it feels like?

MARIELLA: You just get this warm feeling, and if you were

going to interview the Pope, you'd feel like he was your buddy. You'd feel so comfortable. I mean if you were going to meet the president, you'd say, "Hey, Bob, what's up?" And you'd talk to him like if he was just your friend.

JOE: Bill.

MARIELLA: You know what I mean. I'm telling you, it just makes you feel like so confident and you go out dancing and it just completely wipes away every inhibition that you have and you want this feeling tomorrow and you want it the next day. You just want to feel this forever. But then, all of a sudden, boom, it hits you. You got a habit and you're sick and you lose your job and every penny you have. You can't work. You'll go all over New York, Bronx, you'll go anywhere you have to go to get that bag. That's why you have to go into detoxes and rehabs and all that.

JOE: And therapy. Psychiatric treatment too.

MARIELLA: They have to, like, reprogram you to live in the reality and have to deal and cope with life. You can't escape to that bag.

JOE: And that's the reality that you have to live with.

SIMON: Could you give me some idea of what a day is like for the two of you?

JOE: Basically, the day is very boring. And I think that's why we tend to do this crack. That's why, I think, because we're so bored with life or our own lives.

MARIELLA: All we do is, like, sit here and, like, wait. Well, really we're not that bad anymore. We started doing what we had to do. We had to take care of problems that we had with the rent and everything. You procrastinate incredibly. I mean for every little thing. Eugene has been on my back for me to get my teeth fixed since he knows me. He took me to the dentist, actually drove me to the dentist one day, but I had to go somewhere else to get my X-rays. Just to do a simple thing like that. I could be walking around with my teeth in my mouth. But it's like, when I look in the mirror I don't even realize it. When I went up to the detox and I started straightening out and I realized what I looked like without my teeth, it was like, "My God."

JOE: You know, right now I'm at that point where I really don't want it any longer. I'm not as thrilled about doing cocaine any longer.

MARIELLA: But it's scary to go out, like to try to start all over again, to do normal things, to go out and find a job. It's, like, scary after you've been in la-la land for, like, so many years. It's scary, you know, like so that makes you back off a little.

SIMON: What's amazing about that is that anybody listening to this will find it scary to be part of the world that you're living in now.

JOE: They should. Be scared.

MARIELLA: It's so hard to get back. When you try this stuff, you don't think about all the bad things that are going to come. You see a junkie on the corner, oh, ugh, and all messed up, you don't realize that's gonna be you in a year from now. You don't even — you don't connect that whatsoever. And it happens so quick.

JOE: A friend of mine overdosed and when we brought him out of it, he saw me doing my shot. I did half of what was in it, and he sees me squirt the rest of it because I started feeling great. I used to get this tightening in my chest, like if my heart was being squoze inside by somebody's hand. It was painful for a split second, then, boom, all of a sudden, that euphoric feeling would come over me. It's like a warm, warm water flowing over you. All of a sudden, he sees me squirting the rest of it out onto the wall because I knew if I was, if I would have did the rest, I would have died. I knew it, so I squirted the rest. And he says, "What, are you crazy? You could of gave it to me." I couldn't believe it.

SIMON: If somebody said to you, "Try and get through the afternoon without getting something today," could you do that?

JOE: No. I don't think so. It takes a lot more than that. It takes a lot more than that.

MARIELLA: I would love to say yes.

JOE: It takes the individual, actually, even though I say we need help from others and input and stuff, in the final analysis, it's your own decision, it's one's own mind that has to be made up.

MARIELLA: I would love to say yes so much, like, just the way you said that, I would love to say yes. And then put myself to the test and do it for today and then see what happens tomorrow. It's like they say, you have to know when the time is, you have to reach that point. We have reached that point. We're just lingering on right now. Just you saying that makes me want to say yes and really try to do it, really, really, really, with my whole heart and soul, really try to do it. Three or four months ago, I would have said "No way, get the hell out of here." But right now, today, I really want — I wish so much that I could.

Several polls in 1994 revealed that the number-one issue concerning Americans was crime. On a visit to the Lorton Maximum Security Facility of the District of Columbia Department of Corrections, Robert Siegel interviews GARY WINSTON JAGGERS and ANTHONY TIRADO. Jaggers was convicted of murder in the beating deaths of a sixty-five-year-old woman and an eighty-eight-year-old man. Tirado was convicted with his partner of killing a sixty-seven-year-old man in order to steal his Chevrolet. Tirado says that he became attracted to violence and crime when he was twelve and succumbed to peer pressure at school.
April 5, 1994

TIRADO: You want to be "the man," so called in street jargon. You want to be the man. You want to have all the girls. You want everybody to know you. You want everybody to notice you. You want to stand out. You want to be known as a violent individual. I began to develop a pattern of violent behavior. The first time was in school, I beat a kid with his own crutch, and I saw how all the other students in the school feared me.

SIEGEL: But you said you beat this student with his own crutch. That suggests that he wasn't one of the most dangerous guys in the school at that moment.

TIRADO: At that moment, it didn't matter. That incident started from a petty argument over a lunch tray. It wasn't as if he was one of the more well known people in the school. After that first incident, I made sure that if I committed some type of violent act that it would be addressed to somebody who had a big name or somebody who was supposedly in the street jargon "like that." They were the man.

SIEGEL: You came to Washington, D.C., hoping to find a drug dealer to rob?

TIRADO: We didn't. We were unsuccessful in our endeavor to find this drug dealer. Something else came up, you know. I guess now it is what they call car jacking. Back in 1989, the word *car jacking* had no name. In other words, we were carjacking before car jacking actually had a name. In this case, the individual was in the car with the car running, sitting in a parking lot. As the car-jacking statement goes, Just get him, do whatever you do. In our case, he was shot. He was shot, threw him out, and took the car. It was a very malicious act. God only knows I wouldn't do it again. God only knows. I've been incarcerated for a period of five years now. I am locked up for the offense of second-degree murder while armed.

SIEGEL: What if you had known ten years ago that if you were convicted three times of a violent crime, the third time you were going to be in a place like this for life?

TIRADO: If they had that three-strikes-and-you're-out rule, truthfully, I could've cared less because you know that you will suffer some consequences by committing these acts if you are caught. And you will be caught. There's no doubt about it. You will be caught. But at that time and at that young of an age, you don't care. You don't have the slightest idea what consequences you are going to suffer. The penitentiary is somewhere nobody on the face of this earth would want to be. I had no idea what the penitentiary was like. I had no idea.

JAGGERS: I grew up in a household that was dominated by a female. And at that time, I could not muster that type of responsibility that was placed upon me. So consequently a lot of rebellion, a lot of hatred, anger, built up. My first crime was I snatched a pocketbook to obtain certain kind of moneys. Then from snatching a pocketbook, it escalated to a level of real intense violence by grabbing someone, striking them very hard, tearing their clothes off, going through their pockets, taking their wristwatch, to whatever that means.

SIEGEL: Was there always a robbery involved?

JAGGERS: It was always robbery. That was my primary reason, to go out there and to obtain some money. If I see a person in the street, I target them, I size them up, see if they're weak. I look for a certain type of bulges in the pocket. This is an indication whether or not this person may have, in fact, a large sum of money. I follow this person. And usually the person lives in, like, an apartment complex, and I would attack them in the hallway, very violently.

SIEGEL: Were you afraid when you did these things, when you robbed somebody?

JAGGERS: No, I was never afraid. What stimulated me was the act of taking something, someone's money or their wristwatch. That gave me that sense of excitement that I enjoyed at that time. I used to look at people's houses, you know, the structure of the house, how many cars they had parked in their driveway. And this right here was a turnaround, and I was seventeen years of age. I entered this person's house. The person was there. We got into a tussle. And consequently the person died as a result of our tussle. This is what brought me up to this point here. You know, I'm locked up for murder.

SIEGEL: When you were a child, did you see very much violence on television?

JAGGERS: That's one thing I can really truly say that I give my mother credit for. We were never allowed to watch television in a certain period of time. She always instilled upon us the principles of doing your homework first, doing your household chores second, and then if there's time permitted you may have leisure time for recreation such as watching television. So TV itself did not enhance my curiosity to go out to commit crimes. My experience came from being a part of the street itself, watching others commit crimes. That's how I got my social information. That's how it filtered to me.

SIEGEL: And do you have a date for eligibility of parole?

JAGGERS: My date number is 2037.

SIEGEL: That is forty-three years from now.

JAGGERS: Right.

SIEGEL: How old are you now? Thirty?

JAGGERS: Thirty.

SIEGEL: You think about the year 2037 often?

JAGGERS: I think about it a lot sometimes. I more so think about the present. All my energy and attention is focusing on today. I live for today. I let the year 2037 live for itself. If I should live to see the year 2037, it will be a blessing in itself.

Daniel Zwerdling interviews EDWARD HONAKER a week after his release from Virginia's Nottaway Prison. Honaker served nine years for a rape that he always said he did not commit. In 1994 he was freed after a DNA test proved his innocence. October 29, 1994

ZWERDLING: The afternoon you walked out of prison you said something to a reporter that really struck me. You were talking about your freedom, and you said, "The only thing I compare it with is the birth of my first child."

HONAKER: It was just the elation that I felt. In a sense it was sort of a rebirth for me, a resurrection of sorts, maybe. It was just unbelievable, the feeling and the emotions that I was feeling when I was freed. I had every emotion known to man running through me at that time. I was saddened because I was leaving real good friends behind. On the other hand, I was elated to be out after such a long time.

ZWERDLING: What you have been through is one of everybody's worst nightmares, being put away for something we did not do. All of us wonder, if it did happen, how would we possibly handle it? I wonder what sort of mind games you played in prison, or what sort of goals you set for yourself. What sort of work did you do to cope all these years?

HONAKER: My goal was to one day regain my freedom. I never lost track of that. That was my foremost, number-one goal. You have to resolve to make the best of it. It's amazing what the human mind and the human body can adapt to when it has to.

ZWERDLING: But tell me about the sort of things you did in prison.

HONAKER: I worked. I worked in the maintenance shop at the prison. I was the welder there because of my experience. I did a lot of writing, novels and short stories and different things. I did artwork.

ZWERDLING: Do you mind telling me the plot of your novel?

HONAKER: It's about a werewolf is what it is. I'm a Stephen King fan, and it is written in the horror genre. It's about a medicine man whose tribe was wiped out three hundred years ago by the white man. He swore revenge, and he came back as a lycanthrope, or werewolf, and wreaked his revenge on a little, small Virginia town. [laughs]

ZWERDLING: Why are you laughing?

HONAKER: Well, the little, small Virginia town. I guess I was kind of venting a little bit there through the prose.

ZWERDLING: I was just going to say, I'm no psychologist, but it sounds a little bit like you're trying to deal with wanting revenge. You hear interviews with people who are freed after spending years in jail for a crime they did not commit, and they sometimes say, "I'm not bitter, I'm just trying to put my life behind me." Edward Honaker, I can't imagine that you are not furious.

HONAKER: Oh, I am furious. I am still furious to this day. The state of Virginia took so much away from me. They took everything that I had ever worked for. My children were seven, eight, and nine years old when I got locked up, and now they are seventeen, eighteen, and nineteen. They're young adults and I don't know anything about them. I have missed their childhood. My daughter gave birth to my first grandchild in January, and I saw him for the first time in April in a prison visiting room. That is not fair; it's not right. I'm not lying to you, I'm not saying that I'm not bitter, because I am, but I have learned to control the anger. I learned that a long time ago. You can't let it eat at you. You have to do something else with it.

ZWERDLING: What about your feelings toward the young woman who identified you and said that you were the one that raped her?

HONAKER: I don't have any animosity toward her.

ZWERDLING: Really?

HONAKER: I don't appreciate what she did to me. I feel that the victim was coerced by the commonwealth's attorney and by the arresting officer.

ZWERDLING: You've had around a week now to explore what America is like in 1994. What sort of things have you been doing with this first week of liberation?

HONAKER: Just enjoying life, really, doing little things, going to a restaurant for something to eat — with real silverware.

ZWERDLING: With real silverware?

HONAKER: Yes, and a porcelain plate or whatever. I don't have that plastic or metal any longer.

ZWERDLING: Do you ever catch yourself expecting the waitress to tell you it's time to go back to your cell or anything like that?

HONAKER: It's kind of funny you mention that because we had a fifteen-minute time limit to eat in prison, and I've caught myself a couple of times looking at my watch, making sure I didn't overstay. I went to a restaurant the other night and I thought I was going to have an anxiety attack in there, I just felt so out of place. I know they weren't, but I just thought everyone was staring and burning holes in the back of my neck and all. Every time I do something, I haven't done it in ten years and it's like doing something all over again. I got my driver's license day before yesterday, so now I have that.

ZWERDLING: Congratulations.

HONAKER: Thank you. I have a lot of little first things to do yet that I haven't been able to do in a long time.

ZWERDLING: What are you going to do the rest of today?

HONAKER: I'm going to look for a truck, four-wheel drive, and hope that I can find one pretty cheap, and I'm going to see if I can find work.

ZWERDLING: I hope we get to read your novel about the werewolf wreaking revenge.

HONAKER: Well, if it ever does it, I will personally autograph it for you.

JOHN RISDALL is the president of Magnum Research, which manufactures handguns, including the Desert Eagle .50. It costs more than twelve hundred dollars, takes bullets that cost a dollar apiece, and weighs more than four pounds. Magnum Research markets the extremely powerful handgun with a promotional video that shows the pistol in action, blowing up watermelons. Noah Adams asks Risdall about the gun's appeal.
March 31, 1994

RISDALL: Something happens. It's like going bowling. You go bowling, you knock down the pins. In practical pistol shooting, they knock down bowling pins. Target shooters call it "printing paper." You're shooting at a target. The machine-gun shoots that they have every year all over the country are incredibly much fun. They go up and blow up things. You know, I think people go to movies to see things blown up. Well, you can do it yourself. That's the charge. That's the kick. I've always loved fireworks. I go every Fourth of July and I try and go see fireworks. I love the big boom and the explosion and the colors.

ADAMS: Speaking of the movies, your gun was used in *Last Action Hero*, Arnold Schwarzenegger.

RISDALL: Sure. Yes.

ADAMS: In *Cliffhanger*, I have read. In *Menace II Society*. Any other movie I'm missing here?

RISDALL: *True Romance, Demolition Man*, the new Steven Seagal film that's out, *On Sacred Ground*. Things like that. We've worked with most of the action stars in movies today. Sixty percent of movies, year in, year out, use some kind of gun. And then we have the problem of responsible use and display of the guns in the movies, and sometimes that's a real stretch. In *Last Action Hero* — did you go see the movie?

ADAMS: No, no.

RISDALL: There's a scene where Arnold's in a convertible, and he's driving down some L.A. freeway or whatever, or city street, at ninety miles an hour, and he's shooting the gun over the back of his shoulder at some would-be villain. Boy, that's not responsible gun ownership. I mean, it's dreadful.

ADAMS: But how can any of these films be an example of responsible gun ownership, really?

RISDALL: It's difficult with trying to make it box office and at the same time make it real. My problem with TV and the movies is to show the consequences of bad gun ownership, not just the person who's either killed or wounded or crippled, but the family and the hurt that it causes, the ripple effect.

ADAMS: That scene in the movie you were being critical of, Arnold Schwarzenegger firing back from the convertible: aren't some law enforcement agencies around the country very concerned with what they call the collateral damage from Desert Eagle .50, that it is so powerful there's no telling what can happen with that bullet and with bystanders?

RISDALL: There is no bullet that's not dangerous. There are lots of other pistols that have more muzzle energy than a .50 Magnum. It's neither the most powerful nor the most dangerous pistol there is, and our bullets only come in two types, a hollow point and a soft point. Those are no armor-piercing bullets. Those are bullets that once they hit something they stay there, which is why we created them that way for, again, both hunting and target shooting.

ADAMS: When you read in *New York* magazine, as I'm sure you did, "The Desert Eagle is becoming the gangsta gun of choice on the streets of New York. The Desert Eagle is the gun people will boast they own even when they don't," and I've seen the Desert Eagle referred to on television —

RISDALL: Sure. Absolutely.

ADAMS: In *NYPD Blue*, somebody was killed with a Desert Eagle.

RISDALL: Certainly. I saw the episode.

ADAMS: While you're sitting at home and watching that out in Minnesota, and you're seeing what could be real, a depiction of what could be real in New York, what are you thinking about?

RISDALL: Number one, it's fiction. I mean, we could be the gangsta gun of choice just like every gangster drives a Lamborghini too. We are such a small percent of the total population of guns. Even though we do have hundreds of thousands of happy customers out there, it's just not the case.

ADAMS: But, say, as the president of this company, you read about your gun, the .50 Desert Eagle, being used in a holdup and somebody being killed with it.

RISDALL: Sure. It's going to happen. At the same time, what people don't talk about is the good things that guns do. The close to a million incidents every year where an armed citizen confronts some kind of felon with some kind of gun, and that incident doesn't happen and a bad consequence doesn't happen. On the whole, I think guns are doing more good in society than they're doing bad.

ADAMS: If you're putting forth a very practical reason to have this gun, for recreation and for self-defense, why is there so much concern with the way it looks and the way it appears? This is the gun of choice for many of these movies we're talking about. I have read that when the prototypes came back from your factory in Israel that's making these guns, you said that the guns weren't sexy enough, that they just looked too much like a tool. Why is there the image of sex — let's be blunt about it — with this particular weapon?

RISDALL: I think good industrial design can be in anything. I also run one of the biggest advertising agencies in the Twin Cities, and I like to see things that look good. There's no reason why there can't be a good-looking gun, as far as I'm concerned. This happens to be my view of a good-looking gun. At Magnum Research, this is what we think a neat-looking gun should look like. Turns out that movie directors, rappers, hunters, target shooters, happen to agree with us in that we have a distinctive-looking gun. Why have a gun that looks just like everybody else's gun?

ADAMS: But why equate a sexy image with an instrument of destruction? Isn't that a dangerous combination?

RISDALL: Wow! That just may be too deep for me. When we started this company fifteen years ago, this was a gun that was going to be for hunters who walked in the woods, stalked deer, and in the best traditions of America used guns responsibly. Why can't they have a good-looking gun? I don't know. I hope you get a chance some day to shoot the gun. I think you'd find it not an intimidating experience. The .50 Magnum, however, is a gun that is different than the other guns, and for me, my sympathetic nervous system kicks in, and says, This gun is too big. And my deodorant doesn't work when I shoot the .50 Magnum. It's not something I can't physically control, but it makes a very loud noise and the muzzle flash is just huge.

ADAMS: So it scares you a bit.

RISDALL: Any gun should scare anybody. They are lethal, and they need to be handled in the most careful way possible. You just can't tell people that enough. Any gun should be scary.

Daniel Zwerdling looked into a gun buy-back program
that addressed the childhood fascination with weapons.
SANDY RUBEN of Cambridge, Massachusetts, the
proprietor of Sandy and Son Toy Store, describes his offer
to trade with kids who turn in their toy guns: a new
"peaceful" toy or a gift certificate of between one and
seven dollars per toy gun. December 4, 1994

RUBEN: We started the end of September. We probably have
over five hundred toy guns at this point.

ZWERDLING: This program is a wonderful gimmick, at the
very least, but to what extent do you think you're conveying
some sort of serious message to children?

RUBEN: I don't look at it as a gimmick. I look at it as something that we've been doing philosophically for the last nine
years in the store, which is that we try to create an alternative
for children and parents that says that there are lots of wonderful toys out there that don't involve weapons.

ZWERDLING: We've decided to call you now because we
heard that a whole class from a local school was coming. I hear
them in the background. Why don't we talk with one of the
children, or a couple of them, who have brought their guns in
today?

VANESSA: Hello?

ZWERDLING: Hi. My name's Daniel. Who are you?

VANESSA: Vanessa.

ZWERDLING: Hey, Vanessa, how old are you?

VANESSA: Nine.

ZWERDLING: And I take it you are bringing in a gun today to
trade in?

VANESSA: Yes.

ZWERDLING: Tell me about the gun you're bringing in.

VANESSA: It's orange and it's broken.

ZWERDLING: It's orange and it's broken. Is that why you're bringing it in, because it broke?

VANESSA: Yes.

ZWERDLING: So what do you play with your gun?

VANESSA: Five days a week.

ZWERDLING: But what do you do? Do you play like you're a gangster or a policewoman, or what?

VANESSA: Play dead.

ZWERDLING: You play dead.

VANESSA: Yes.

ZWERDLING: OK, well, listen, Vanessa, thanks a lot, and let me talk with somebody else who's trading in their gun.

VANESSA: OK. [*To classmates:*] Anybody want to use the phone?

DARREN: Hello?

ZWERDLING: Hi. What's your name?

DARREN: Darren.

ZWERDLING: And what gun are you bringing in today?

DARREN: Three Super Soakers.

ZWERDLING: Why are you bringing them in?

DARREN: Because they're broken. I don't need them anymore.

ZWERDLING: Ah. You know, some adults say that when people your age play with guns it makes you think about violence, and maybe it will even lead you to acting violent one day. What do you think about that?

DARREN: Well, with some kids they think about that, but I don't think about buying guns because I know the difference between a toy gun and a real gun.

ZWERDLING: All right. Well, listen, thanks a lot, Darren. Thanks for talking to us.

DARREN: OK. You're welcome.

AMANDA: Hello?

ZWERDLING: How are you doing today?

AMANDA: Good.

ZWERDLING: And what kind of gun are you bringing in to-day?

AMANDA: A Super Soaker.

ZWERDLING: A Super Soaker. Boy, everybody seems to have these Super Soakers. How far can they shoot water?

AMANDA: Some of them shoot, like, a thousand miles, but mine, it only shoots fifty miles.

ZWERDLING: Fifty miles. Wow, that's pretty far. You're the second girl I've talked with today who has brought in a toy gun, and when I was your age I didn't know any girls who played with toy guns.

AMANDA: Oh, I always play with the toy guns.

ZWERDLING: And what about other girls you know? Do they play with toy guns too?

AMANDA: Yes.

ZWERDLING: And why are you bringing in your Super Soaker today?

AMANDA: Because it's broken.

ZWERDLING: I think I'm starting to understand who's bringing in their guns today. All right. Well, listen, Amanda, thanks a lot.

AMANDA: All right.

ZWERDLING: Sandy?

RUBEN: Yes.

ZWERDLING: When I ask the kids why they are bringing in their guns, they don't say it's to promote peace in the world, they say it's because they're broken.

RUBEN: For some, it's just, "This is a broken toy and let's go get a new toy in exchange for it."

ZWERDLING: And that doesn't bother you, that they're being so, you know, cold and calculated about this trade?

RUBEN: No, because I think they can still act out violent play with a broken gun, and I'm just as happy not to have it in the household.

At the end of July, two men were murdered in Pensacola, Florida, at a medical clinic where abortions are performed. One of the men was Dr. John Britton, who performed abortions. The other was James Barrett, a retired military man who was escorting Dr. Britton to the clinic. An antiabortion protester named Paul Hill was arrested for those murders and later convicted. In 1993, another physician, Dr. David Gunn, was murdered by an antiabortion activist in Pensacola. The Pensacola murders continued an escalation of antiabortion violence since the 1980s: bombings and arson attacks, beatings of clinic employees. In Pensacola, Linda Wertheimer asks four people who are active in the community why their city has been the scene of such violence. The four are ROSALIND FISHER EMERSON, an administrator at the University of West Florida; JOHN GRIFFING, who heads the chamber of commerce; Dr. LANGDON GARRISON, district superintendent of the United Methodist Church; and KATHLEEN LOGAN, an administrator at Baptist Hospital. August 26, 1994

EMERSON: I think sometimes when one thing happens in any town, it provides an impetus for other people to do it again. Kind of like, "Ooh, he got away with it. I'm gonna do it, too." And that it has a tendency, in many cases, to draw people from other areas to come in and pick up on that theme. I think this could as easily have happened in Virginia Beach, in Sacramento, California, anywhere.

WERTHEIMER: But it hasn't happened in this way in other places.

GRIFFING: I don't think you can say that Pensacola is any more violent when you look at overall statistics as far as crime is concerned. But when it happens and is associated with such a controversial issue, that's why we're in the spotlight. It's because those murders were associated with this particular issue. I don't think it's because we're a violent town because we're not.

GARRISON: I don't have an answer to your question either, and that's the reason for our concern. The first time this happened, the first killing, the ministers of the community came together, discussed it, issued a statement. We felt that was the end of it. Now that it's happened the second time, when we got together as religious leaders it was more than a statement we wanted to issue. We wanted to find reasons and then begin to deal with the basic causes.

GRIFFING: I think it might be easier to predict an earthquake, or it might be easier to predict a hurricane than it is to predict something like this. It's like a natural disaster. I don't know that there was anything in particular that we could do because it was just so hard to predict.

EMERSON: I'm not sure I entirely agree with that. I think that there is a certain amount of apathy, that people just said, "Well, you know, this is a terrible thing, but it won't happen again. Lightning doesn't strike the same place twice." And that just wasn't true. We looked at it as something very sad that had happened, something that was terrible, but it was an individual problem. It was not everybody's problem. For the first time I think we're saying, "Wait a minute. This affects me."

WERTHEIMER: When Paul Hill spent almost a year standing out in front of an abortion clinic, saying, "These people should die. We should be able to shoot them," people apparently listened to it and just took it for hyperbole. Now we can look back and say that was a mistake, but should you have looked at it when it was happening, and said, "This is serious"?

LOGAN: Absolutely. That's where we erred, in not taking seriously all the things that he was putting forth. If you could look at some of the videotapes now that were taken during the last year, you could see that this was a problem that was bound to burst, so to speak. Something was going to happen. It's like being a parent, having kids in your family. Your kids are going to push and push and push the limits, and, unless you draw the line, they're going to keep pushing.

WERTHEIMER: When you think about ways in which these events have impinged on the community — I mean, among other things I would think something like this would be bad for business in Pensacola.

GRIFFING: I'm not sure how you measure that this quickly after these sort of incidents. I can tell you that we have an average of twelve hundred people a day who come through our visitors center. That traffic has not stopped.

WERTHEIMER: But presumably your level of concern has risen.

GRIFFING: Yes. We know that it could have an impact some time in the future, but, in the short time that we've been able to assess it, it's been business as usual from the business perspective.

In August, Idaho had thirteen blazes under way at once, with thousands of firefighters helping out. Noah Adams talks with a former smoke jumper and *All Things Considered* commentator CLAY MORGAN, who was working on a novel at his home in McCall, Idaho, just by Lake Payette, where he could see the smoke of the forest fires from his living room window. August 24, 1994

MORGAN: The visibility in the morning is down to less than a quarter mile. But about one o'clock, a south wind comes up. Everything gets crystal clear. But that wind blows up the fires, and many days since August 3 we've had these huge smoke columns, fire columns, going up high into the atmosphere. They're very impressive, very awesome in the old sense of that word.

ADAMS: And you can actually, from your home there, see columns of fire?

MORGAN: Oh, man. The Blackwell complex [the largest series of fires in 1994] started almost on the lake, and the first day it was like an atomic bomb going up, the material going up into the sky and a big cap forming, and then it ices off on top because it gets so high, and thunder and lightning start rolling around inside of it, and there's so much material going up into the sky that the fire scientists were saying they were worried that the energy from the fire would reach an equilibrium with the weight of the material in the column. They worried for a while about "column collapse," they called it, where the column would fall back down on itself and push the fire out with winds in all 360 degrees. Sometimes it looks like an atom bomb. Sometimes it looks like Mount Saint Helens, like the earth has opened up, and you cannot believe the scene here some days. We have 120,000 acres burning right around McCall.

ADAMS: Don't you fear that it could turn towards your house?

MORGAN: If the winds turned around, that would be a shift in weather and would probably mean, you know, Canadian cold front coming down which would bring rain with it, or off the Alaskan Gulf, so right now there's no worry about McCall.

ADAMS: Are you sleeping comfortably?

MORGAN: It's very clear in the evenings, and you can sit and watch these spruce trees torch off, and they're fantastic to watch. Just like the Fourth of July. You can sit out on the deck and watch them. And then at two in the morning you get up and close the windows because you know the smoke's coming back.

ADAMS: You mean in the dark you can see the spruce trees lighting up?

MORGAN: Oh, yes. It's on the mountain side just northeast of the lake. You can go to Shore Lodge and sit down and have drinks and watch this amazing show, and watch these old airplanes, PP-4Ys and DC-4s bombing, and great big Sikorsky helicopters dipping buckets right out of the lake and dropping bucket loads on the spot fires. It's fantastic.

ADAMS: How long has it been since you were involved in fighting these fires yourself?

MORGAN: My last smoke jump was 1987, so it's been a while now.

ADAMS: And do you get a bit eager, anxious?

MORGAN: Yes, I've been spending time out there at the smoke jumper loft this summer quite a bit and even have worked as a driver for the forest in the last week. I'd love to go back out there and jump again.

ADAMS: Why wouldn't you? Are you out of shape?

MORGAN: Yes. Am I out of shape! I could get back in shape for it. It's just that, you know, I'm a writer and one of the reasons I stopped jumping was that I began to make enough money writing that I, you know, didn't also have to jump, and taking out five months every year to go jump stopped the writing for me, and I have to pick it all back up again.

ADAMS: I'm surprised that I don't hear you talking about the thrill of smoke jumping, the adrenaline rush. I don't hear you saying you miss that. You really wouldn't want to do it again?

MORGAN: Oh, no, I do miss that. That's the best part of it, the jump. You never know exactly where you're going. You size up the situation, you pick out a landing spot, you jump, you hope you make it, and then you've got this fire to fight, and if you're a jumper it's usually way out in the wilderness somewhere where no one else can get to. It's a wonderful experience. Once you get to a certain age, you start to dread the pack-offs. You have to pack off, oh, I think an average 100 to 110 pounds, you know, two-thirds of your own body weight and with no trail often for quite a ways, and that can just really wear you down. I really think more jumpers get hurt in the pack-offs than they do fighting the fire or making the jumps.

ADAMS: You mean you got to walk out?

MORGAN: Often you have to walk out.

ADAMS: How far would that be?

MORGAN: It can be to a helispot a quarter mile away or it can be a five-mile pack-off without a trail. I've had pack-offs that took me two days to complete, that's back in the old days, but that'd be the only thing I'd dread going back to right now.

....

The Barcys of Dayton, Ohio, were a family heavily dependent on welfare. DIANE BARCY, twenty-nine, had
two children on the federal welfare program, Aid to
Families with Dependent Children, AFDC. She lived in
publicly assisted housing and was expecting another
child. Her ex-husband, DON BARCY, thirty-five, lost his
job as a short-order cook and fell behind on child support
payments. He and his second wife, MISSY BARCY,
twenty-seven, had a newborn, their first child together
but her fourth. The Barcys describe their lives and
thoughts on welfare to Robert Siegel. May 4, 1994

DIANE: I was on and off AFDC ever since my first child was
born, because I was sixteen when I had her and I couldn't make
it on my own, and I got married early and he's been fluctuating
between jobs the whole time we were married and we just
needed extra help.

SIEGEL: Then, four years ago, you had Joey and the welfare
department asked you who his father was?

DIANE: They wanted me to name Joey's dad, and it was like
I named the two that I thought was his father. I named Brian,
the guy from out of town, and I named Don. They had to go after
both of them with court papers to have them both come in and
have blood tests taken.

SIEGEL: When you say you named two, you said either one
of these men could be the father.

DIANE: Right. Well, it was the only two that could have been
the fathers.

SIEGEL: And then they did the tests.

DIANE: Right, downtown did.

SIEGEL: Big surprise to you after that, huh?

DIANE: Oh, I was hoping the other father was, but it came out to where it proved to me that I wasn't out being a slut puppy or whatever and got pregnant with another guy's baby when I got pregnant at home with my husband. So that made it look good on me, but —

SIEGEL: Well, it made it look good, but as you say, you were seeing the other guy at that time and it could as easily have been him.

DIANE: Well, yes.

SIEGEL: But it was the welfare people who insisted on that, to figure out who should get hit with the child support.

DIANE: Child support.

SIEGEL: Why do you want to stay home with the children instead of getting a job?

DIANE: In the last two months we have had a hostage situation. We just had a killing, a homicide over here last weekend. We've got drive-by shootings. Nobody can pay me enough to leave my thirteen-year-old alone here. I went to school back when Jessie was in Head Start, eight years ago when she was five, but I was so young and so scared of that big test and going over to a strange school that I wouldn't go do it. This year I told them that I want to get through with it, and the teachers have been helping me, they've been throwing little tests at me.

DON: My mother and father broke up when I was real young, and my father was raising us and he had a mental breakdown. So for about two months, I was in charge of the family, which was me and three other children.

SIEGEL: At age —

DON: Sixteen. I went to work at McDonald's, worked days there while they were in school and then came home and I was daddy and mommy, clothed them and kept them. I had someone coming over visiting, make sure everything's all right, but I was pretty much in charge of everything. I had to go to work and get the kids up to school and then go to work and be home by the time they got home. And my youngest brother was seven when it started.

SIEGEL: So at the end of it all, you didn't have a high school diploma.

DON: No, I still don't.

SIEGEL: In two and a half years, your baby will be three and your wife might lose her AFDC grant if she doesn't go to work or to school. Do you think you'll have another baby at that time?

DON: No. She had her tubes tied.

SIEGEL: No more.

DON: No more. She's had four kids in just about four and a half years. So she wasn't even going to have a last child till we got together and got married, and she thought, Well, I always said I wanted a son of my own. That was before I knew that I had a son. So we went ahead, and she got pregnant, very surprisingly actually.

SIEGEL: This was an unplanned child that you had.

DON: Right, right. We took everything as it came, but the day after she had Michael, she had her tubes tied.

MISSY: I've been on AFDC since my daughter was born. She's five years old, so I've been on it for five years. I've not had any problems with it. It's helped me out a lot. Being on AFDC, you're subject to be in low-income housing. I've been through that. I've been in a low-income housing project. That's not the most thrilling place to live. I had two crack houses beside me on each side. And that's how I met my husband was when I was living in a project. We get $341 a month in AFDC, from WIC [Women, Infants and Children]. We get formula for the baby. And now that he's getting older, we get juice for him. And Timmy, the three-year-old, he gets a gallon of milk a week. He'll get a dozen eggs every other week, two boxes of cereal a month. I mean, they tell people to get off WIC and everything, but you're handed things like this, you know. Why should they get off welfare when they're getting all these handouts? But this is all for the children. I guess there are women that go out and they get pregnant and keep having babies so their grants will keep going up and going up and going up. And that just hurts the people that really need the benefits the most.

SIEGEL: How would it have affected your life had there been a rule that said after two years on welfare you've got to get off, period?

MISSY: It would have affected my life a lot because by then I had him, and he wouldn't have the medical benefits that she's got.

SIEGEL: Would you have had him if two years after Holly was born you were off?

MISSY: I can't say that I wouldn't have had him because he was unplanned anyway. I'd still have my kids. Even if I wasn't on AFDC, I'd still have my kids because my kids, you know, that's my life.

SIEGEL: What do you mean by that when you say that's your life?

MISSY: My kids are important to me, and I would rather be home when she comes home from school because my mom did that for me in case something great happened at school and she wants to come home and she wants mommy there to say, "Hey, this happened." I want to do that for them. You know, she's my life. If it wasn't for her, I wouldn't get the AFDC.

Dr. BENJAMIN SPOCK, the most famous baby doctor of the century, published *Baby and Child Care* in 1946. It became a bible for parents around the world, selling forty million copies in thirty-nine languages. In 1994, at age ninety-one, Spock published *A Better World for Our Children: Rebuilding American Family Values.* As he tells Susan Stamberg, Dr. Spock is most concerned about the world we are leaving to our children and does not think that his permissive guidance on child-rearing created spoiled children. September 27, 1994

SPOCK: "Children are not what they used to be. They interrupt their parents. They grab the best food at the table. They're quite disrespectful of their parents." Well, this was Socrates in the fifth century. The fifth century B.C.!

STAMBERG: I bet it was better then than now. [*laughs*]

SPOCK: I don't know.

STAMBERG: Dr. Spock, you point to a number of problem areas. One of them is that you say we're putting too much pressure on our kids. We're making them too competitive. We're too competitive as parents, and we're doing the same number on our children.

SPOCK: Right. American society is doing that to American adults, putting the pressure on them. The work, the job, is by far the most important thing; family has to be sacrificed if necessary. It gets passed on from the society to the parents to the children. Children immediately sense when their parents are under tension.

STAMBERG: For years — since 1946, actually — we've been turning to you for practical advice as to what to do with our children. Let me do that with you right now. What are some specific steps that families can take in order to strengthen the family unit?

SPOCK: A great deal of respect, not only between the adults, but a respect for the children by the adults, I think that's the first thing for people to recognize. That comes up in such things as what kind of discipline do you believe in. Do you believe in hitting kids? Humiliating kids? Isolating kids? The answer is, you try to treat them in a respecting way, the way you would treat your good friends. Children should be encouraged to be helpful and kindly right from the beginning, at least from one or two years of age. Too many parents say, "Oh, it's quicker for me to do it myself than to ask the child to help." That misses the point. Children should feel that it's their privilege to be helpful. Children love to be helpful. Children, more than anything else in the world, want to be more grown-up, and the place to start is letting them set the table or clear off the table, back at two and three years of age.

STAMBERG: You have written eight words, in your most-read book, *Baby and Child Care* — the very first words in that book, that mean more to the parents of the world maybe than any other eight words ever written. They are "You know more than you think you do."

SPOCK: Those are amazingly popular words. I put them in because I thought it was a good idea, but I didn't really expect people to take them as seriously. [*laughs*]

STAMBERG: But do you think it's still true, Dr. Spock?

SPOCK: Yes, it still is true, or should be true, that parents trust themselves. I've seen so many cases where the parent says, "Charlotte, dear, it's half an hour past your bedtime." Instead of saying, "Oh, Mother, I'm sorry," Charlotte says, "Why do I have to go to bed at that time? None of my friends have to go to bed at that time! Last month you let me stay up an hour after my bedtime!" It makes for unhappiness both in the children and the parents to have parents unsure of themselves. Parents nowadays in America are very hesitant, scared to be definite, scared to be firm, and what it does is it makes for children who are pesky, and they argue every single point unnecessarily. I think that makes child-rearing much less pleasant than it could be.

STAMBERG: Thank you for helping make us feel more confident. How are you feeling, Dr. Spock?

SPOCK: I'm having to admit that I'm old, and that I'm frail in a number of ways. I've always despised people who acknowledged too easily that they were sick or wanted to tell people about their illnesses, but when you ask me now, I feel it's a little more important to be honest, and say, "Yes, I've got a lot of health problems." But I'm holding them at bay with a very strict macrobiotic diet, and I'm holding them at bay with exercise, not only swimming, but walking. We walk at least once a day for half an hour. So you can hold the Grim Reaper at bay, but you've got to be serious and consistent about it.

ENDERS

....

In the Christmas shopping season, talking G.I. Joe and
Barbie dolls were, as usual, best-selling items. But some
dolls had been unusually altered. Reports surfaced of
G.I. Joes who talked like Barbie, saying, "Let's go to the
beach" and "Let's go shopping." And there were Barbies
who bellowed like G.I. Joe. The switches were the work
of a group called the Barbie Liberation Organization.
In a satellite interview, a BLO spokesman with the nom
de guerre MR. G.I. JOE tells Scott Simon about the
clandestine group's actions. January 1, 1994

MR. JOE: We have corrected approximately three hundred
dolls. We have operatives all over the country who purchase the
dolls and send them to our central hospital facilities, where our
BLO surgeons perform the operations, which consist of elec-
tronic cutting and pasting. We take the components from the
G.I. Joes, put them in the Barbies, and we take the Barbies'
components and put them in the G.I. Joes. We then repack the
dolls carefully, send them back to the original person who purchased them and they put them back on the shelf.

SIMON: I think the last time I checked, a Barbie doll was
going for something like thirty-five dollars, and a G.I. Joe must
be the same. This is adding up to a lot of money.

MR. JOE: It is, but some members of our organization feel
very strongly about this and as a result have been rather generous with their own personal funds.

SIMON: Feeling strongly about what?

MR. JOE: We are actually protesting the violent and sexist
nature of these toys. People are shocked to hear a Barbie saying
something like "Vengeance is mine" or "Mutants must rule,"
and we think that that reveals the real hypocrisy behind the
production of these toys.

SIMON: Mr. Joe, you have a couple of altered dolls there with you?

MR. JOE: I most certainly do.

SIMON: Now, we'll, of course, stipulate that for all we know you're holding up a Barbie and she's talking like Barbie and you're holding up a G.I. Joe and he's talking like G.I. Joe. But you maintain they've been switched.

MR. JOE: They certainly have.

SIMON: Could we hear G.I. Joe?

MR. JOE: This particular model is the G.I. Joe Stalker Ranger, and he's got a rather evil grimace on this face and some guns that are larger than even his body. Here he is:

G.I. JOE DOLL: "Let's have a dance contest." "Ken's such a dream." "Your school clothes are hot." "It's so much fun to shop with you."

MR. JOE: So that was G.I. Joe.

SIMON: Not exactly as I remember him, I must say.

MR. JOE: No, I think he's been improved quite a bit.

SIMON: Could we hear Barbie now?

MR. JOE: You certainly can. Here she is:

BARBIE: "Vengeance is mine." "No escape for the guilty."

SIMON: You know, it suits her somehow.

MR. JOE: Yes, I think it goes pretty well. "Vengeance is mine" and "No escape for the guilty" — we found those quotes to be particularly satisfying for our organization.

SIMON: Now, I must tell you, Mr. Joe, so far as we know, no consumers have filed complaints so far, and one of our producers talked with a family who received an altered G.I. Joe today and they're delighted.

MR. JOE: Yes. As a matter of fact, nobody we know of really wants to return them. They seem to really like their new doll. We think that our program of putting them back on the shelves, which we call "shop-giving," benefits everyone. The storekeepers make money twice, we stimulate the economy, the consumer gets a better product, and our message hopefully gets heard.

Inspired by the writing of the sixties poet and novelist Richard Brautigan, a seventeen-year-old resident of Carpenteria, California, legally changed his name to the title of Brautigan's most famous book. Formerly Peter Eastman, Jr., the teenager explains to Noah Adams why he took the name TROUT FISHING IN AMERICA. March 4, 1994

AMERICA: I chose that name because I thought it was an interesting name. One of my main reasons for changing my name is because my father, his father, and his father are all named Peter Eastman. So I'm saying I'm my own person.

ADAMS: As I recall the book, there is a character named Trout Fishing in America Shorty.

AMERICA: Yes. He is drunk in the wheelchair, and Brautigan makes references to the autopsy of Trout Fishing in America, and he speaks of Trout Fishing in America as a person, but that's not really why I decided to change my name.

ADAMS: So you went to your father, and said, "Gee, Dad, I like this book a lot and, and I'm graduating from high school, and I want to change my name to Trout Fishing in America," and what did he say?

AMERICA: He said, "If you want to do that, I'm behind you." He was kind of sad about it, a little bit, but he realized I want to be someone, and he accepted that.

ADAMS: Accepted to the point where he was willing to pay the $182 filing fee.

AMERICA: I asked him if he would pay that as a graduation present, and he agreed.

ADAMS: In actual use, when you use a name like Trout Fishing in America, how will that actually work?

AMERICA: "Trout" would be my first name.

ADAMS: Right.

AMERICA: "America" would be my last name, and "Fishing in" is my middle name.

ADAMS: I can just imagine a lot of difficulties: you go into a bank to get a checking account and have to have personalized checks, trying to go through this story over and over again for people.

AMERICA: I'm not too worried about it. Maybe I will be, but not at this point.

ADAMS: But do you think it would be strange checking into a hotel, asking for an airline ticket?

AMERICA: No, I mean, it's my name. I don't feel weird about it.

ADAMS: Well, good luck to you. It — it'll be an adventure, won't it?

AMERICA: Yes, you could say that.

Alone with the President is a collection of White House photographs of presidents and visiting celebrities, starting with the Kennedy White House. Official White House photography has escalated to the point at which the Reagan White House produced one and a half million photos, more than five hundred a day. Robert Siegel talks with the writer JOHN STRAUSBAUGH, who combed presidential libraries and emerged with a sampling of presidents shown performing the routine ceremonies of office: the Easter Seal twins stand on their heads for Lyndon Johnson; Gerald Ford meets George Harrison; the Carters meet the Pope; and, above all, Richard Nixon receives Elvis Presley. February 21, 1994

STRAUSBAUGH: It is the most-requested photo of any president ever taken. That's because it's not a photo of a president, it's a photo of Elvis Presley, who happens to be standing next to a president.

SIEGEL: [*laughs*] Right. "Who's the guy next to Presley?"

STRAUSBAUGH: In fact, someone asked a *New York Times* reporter once in the Nixon Library, "Well, I know who the King is, but who's that president standing next to him?"

SIEGEL: Tell us the story about this remarkable set of photographs of President Richard Nixon and an unusual-looking Elvis Presley. What was he doing there? What was happening?

STRAUSBAUGH: Elvis was a big collector of cop memorabilia and paraphernalia. He got the notion that he wanted a federal drug enforcement agent's badge, so he applied, and the deputy director of the Drug Enforcement Agency — I think half jokingly — told him, "Well, the only person who can just sort of hand you a drug enforcement badge is the president of the United States." The King heard that, got on a plane, flew to Washington, and appeared at seven in the morning at the northwest gate of the White House, saying, "I want to meet the president." He thought he was traveling incognito, so he approached them as Dr. John Carpenter, which was the name of the character he had played in a movie called *Change of Habit* the year before, but it was the King. Everybody recognized the King.

SIEGEL: What is that that he's wearing around his waist, by the way? Do you have any idea?

STRAUSBAUGH: That thing that looks like a license plate? That's Elvis's belt buckle. He loved those big, license plate–size belt buckles.

SIEGEL: He didn't think small, did he?

STRAUSBAUGH: Not at all. He was wearing a purple cape and rings on every finger. I don't think anybody was fooled that this was not the King among them.

SIEGEL: Now, it's understandable that a celebrity of such extraordinary fame would have met the president of the United States. However, seeing the television actor Chuck Connors a couple of different times isn't quite so easily understood.

STRAUSBAUGH: One of the things that kept surprising me, as I looked at tens and tens of thousands of photographs, were the secret schmoozers like Chuck Connors, whom one would not have expected to see meeting with JFK at the White House and later at Nixon's California White House at a party for Leonid Brezhnev, of all people.

SIEGEL: This was the general secretary of the Soviet Communist party, who came to visit, and his one request was to meet Chuck Connors?

STRAUSBAUGH: He was a great fan of Chuck's TV show *The Rifleman*, and they were best buddies for, I think, about a twenty-four-hour period and ended with a big bear hug on the airstrip as Brezhnev was leaving the country.

SIEGEL: One of my favorite shots in your collection is actu-

ally not of the president but of Nancy Reagan, flanked by several
visitors to the White House, some of whom I don't recognize at
all. One of them is Bruce Jenner, the decathlete; another is Tom
Cruise; and another is Cher, with quite a head of hair on her.

STRAUSBAUGH: Cher has this enormous bush coming up
out of her head. One of the things that strikes you is the way
people dress when they go to the White House. If you or I were
to go to the White House, we'd put on a suit and tie or formal
dress, but celebrities go as their celebrity images. They tend to
dress as themselves. So Cher was flamboyantly dressed when
she was there. Willie Nelson went in a kind of bad muscle shirt
with his arms hanging out of it. People dress as themselves
when they go to the White House. It's a very interesting phenomenon.

SIEGEL: Something else that you include a couple of times in
the book is the memo that a president would receive to prepare
him for the visit from the celebrities. There's one with the
Carpenters. Is it President Nixon they're visiting?

STRAUSBAUGH: It's Nixon.

SIEGEL: Yes, this is from Ken Cole of the White House staff
to the president: "Subject: Photo with the Carpenters. Tuesday,
August 1, 1972. I. Purpose: To greet a young, talented, all-
American recording group."

STRAUSBAUGH: There you go. "All-American recording
group." And the photo is amazing. They look like space aliens.
They have this very glassy-eyed stare.

SIEGEL: Did Richard Nixon, who's being briefed so minutely
on who these people are, what he should say, what they're
likely to say, have the faintest idea whom he was meeting with
in these photos?

STRAUSBAUGH: I sincerely doubt it. He said years after
meeting the King that he had very little idea of who Elvis Presley was that day he shook hands with him. He was aware that
the girls had bought one or two of his records, but beyond that,
he says, he did not know who Elvis Presley was, so I suspect he
didn't have much of an idea of who the Carpenters were.

With Christmas approaching, Neal Conan addresses the dilemma of shoppers stumped by what presents to buy their loved ones. Conan consults an expert, DAVE BARRY, a nationally syndicated humor columnist and the author of *Dave Barry's Gift Guide to End All Gift Guides*. December 16, 1994

CONAN: I should point out right away that this book is not a joke. In fact, I don't think I've ever read a book that repeats the phrase "I swear, I'm not making this up" more than this one.

BARRY: That's actually a tip for young writers. If you use a phrase like that over and over again, you don't have to think of other stuff. But no, the whole point of this book is that these are gifts that you can actually buy and give to somebody. This is a classic case of "it's better to give than to receive." You would not want to receive these gifts.

CONAN: I have to mention the book is nonfiction right away, because frankly, some people's credulity might be strained by, for example, the Bug Gun.

BARRY: You can get that from Archie McPhee, which is an outfit in Seattle, but it's a gun that has a little spring kind of deal on it, and you put an insect in it and you pull the trigger and it fires the insect across the room. So, like, for people who've been throwing insects manually, this is a real blessing.

CONAN: Well, the Bug Gun at least, is advertised by Archie McPhee, as a gift, but how do you explain the inability of the marketing folks at Armour to realize that people are just dying to find a can of pork brains in their Christmas stockings.

BARRY: It's not just pork brains; it's pork brains in milk gravy, which to me is the touch that makes it just scream "Holiday!" right at you. Those out-of-town guests come to stay, you open up a can of your pork brains and milk gravy, and watch them clear out of the room.

CONAN: And if your loved one enjoys fishing or hunting and has a fatal coronary after opening one of these thoughtful presents, there's even what you describe as the ultimate gift concept for the sportsman.

BARRY: Yes, there's this outfit called Canuck's Sportsman's Memorials in Des Moines. They will take the cremated ashes of a sportsperson and use them in various creative ways, such as, put them in a duck decoy; or they'll put them in a fishing lure so your sportsperson could, for the rest of his life, be swallowed and spat out by large-mouthed bass; or, they will even — this is my personal favorite — load the sportsperson's ashes into a shotgun shell, take it out into the woods, and shoot it at something, like I guess a wild animal of some kind. And isn't that a way to be remembered, don't you think?

CONAN: What a way to go.

BARRY: Yes.

CONAN: There are a couple of other hunting-related items: the venerable Duck Butt — and I do have to mention that we here on *Morning Edition* actually ripped the lid off that Duck Butt scandal a year ago — but I have to stand in awe of the giant fiberglass goose.

BARRY: Yes, well, the Duck Butts, they're duck decoys but instead of the duck in a horizontal position, this is just the butt of a duck sticking up. Presumably the duck is down with its head underwater, eating whatever it eats, so that ducks flying overhead will say, "Hah. This can't be a decoy 'cause look, there's its butt." I suggested using Duck Butts in punch bowls. Nothing would make a punch bowl more festive than Duck Butts floating around in it. Then the manufacturer said that could be a problem in that the alcohol in the punch might dissolve some of the paint and it could be toxic.

CONAN: People put alcohol in that punch?

BARRY: Yes, apparently they do, especially with Duck Butts in it, but my feeling is that anybody who drinks from a bowl with Duck Butts in it deserves to die. But the giant fiberglass goose is absolutely my favorite, all-time, gift guide item. It's a huge — about eight feet long, about six feet high — replica of a goose, made out of fiberglass, with a little hole in it for the hunter to look out. According to the manufacturer, the hunter "and his dog" can crouch inside this gigantic thing. It costs $385, and will not be noticed by geese flying overhead so they'll come down and land. But my feeling is — I'm not saying geese are rocket scientists, but if I'm a goose and I'm up there and I see a goose down there that's got to weigh a thousand pounds, I'm staying away. You know what I'm saying? By the way, we used the fiberglass goose on Miami Beach. There's a photo of this in the book, and we found that you could put it on the beach, right next to a sunbathing woman, and kind of crouch in there and hardly be noticed at all.

CONAN: We here in Washington have a whole group of people on our Christmas lists who we suddenly need, well, something special for this year. Any suggestions for Newt Gingrich?

BARRY: There's one item that Newt might like. It's the Internal Revenue Service Christmas Tree Ornament. It costs eleven bucks. You can get it from the Treasury Historical Association. It's a beautiful brass replica of the first ever 1040 Form, a 1913 tax form, and at the bottom it says, "Eighty Years of Income Tax." If that doesn't say "Holidays" to you, I don't know what does. Newt might like that.

CONAN: I was also looking for something for Bill Clinton, but you don't include a single item that's reversible.

BARRY: [laughs] A little vicious holiday humor there, Neal.

CONAN: I can't let you go without following up on a news item. In honor of your love of opera, the opera company in Eugene, Oregon, has issued an invitation for you to play a part in an upcoming production of *Gianni Schicchi*. It's a nonsinging part. In fact, it's a nonliving part —

BARRY: It's a dead part.

CONAN: I think your big moment comes when they stuff your body into a box —

BARRY: Yes, this is actually kind of appropriate because this happened when I wrote a column suggesting that opera could be fatal to human beings. There's an animal called an okapi, an African animal that was in a zoo in the Netherlands. Some opera singers were practicing near the zoo, and one of the okapis keeled over and died from stress from hearing the opera. My feeling was that these are mammals, we're mammals. I think the surgeon general, when we get one again, should warn people. Maybe there should be a warning actually printed on Luciano Pavarotti that listening to this person could kill you. So now they've invited me to be in an opera out there, where I play a dead person. My only concern about that is, since there was a lot of hostility from the opera community when I wrote that column —

CONAN: No —

BARRY: They might go ahead, put me in the box, and just bury the box, you know what I'm saying? And then say later on, "Well, we didn't know it was a real person," or something like that.

CONAN: Well, as angry as they might be with you, the one thing they wouldn't do is rewrite Puccini.

BARRY: No, no, whoever he is.

Riverdale, U.S.A., is the fictional hometown of the comic book characters Archie, Veronica, Betty, Reggie, and Jughead, who have been stumbling through high school for decades. For reasons best known to the cartoonist BATTON LASH, they are visited by another Marvel Comics character, a brute named the Punisher. Scott Simon asks Lash about the thinking behind the issue called *Archie Meets the Punisher*. July 9, 1994

SIMON: Did Archie need the Punisher, or did the Punisher need Archie?

LASH: Apparently, Archie needed the Punisher. In comic shops, unfortunately, the clientele is into real adventurous, sock-'em superheroes. That sort of stuff. Archie Comics decided that they really wanted to pull the new reader in, and they decided they had to go big guns, no pun intended.

SIMON: Mr. Lash, with all due respect to your work, there was a part of me that was a little saddened to read this because the implicit message is, you can't hold an audience except with violence.

LASH: I hate to say "violent" because I didn't write this as a violent story. I wrote this more as a lighthearted romp, if you want. The violence in *Archie Meets the Punisher* is all off-screen. You don't really see people getting blown away like you do in the usual Punisher comics.

SIMON: Had you written for the Punisher or, for that matter, Archie before this?

LASH: No, no. I had always done my own weekly comic strip. About attorneys, believe it or not.

SIMON: You grew up reading Archie and Jughead?

LASH: I grew up reading everything, and, ironically, it was the introduction of the Punisher twenty years ago that kind of got me to stop reading comics because a character like that was very alien to the lighthearted comics I read when I was a kid.

SIMON: Let me explain about the Punisher. He's got a skull-and-crossbones symbol on his chest. He carries what looks to me like an Uzi. And he uses it.

LASH: Yes, the Punisher watched his family get gunned down on a picnic and never got over it. It's twenty years later, and he still hasn't sought out help.

SIMON: Mr. Lash, do you have a favorite line that you wrote for this comic?

LASH: I do have a favorite scene, which was when the Punisher enters Riverdale High to get into the dance. He's walking through the school, and this is the first time he's been in a high school in a long time where there weren't bars on the window, and he comes across a locker and notices some graffiti, a little heart that Betty had written that says "Betty Cooper and Archie Andrews Forever." This gets to the Punisher. He's determined to save this town from the syndicate setting up a drug network there.

SIMON: To keep Riverdale clean?

LASH: Keep Riverdale clean, right.

SIMON: Mr. Lash, it's none of my business, but a personal question.

LASH: Sure.

SIMON: Are you a Betty man or a Veronica man?

LASH: I'm a Miss Grundy man.

SIMON: The teacher?

LASH: The teacher.

SIMON: Oh, is that the politically safe answer, Mr. Lash? Congratulations. Yes?

LASH: No, when I was a kid, I always felt bad for Miss Grundy, saying, "You know, she doesn't seem that bad. Why are all the kids picking on her," and there's something about that nose. The nose and the little hair bun was very cute to me.

SIMON: Without giving away the plot, you give her sort of a just reward after all these years.

LASH: If you call being kissed by the Punisher a reward. I don't think many people would agree with that.

The town of Herman, Minnesota, 150 miles west of Minneapolis, has a population of 474, of whom 78 are single men between the ages of twenty and fifty. There are only about 10 single women in the same age range, and all 20 females in the high school's graduating class of 1995 said they planned to leave Herman to find jobs. Faced with a critical shortage of women, and the prospect of it worsening, the town decided to take action, as the bachelor RYAN RILEY, a dispatcher in the local sheriff's office, explains to Bob Edwards. July 20, 1994

EDWARDS: first of all, what is it about the town that drives women away?

RILEY: It's the fact that there are no opportunities for gainful employment, other than working on a farm or in a farm-related business.

EDWARDS: So it's the quality of the job market, not the quality of the bachelors?

RILEY: Yes, exactly.

EDWARDS: Well, what's the town of Herman doing to attract women?

RILEY: Right now it has an economic development corporation which is giving people from out of town opportunities to apply for small-interest loans and to open up their own businesses.

EDWARDS: What sort of response have you gotten so far?

RILEY: It's been pretty large. It's got two parts to it, the economic point of developing new businesses for Herman, and the second point of getting wives for these bachelors. So you come down to the local liquor store any Friday or Saturday night and it'll be packed because the people come from out of town.

EDWARDS: How do you and the other bachelors feel about being the focus of so much attention?

RILEY: Personally, I don't pay too much attention to it. The other bachelors, they're low-key about it, but they kind of enjoy it.

EDWARDS: Are the bachelors of Herman the marrying sort, or do they just want companionship?

RILEY: It's really hard to say. A lot of them are looking to be married, and the other half will just say, "Well, yeah, I'd like a companion."

EDWARDS: How about yourself? Have you volunteered to be the Herman, Minnesota, poster boy for this campaign?

RILEY: I've heard that a lot. People have said we should get a calendar or something. No, I don't plan on doing too much down there in Herman. I'll work on my job and then graduate from college, and I'll be forced to move out because there won't be any opportunities for myself around there.

Some fans of the Boston Red Sox turn to the supernatural to explain their team's super-misfortune. The Sox have not won a World Series since 1918, a drought exceeded only by those of the Chicago Cubs and White Sox, whose misfortunes are generally attributed to ineptitude. The theory of a mystical obstacle to Boston's hopes rests on "The Curse of the Bambino." In 1920, the Red Sox traded Babe Ruth (the Bambino) to the New York Yankees, a misstep of magical dimensions. The Yankees became dynastic champions; the Red Sox never again won a World Series. The Sox fan ALAN SHAWN FEINSTEIN purchased the original 1919 contract that sent Ruth to New York and, as he explains to Scott Simon, offered to give the contract to the Red Sox if they promised to burn it at home plate at Fenway Park on opening day, 1995. Amidst other concerns regarding the start of the 1995 season, the Red Sox ultimately declined the offer. July 9, 1994

SIMON: And you figure that would do it?

FEINSTEIN: I don't know, but it's certainly worth a try. The legend of this Curse of the Bambino seems to grow stronger every year.

SIMON: Now, that's quite a piece of history, that contract. May I ask how much you paid for it?

FEINSTEIN: Yes. I paid ninety-nine thousand dollars for it, and now I'm willing to give it to the Red Sox.

SIMON: What do the Red Sox say?

FEINSTEIN: The Red Sox haven't said anything yet, but they just received my offer last week. So it's still early.

SIMON: I guess the problem they might have, and I'm projecting now, is that to accept your offer would be for them to accept that they have been the subject of a curse.

FEINSTEIN: Yes. I think most people don't believe literally in curses, but it seems that the longer the Red Sox go on without winning, the idea of this curse seems to loom over them.

SIMON: My stepfather is a historian, not to mention a former minor league ball player with the Tucson Toros. The historian part of him would be appalled at the idea that you're going to take an important piece of baseball history and torch it.

FEINSTEIN: I know, and I sympathize with people who feel that way. Purists, and there are many of them, feel this is history, you don't destroy history, but it's my feeling that if this can be used to turned the Red Sox around, I would be willing to try it.

SIMON: While I have the chance, given your area of expertise, do you have any idea what might be troubling the Cubs?

FEINSTEIN: No, no! I have enough trouble here in Boston without looking at Chicago.

....

In 1934, STEPHEN VAN NEST POWELSON won a
national prep school classics competition, and the prize
money made it possible for him to attend Harvard
despite his father's bankruptcy. As repayment of his
debt of gratitude to the classics, Powelson became a
Homeric rhapsodist. In 1978 he began committing
Homer's *Iliad*, in ancient Greek, to memory. Sixteen
years and 14,000 lines later, Powelson was only 893 lines
short of memorizing the entire work. As he tells
Robert Siegel, while memorizing or reciting the *Iliad*,
he visualizes every scene. April 29, 1994

POWELSON: I memorize not only the words of the *Iliad*, but
I memorize the action. I know when somebody does something
with his left hand or with his right hand, or when he nods his
head or shakes his head, and I have the impression that if,
through some misfortune, all the words in my mind fell out, I
could still sit down and write out an account of the *Iliad* in
detail and in proper sequence.

SIEGEL: This entire task seems to be one that has required
great discipline and regular attention. This requires a very or-
derly approach to do what you've done.

POWELSON: That is true. People ask me, "Can anybody do
this?" And I say yes, anybody who has a moderately good memory. Only three things are required. One is an intense will to do
it; second is the discipline to keep at it and keep practicing; and
the third is a touch of madness.

SIEGEL: And, I should think, somewhere, an obliging spouse
would come in handy, someone who could tolerate your constant recitation.

POWELSON: Yes, but I must say that my wife benefits from

it in this sense: She never has to take a sleeping pill. If she has trouble getting to sleep, she just asks me to recite and off she goes to sleep.

SIEGEL: [*laughs*] I'm just curious. Had it not been for your going to college based on your proficiency in the classics, is there any other nonclassical work, apart from a Homeric epic, that you might have considered giving this much of your life over to? Is there any other work of literature that you could imagine somebody spending four hundred hours memorizing?

POWELSON: No, but a friend of mine, Bill Murphy, who used to be an English teacher, knows a couple hundred lines of *Paradise Lost*, and I once suggested to him that we form a team and go around, he reciting *Paradise Lost* and I reciting Homer, and he said no, he wouldn't. I said, "Well, why not, Bill?" He said, in that case, his performance would look like a two-base hit compared with my Homer.

[*Stephen Van Nest Powelson died on December 26, 1994.*]

As women's figure skating, the most popular event of the Winter Olympics, was about to begin in Lillehammer, Norway, LAUREN MACDONALD SHEEHAN discusses a vital, if nonathletic component of the competition: the skaters' costumes. Sheehan is a former figure skater who has been designing skating outfits for nearly twenty years. Her clients include 1992 Olympic gold medalist Kristi Yamaguchi, the 1988 Olympic bronze medalist Debi Thomas, and, in 1994, the French skater Surya Bonaly, as well as the American skater Scott Davis. Sheehan tells Bob Edwards that it's a lot harder to design skating outfits today than it was when she started out. February 23, 1994

SHEEHAN: If the ice skater and the ice skater's mother liked the costume, that was enough. Now you have to please a coach, a choreographer, a sponsor who might be helping monetarily, judges. Every little silly thing about ice skating has become important: how you wear your hair, how you conduct yourself in public. Seventeen years ago people didn't follow people around with television cameras. It's amazing how much it's changed, and it's affected everything, even the costuming.

EDWARDS: Well, ultimately it's the judges that are important, right? Unless you're looking for endorsements later, in which case I could see where the costume might be useful.

SHEEHAN: A new client that I have, Surya Bonaly from France, who is the French national champion and has been four-time European champion, has not been popular in the United States due to her style. She has a style like a gymnast. When she met with me, we had a disagreement about color. I didn't like the fact that she was choosing these very, very pastel colors that were such a huge contrast with her skin tone. You didn't even see her face. It made her look so dark you couldn't even really see her on television. She said to me, "But this is what the American judges want me to look like." And it broke my heart because this girl can turn herself inside out trying to please the American judges and they'll find something else to criticize. I don't think they're ever going to like this girl. The U.S. judges are always going to be in favor of the U.S. skaters. It's a very political sport. I have mixed feelings about whether it should even be in the Olympics.

EDWARDS: Katarina Witt's costume got a lot of attention at the 1988 Winter Olympics.

SHEEHAN: Yes.

EDWARDS: And they don't want to see anything like that again, right?

SHEEHAN: Well, oooh —

EDWARDS: I mean the skating people. [laughs] The rest of us, well —

SHEEHAN: The thing is, the costume that she wore inspired the "Katarina Rule," and, again, this is my opinion, I don't think there was a thing in the world wrong with that costume except that it dropped feathers on the ice. It was not too revealing. It looked like a Las Vegas showgirl, but that depicted the music she was skating to. The coach of Elizabeth Manley, who was competing for Canada, who ultimately was second overall, skated after Katarina, and Elizabeth Manley's coach, rightly so, was concerned about the feathers on the ice, and there was a lot of criticism about that. I thought her costume was really pretty, but I would not have used feathers because it's terribly difficult to get them to stay on. I agree with the ruling. I don't think you should be able to drop feathers on the ice and get away with it, but I find it very upsetting that now they have opened the door to taking points away from a performance based on costume. Part of that ruling says that a costume is not to be overly theatrical. That is so subjective. I hate to see a performance have points taken away because some judge doesn't like the costume.

EDWARDS: But she lost more than feathers, didn't she?

SHEEHAN: See, they're talking about two or three different events. There was an event where she was doing a camel spin and exposed one breast and shocked the world. She wore another costume where she had her navel exposed, and now the ruling says that you can't wear a costume on a female that has a bare midriff.

EDWARDS: Now, there go the Dallas Cowboy cheerleaders.

SHEEHAN: [laughs] Exactly. And then there's Tonya Harding's costume that she wore when she won the U.S. National Championship. I've been very outspoken about my dismay that she appeared on the ice in that thing. It was very revealing and terribly cut away, and I heard on fairly good authority that she's not going to wear that again at the Olympics. I wasn't really surprised that Tonya wore it. I was surprised that the people around her let her wear it.

EDWARDS: Do they have rulings like that for the men?

SHEEHAN: Yes, there are rules for the men. The men are not allowed to wear anything without sleeves. They don't really state exactly why, but everyone's guess is they don't want to see hairy armpits hanging out. They're supposed to have their legs and arms covered, and that's really about it for the guys. And the girls — I did a unitard for Debi Thomas that she wore in the Olympics in 1988, and that also was outlawed with the Katarina Rule. They felt it was too masculine and they want the girls to be wearing skirts. There's a rule that they have to have a skirt that covers front and back.

EDWARDS: Too masculine? Now, that's interesting, because they want a little show business, but only so much. Isn't that right?

SHEEHAN: It's a media sport, and yet the officials and the judges are quite conservative, and I think sometimes their fear is that this is trying to be an Olympic sport, and they don't want the costuming and the theatrical side of this to outweigh the technical side. They're trying to pull the reins in a bit just so they can keep it a little more conservative and a little more uniform.

EDWARDS: But if you don't hit the triple jumps, it doesn't matter what your costume is.

SHEEHAN: That's exactly it. If you're sitting there on all fours on the ice, nothing's going to help you. I thought Brian Boitano's costume was beautiful. It fit his music, and he looked great in it, but it certainly couldn't save him from a bad performance. So a costume's only important to a certain point.

The Reduced Shakespeare Company performs *The Complete Works of William Shakespeare (Abridged)* in a two-hour, three-man production that is funny, smart, and slapstick. They also stage an abridged history of America. The RSC has performed in London and New York and has produced a radio series for the BBC World Service. During their engagement at the Kennedy Center in Washington, D.C., AUSTIN TICHENOR, REED MARTIN, and MATT CROKE tell Robert Siegel about the troupe's beginnings and their approach to Shakespeare. June 23, 1994

TICHENOR: It began in 1981 when Daniel Singer decided he had always wanted to run a theater company. There are these things called Renaissance fairs in California, and he decided he would do a reduced version of *Hamlet* to take to these Renaissance fairs, about a twenty-minute version. It had to be Elizabethan and vaguely Renaissance-ish, and they went out there, and the version of Hamlet was such a hit that they decided to do a version of *Romeo and Juliet*. The company learned early on that if you make it loud and funny and physical, more people will throw money in your hat at the end of it. That was a very valuable lesson in capitalism which the company has stuck to over the years. From there, somebody said, "You should do the whole, complete works of William Shakespeare," and they said, "Well, all right. We've done two plays. There's only thirty-five more. How tough can that be?"

SIEGEL: How would you describe your attitude toward Shakespeare in the complete works?

MARTIN: Well, we've never met him. We understand he was a nice enough guy.

CROKE: Yes.

MARTIN: His plays are pretty keen. We actually do admire the work of Shakespeare for the most part. We don't think all of them are masterpieces by any means, but I think what we do in the Shakespeare show — we're not making fun of Shakespeare, we're making fun of the way Shakespeare is performed. He's become high culture, where in his time he was popular culture.

CROKE: Shakespeare was a showman. He put on the plays people wanted to see, and now he's handed down to us as a genius and it gets a little stuffy. So we're not doing him any injustice. It's very much a theater experience.

SIEGEL: I read in the Playbill that you think that Shakespeare would appreciate your performances.

MARTIN: Yes. We think he would even go bowling with us after the shows on Thursdays.

CROKE: We think so, yes. We're not sure.

TICHENOR: Essentially we just want to put the shake into Shakespeare. Cut out all the unimportant poetry that nobody understands. Get right to the sex and the killing. That's what we're about. It's our mandate, really.

SIEGEL: Now, as you said, this all began in performing a shortened version of *Hamlet*, a twenty-minute version of *Hamlet* is what you started with.

TICHENOR: Well, Hamlet is Shakespeare's greatest play. To give it anything less than twenty minutes would be sacrilege.

MARTIN: Oh yes, that would be so disrespectful to the genius of Shakespeare.

SIEGEL: But you have attempted to push the envelope on this score, to make it even shorter than twenty minutes.

TICHENOR: Well, we do *Hamlet* fast. We were watching the Olympics, and we were thinking, Well, I wonder what the world record for *Hamlet* is? We discovered it was in at around forty seconds. We thought we could do it faster than that, and we actually set the record at thirty-eight seconds. Then we were just mortified. We found out that there was an East German troupe that had apparently done it in seventeen seconds, which we thought would have been impossible, but their Ophelia tested positive for steroids, so we still hold the record. We could do that for you if you'd like.

SIEGEL: I think everyone in the country probably would like to hear a go for the record here.

TICHENOR: I think the record is thirty-eight seconds. We're not going to promise anything, but we'll make it close.

CROKE: OK, I'm all set. You ready? Everybody oiled up?

MARTIN: All right, here we go.

TICHENOR: O, would that this too too solid flesh would melt.

MARTIN: My lord, I think I saw your father yesternight.

TICHENOR: Would the night were come.

MARTIN: Night.

CROKE: Mark me.

TICHENOR: Something is rotten in the state of Denmark.

CROKE: Revenge my murder.

MARTIN: My lord, this is strange.

TICHENOR: There are more things in heaven and earth, so piss off. To be or not to be, that is the question.

MARTIN: Good my lord!

TICHENOR: Get thee to a nunnery. Speak the speech trippingly on the tongue. I'll take the ghost's word for a thousand pound. Now, mother, what's the matter?

MARTIN: Help.

CROKE: Help, help.

TICHENOR: How now, a rat!

CROKE: Dead for a ducat, dead.

MARTIN: Now, Hamlet, where's Polonius?

CROKE: At supper?

TICHENOR: Where's my father?

CROKE: Dead.

TICHENOR: Sweet Ophelia! Alas, poor Yorick! But soft, here comes the queen.

MARTIN: Lay her in the earth.

CROKE: Sweets to the sweet.

MARTIN: Hold off the earth awhile.

TICHENOR: It is I, Omelette the cheese Danish.

MARTIN: The devil take thy soul.

CROKE: One for me. O! I am slain!

MARTIN: O, I am poisoned.

TICHENOR: I follow thee, the rest is silence. Time!?

CROKE: Thirty-four seconds. [*cheers and hoots*]

SIEGEL: That was a moment of history, made right here on the program.

TICHENOR: You are there.

SIEGEL: Now, you have not limited yourselves to the works of Shakespeare?

TICHENOR: No, we have not. We've become the bad boys of abridgment all over the world.

MARTIN: It is true.

TICHENOR: We've abridged for the BBC. We've abridged *Gone With the Wind*. We've abridged *Glen Row*, which is the most popular Irish soap opera. We've abridged American history in our new stage show.

SIEGEL: You've abridged American history? Starting where?

TICHENOR: Starting with the big bang and going up all the way to Paula Jones, which is more or less —

MARTIN, CROKE: [*in unison*] The same thing.

SIEGEL: I heard in the last of your six-show series on the BBC World Service your remarks about Her Majesty Queen Elizabeth II. You made some disparaging remarks, and then you had an audio footnote disclaimer. I'm just curious how the BBC took to your irreverent humor and what the experience was like doing this on the air.

CROKE: Well, so are we, actually.

TICHENOR: As far as we know, they just gave us the go-ahead to make the program and then never listened to it. So we did whatever we wanted, and we think one of these days somebody at the BBC is going listen to it and we're going to be in big trouble.

MARTIN: Particularly since they've already been aired on

World Service. But the British seem to take very strongly to what we do, both in the Shakespeare show and in the history show. In the Shakespeare show, we think they're flattered that we would spend so much time on their national playwright, and also because we do Shakespeare the way they think three stupid Americans would do Shakespeare.